Technological Change: Its Conception and Measurement

Prentice-Hall Series in Mathematical Analysis of Social Behavior

James S. Coleman and James March, Editors

PRENTICE-HALL INTERNATIONAL, INC.   London
PRENTICE-HALL OF AUSTRALIA, PTY. LTD.   Sydney
PRENTICE-HALL OF CANADA, LTD.   Toronto
PRENTICE-HALL OF INDIA (PRIVATE) LTD.   New Delhi
PRENTICE-HALL OF JAPAN, INC.   Tokyo

Technological Change: Its Conception and Measurement

Lester B. Lave

Assistant Professor of Economics

Carnegie Institute of Technology

PRENTICE-HALL, INC.   ENGLEWOOD CLIFFS, NEW JERSEY

To my parents

Preface

During the post war period, economic writing has shifted somewhat from Keynesian concerns with full employment to questions of growth and development. With the increasing focus on what makes economies grow came the realization that the difference between rich and poor, between developed and underdeveloped nations involves more than the number of complex machines. In the mid 1950's this realization became crystalized into overt dissatisfaction with the neo-classical explanation of increased productivity resulting primarily from increases in capital per laborer.

In 1957 Robert Solow presented an elegantly simple paper. He called all increases in output per man, that couldn't be explained by increases in capital per man, technological change. Then, postulating an aggregate production function for the economy, he decided how much of the increase in productivity could be explained by increased capital and derived an index of technological change. Although Solow claimed that the paper provided no more than "an oblique approximation," it seemed to be the rod in a supercharged atmosphere that drew an enormous reaction. Economists rushed off to prove Solow wrong, to argue with the aggregate production function, to prove that it was really Cobb-Douglas, to argue about technological change, and so on. Solow himself became caught up in the flood, changed his views in subsequent papers, and stayed as a principal combatant throughout.

The massive reaction precipitated by the 1957 paper continues. Indeed, it seems to be still growing. Major areas of economic theory have had to be reworked, and changed to a greater or lesser degree.

In 1963 the body of this work seemed ill-related, ill-understood, at least by part of the profession and in danger of needless duplication. Richard M. Cyert of GSIA encouraged me to extend the work of my dissertation. In the ensuing two years, GSIA, Dean Cyert, and my colleagues provided support and encouragement.

This book has benefited from numerous critics, both principals in the battle and innocent bystanders who couldn't refuse assistance. While acknowledging their help, I must confess that there remain a number of disagreements. The views and errors are mine. Some of the debts are acknowledged in specific chapters; although it is not specifically noted, G. L. Bach, Myron Joseph, and Leonard Rapping contributed to Chapter 11. A tremendous intellectual debt is due Robert Solow and Evsey Domar. I was able to consult both at the beginnings of this work and have found their writings of inestimable help. The entire manuscript received the attention of Murray Brown, Michael Lovell, Martin Bronfenbrenner, and William McD. Herr. Thoughtful criticism was also provided by Gary Bowman, Otto Davis, Hendrik Houthakker, Charles Lave, Arnold Lieberman, Fred Rueter, Murray Silverman, and Roman Weil. Rueter did triple service as coauthor, critic, and with Bowman index compiler.

The writing benefited from the editorial help and patience of Ruth Westheimer and my wife. Secretarial assistance was graciously provided by the Mrs. Jean Patterson, Virginia Bloom, and Stina L. Hirsch; anyone who has prepared a manuscript will recognize how inadequate a payment this recognition is for the work involved. Finally, my wife contributed patience and encouragement.

LESTER B. LAVE

Contents

Part Two: Technological Change and Economic Theory

List of Tables and Figures

Technological Change: Its Conception and Measurement

The Measures
and Measurement
of Technological
Change

CHAPTER ONE

Introduction: Growth and Technological Change

Around 1800 economists described economic growth as the process whereby a nation transformed its economic surplus into capital accumulation. They argued that capital accumulation could not continue indefinitely: stagnation would slowly strangle economic growth with a subsistence real wage, low profits (and therefore a low return to capital), and high economic rents. These conclusions were based on three assumptions: the law of diminishing returns, the Malthusian principle of population, and implicitly, an invariant state of technology. This view of the future earned economics the nickname of "the dismal science."

Had these economists been asked for advice on a development program, they would probably have answered, "Don't bother." An increase in the real wage would lead to faster population growth. Indeed, wages could not remain above the subsistence level for long. The only events that might result in a wage above subsistence, temporarily, were war, famine, and plague[1].

[1]"Although . . . under the most favorable circumstances, the power of production is still greater than that of population, it will not continue so; for the land being limited in quantity, and differing in quality, with every increased portion of capital employed on it there will be a decreased rate of production, whilst the power of population continues always the same . . . ." (p. 56)

"With a population pressing against the means of subsistence, the only remedies are either a reduction of people or a more rapid accumulation of capital. In rich countries, where all the fertile land is already cultivated, the latter remedy is neither very practicable nor very desirable, because its effect would be, if pushed very far, to render all classes equally poor." (p. 56.) Ricardo, David, *The Principles of Political Economy and Taxation* (New York: Dutton & Co., 1911 edition).

However, these gloomy predictions are not corroborated by contemporary reality, at least in the so-called developed countries. Real income per worker is many times its 1800 level. The increase in per capita income in the United States has averaged more than 2 per cent per year since 1870. In fact, the United States economy might best be characterized by the words; prosperity and progress. Currently, per capita income is about $2400 and median family income is more than $6000. If the present rate of growth continues, by the turn of the century per capita income will average more than $5000 and median family income will exceed $14,000.

How did the classical economists err so badly? Is it the three assumptions which fail to describe reality, or the analysis that went awry? The answers to these questions will help to distinguish current from classical economics as well as provide some insight into the current economic situation.

Had Ricardo been asked whether increased productivity were possible, he would probably have answered that productivity would increase if capital per worker, including land per worker, were increased.[2] Pressed for a quantitative answer, it is doubtful he could have replied. Assuming a Cobb-Douglas[3] production function and no complications, one might say that output will rise 1 per cent for every 3 per cent capital increases, holding labor constant. This ratio is simultaneously an estimate of the elasticity of output with respect to capital and the share of capital in income. Using this ratio, a preliminary explanation of the observed increase in per capita output is possible.

Between 1909 and 1949, employed capital per man-hour in the private, nonfarm sector of the United States economy rose by 31.5 per cent.[4] By the preceding argument, this increase in capital should have given rise to an increase in per capita output of about 10 per cent. The data showed that output per man-hour in this same sector and over this same period rose not by 10 per cent, but rather by 104.6 per cent. What caused the 90 per cent increase in productivity that is unexplained by the increase in capital per worker?

With a magnificent wave of his hand, Solow named this 90 per cent *technological change*.[5] In one mighty blow, Solow cut the Gordian knot and banished poverty from our midst. No wonder the classical economists were wrong; 90 per cent of the increase in productivity was neglected. The classical world is one where productivity increases result from painstakingly saving part of one's subsistence wage and carefully transforming it into capital.

---

[2]"In that case (capital increasing faster than labor over a period), wages during the whole period would have a tendency to rise, because the demand for labour would increase still faster than the supply." (Ricardo, p. 55.)

[3]See discussion in Chapter 2.

[4]Solow (1957, p. 315).

[5]Both Solow's conclusions and method actually appeared in the literature much earlier; the former in Abramovitz (1956) and the latter in Tinbergen (1942).

How different is this economy that gives away 90 per cent of the increase in productivity free as "technological change!"

What is this mysterious factor, *technological change*? Solow notes that he is ". . . using the phrase 'technical change' as a shorthand expression for *any kind of shift* in the production function. Thus slowdowns, speedups, improvements in the education of the labor force, and all sorts of things will appear as 'technical change.'" [6] In view of the subsequent literature, Solow might have added to the factors affecting "technical change" nonconstant returns to scale, non-neutral technical change, interindustry shifts of resources, aggregation biases, and many many more. There are several factors that might give rise to an apparent shift in the relationship between output per laborer and capital per laborer; Solow devised a name, perhaps misleading, to cover this group. Domar (1961) thought that a more appropriate name was "the residual," that is, that part of increased output per man which is left over after increases in capital per man are accounted for.

The "residual" is clearly defined: the increase in productivity not explained by increases in capital per man. But it is not well understood. The Solow measure is intended to do no more than provide ". . .some crude but useful conclusions." [7] There is no hint of a causal mechanism, no suggestion that policy conclusions may emerge except under the strong assumption that economic forces will continue as they have in the past.

This book is concerned with the definition and measurement of this mysterious factor. The importance of this force is easily seen in the fact that it represents approximately 90 per cent of the increase in productivity. The importance of attempting to measure and understand what makes up this factor might be seen in the observation that technological change has not always proceeded at the same pace in the United States, and that it is currently proceeding at very different paces in different countries. The range of measured technological change goes from 4 or 5 per cent per year for some short periods, to zero or even negative numbers for others. In order to understand the future and to make intelligent predictions about, as well as helping, the growth of the United States and other economies, an understanding of technological change is essential.

Organization of the Book

Part 1, comprising the first eight chapters, pertains primarily to the various measures of technological change which have been devised and the conclusions to be drawn from them. A review of the more important definitions

[6]Solow (1957, p. 312).
[7]Solow (1957, p. 312).

of technological change is given in Chapter 2. In Chapter 3 the differences between these definitions is discussed and an attempt is made to integrate them.

Given the conceptual framework of the first three chapters, the results of actually calculating technological change are presented in Chapter 4. Chapter 5 is an effort to measure technological change in the agricultural sector of the United States economy over an entire century.

A further elaboration of the difficulties inherent in measuring technological change is given in Chapter 6. This chapter includes a discussion of the effect on the technological change index of: 1) errors of measurement in the data series, 2) the economy failing to stay in long run equilibrium, and 3) using value added rather than total value in measuring output.

Chapters 7 and 8 are focused on the aggregation problem: What are the effects of aggregating the data and which method of aggregation is most appropriate to an index of technological change?

The evolution of the idea of technological change and its effect on economic theory is summarized in Part II. Modern macroeconomic theorists are not likely to make the same mistakes as the classical economists; technological change is included in more and more of their models. A few of these are presented in Chapter 9.

The significance of the technological change concept with respect to economic theory is discussed in Chapter 10. The pure theory of international trade is challenged and empirical estimates of the accelerator are considered.

In Chapters 11—13 an attempt is made to relate technological change to public policy. Chapter 11 is concerned with the inefficiency of agriculture in the Appalachian region and with what might be done to mitigate the problem. A hypothetical economy is described in Chapter 12 in an attempt to illuminate some of the problems in the development literature and to illustrate how technological change might prove baneful to a development program. In Chapter 13 an employment model is constructed, involving diverse manpower and equipment, which is discussed in the light of inflexibilities and technological change.

Chapter 14 is an attempt at a comprehensive bibliography of the literature on technological change. The breadth and scope of this literature has been expanding enormously in the past few years; about half the entries appeared in 1963 or 1964. The scope of current research is indicated in *Current Projects on Economic and Social Implications of Science and Technology* compiled by the National Science Foundation.

CHAPTER TWO

The Models Measuring Change

The Arithmetic Index

The arithmetic index (see Abramovitz [1956] and Kendrick [1961]) is perhaps both the most common and the most misunderstood measure of technological change. In national income accounting terms, the product of an industry or sector is the sum of the rent to capital and the wage to labor as shown in equation

$$Y_0 = W_0 L + i_0 K \qquad (1)$$

W_0 is the average wage at time zero and i_0 is the average return to capital at time zero.

Equation

$$\frac{Y_1}{Y_0} = C_o \left(W_0 \frac{L_1}{L_0} + i_0 \frac{K_1}{K_0} \right) \qquad (2)$$

shows the percentage growth in output over a time period, holding wages and capital's return fixed. That is, the percentage increase in output is a weighted sum of the percentage increases in labor and capital. In general the increase in output will be greater than the changes in labor and capital would indicate. C_o is introduced to account for an increase in efficiency; it is a measure of technological change. Thus, a measure of technological change is implicit in national income accounting.

7

The simplicity of this approach has many advantages that aid understanding and exposition. Given perfect competition and a linear homogeneous production function, equation (1) can be viewed both normatively and descriptively; it is both an efficiency and distribution statement. Competition guarantees that labor and capital will be paid their marginal products: W_0 and i_0. Under these assumptions (and some others about externalities), equation (1) may be viewed as an exact descriptive statement of the economy and a guarantee that the economy is at a Pareto optimum.

To get from equation (1) to equation (2), consider what the output in period 1 would be if the inputs of period O were used. If period 1 output is greater, there must have been a change in efficiency which is measured by the ratio of outputs in the two periods.

Since (2) comes so directly from national income accounting, some economists have assumed that:

> The output-per-unit-of-input method avoids the specification of a production function ... the only assumption underlying the production function is that of no economies of scale. [Barzel 1963 p. 396]

However, in addition to these requirements, Domar points out other assumptions implicit in the approach; for

> the marginal products of the inputs are changed only by the "other forces" and always in the same proportion, so that their ratios remain constant and independent of the ratio of the quantities of the inputs, however fast capital may grow relative to labor. [Domar 1962 p. 601]

In other words, it is assumed that W and i are changed only by technological change. Yet, what could be more at variance with neo-classical theory than that a change in the capital-labor ratio should not change the relative marginal products of the two? Thus, the assumption that is critical here is that capital and labor increase in approximately the same proportion and that W and i are affected only by technological change.[1]

Over a short period of time, assuming that prices are affected only by technological change might be a reasonable approximation, although over a longer period it clearly is not. Kendrick (1961) attempts to circumvent this problem by changing the price weights. However, the interpretation of the implied production function now becomes completely muddled. With constant prices, the implicit assumption is that, at the point where the economy is operating, the isoquant is shifted out along a ray from the origin. However, with changing prices the picture is one of movements along a ray and subsequent sideward movements along the isoquant. The technological change measure, which is a measure of the amount of shift along the ray, now becomes difficult to interpret.

These concepts are illustrated in Figure 2.1. In period 1 (point 1 on the

[1]Implicit in the discussion is the "neutrality" of technological change to be discussed at this point.

diagram) the economy is at point 1 with given price and capital labor ratios. By period 2 a movement has taken place which has preserved both ratios. The technological change index of 1.5 is valid since no underlying assumptions have been violated. Had the economy ended up at 2′ there might have been some difficulty in getting a good measure of technological change. Since both ratios would have varied, the measures should be questionable, using either constant or current prices. In this case, the measures of technological change would be 1.6 and 1.8 respectively. On the other hand, the path might be thought of as having two parts. First, the economy shifts to 2; then it follows the isoquant to 2′. If the path is broken up in this way, it is clear that the proper measure of technological change is the one from 1 to 2: $C = 1.5$.

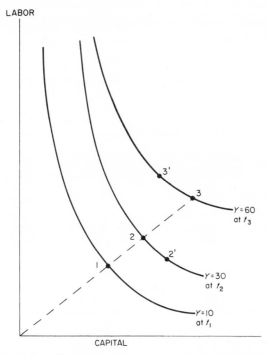

Figure 2-1. Illustration of the Technological Change Index

In going from 2 to 3, the capital–labor ratio is preserved, while prices vary due to a nonparallel shift in the isoquant. The measure of technological change is independent of the price weights since capital and labor shift proportionally and $C = 1.33$. In this case the nonparallel shift of the isoquant prevents an exact measure of the change. The measure depends on the relevant capital–labor ratios.

In the shift from 2′ to 3′ the price ratios are constant while the capital–

labor ratio is varied. In this case the use of constant prices results in zero technological change, while current prices yield a change of .857. Again, there is no exact measure of technological change possible.

Finally, in the shift from either 2 to 3′ or 2′ to 3, none of the properties remain constant: the ratios vary and the isoquant shift is not parallel. The measures given by the different prices show little consistency. This situation is inherently poor and there are only better approximations, not correct measures, of technological change.

In all these shifts, except the ones holding the capital–labor ratio fixed (1 to 2 and 2 to 3) the results are different for current prices than they are for constant prices. A movement along an isoquant from 3 to 3′ gives a shift of .96 in constant prices and .90 in current prices. The reverse movement from 3′ to 3 gives shifts of 1.00 and 1.07. The assumption that price changes result only from technological change is dramatized in this example. Of the various movements shown in Table 1, only the shift from 1 to 2 satisfies the above assumptions.

Table 2.1   Arithmetic Technological Change

Period	Y	K	L	$\dfrac{W}{i}$	Between m and n		C_m (Period m Prices)	C_n (Period n Prices)
1	10	12	8	1	1	2	1.5	1.5
2	30	24	16	1	1	2′	1.6	1.8
2′	30	30	10	2	2	3	1.33	1.33
3	60	36	24	3	2	3′	1.28	1.2
3′	60	30	30	2	2′	3	1.11	1.0
					2′	3′	1.0	0.857
					3	3′	0.76	0.90
					3′	3	1.0	1.07

$$C_j = \frac{Y_m}{Y_n} \frac{1}{W_j \dfrac{L_m}{L_n} + i_j \dfrac{K_m}{K_n}}$$

Since there is no evidence that one set of prices is preferable to another, it might be argued that changing the price weights just adds another element of confusion to the problem. However, insofar as producers engage in maximizing behavior, the relevant variable is that of current relative prices. The problem would be solved if all prices shifted by the same factor, thus leaving relative prices unchanged. But all price shifts are not similar so that the use of constant prices tends to distort the efficiency of current production decisions. Unfortunately, the index number problem has reared its head and no general solution is possible.

The Dynamic Input-Output Index

Not much will be said about this particular measure. Leontief (1953) has used it over such periods as 1929–1939, but its use has not been general for two reasons. First of all there are the nearly prohibitive assumptions involved in setting up an input–output table. Added to these are additional ones required for dynamic stability. Finally, there is the problem of the amount of computation required to derive the two tables and the index.

The Geometric or Solow Index

Robert Solow (1957) derived a measure of technological change from very general assumptions. The derivation is characterized by the assumption of an aggregate production function of two factors that exhibits constant returns to scale. This function is

$$Y = A(t)f(K, L) \tag{3}$$

Solow also uses the standard assumptions that the function be homogeneous, that the economy be perfectly competitive, that there be no errors of measurement in the data, and that there be the stringent assumption of neutral technological change (isoquants shift out parallel to each other). The technological change between two periods is then given by equation

$$\frac{\Delta A}{A} = \frac{\Delta Y}{Y} - W_K \frac{\Delta K}{K} - W_L \frac{\Delta L}{L} \tag{4}$$

where Y, K, and L are defined as the aggregates for society and W_K and W_L are the elasticities of output with respect to capital and labor. The formula can also be written intensively (with the data in "per labor" units)

$$\frac{\Delta A}{A} = \frac{\Delta y}{y} - W_K \frac{\Delta k}{k} \tag{5}$$

where y and k are Y/L and K/L respectively.

Equation (4) has a relatively straightforward interpretation; it is that technological change is equal to the change in output not accounted for by the changes in capital and labor. Whatever part of output is not explained by increases in capital and labor must be assigned to technological change. The terms which delineate the influences of capital and labor are also easily interpreted. Each term is the change in a factor weighted by the elasticity of output with respect to that factor.

Under Solow's assumptions, the share of a factor in output will be equal[2]

[2] $$\frac{\frac{\partial Y}{\partial K}K}{Y} = \frac{\frac{\partial Y}{Y}}{\frac{\partial K}{K}}$$

to the elasticity of output with respect to that factor. Thus, the change in the factor is weighted by the share of the factor in output. The formula is an example of neo-classical theory applied to an aggregate production function and the measurement of technological change.[3]

The geometric or Solow index is illustrated in Figure 2.1. The technological change indices are shown in Table 2.2. The proper measure of factor shares from the derivation is the one of current shares; the index involving constant, period 1 shares will be used later.

Table 2.2   Geometric Technological Change

Period	Y	K	L	$\dfrac{W}{i}$	W_K	Between — and —		A in Period 1 Shares	A in Current Shares
1	10	12	8	1	.6	1	2	2	2
2	30	24	16	1	.6	1	2′	2	2
2′	30	30	10	2	.6	2	3	1.5	1.5
3	60	36	24	3	.33	2	3′	1.5	1.625
3′	60	30	30	2	.33	2′	3	1.4	1.133
						2′	3′	1.2	0.667
						3	3′	1.0	0.89
						3′	3	0.96	1.067

$$A(2) = 1 + \frac{Y_2 - Y_1}{Y_1} - W_K \frac{K_2 - K_1}{K_1} - W_L \frac{L_2 - L_1}{L_1}$$

Technological change is neutral in the shift from period 1 to period 2. When technological change is no longer neutral, as from period 2 to period 3, the formula yields an approximation of the true amount of technological change. Note that when factors increase proportionally, as from period 2 to period 3, it makes no difference which weighting scheme (current or constant shares) is used.

The shifts from 3 to 3′ and back should give technological change indices of 1.0. That they do not indicates a difficulty in the analysis: the derivation is strictly true only for infinitesimal changes. When the changes are finite, the correct ratio is not $(Y_2 - Y_1)/Y_1$, but $(Y_2 - Y_1)/Y_j$, where Y_j is somewhere between Y_1 and Y_2. The larger the shifts, the larger the error stemming from this incorrect divisor is likely to be. However, for the data to which the formula is generally applied, this error tends to be negligible.

Domar (1961) gives a more general interpretation to the Solow measure. He considers the measure of technological change to be an index number of the sort generated by the arithmetic index described above. In the Solow measure factor changes are combined geometrically (weighting by the elas-

---

[3]Problems with aggregation are relevant here and might be crucial to the analysis.

ticity of output with respect to each factor) rather than arithmetically (weighting by prices). This difference in weighting produces indices with different characteristics: in the arithmatic index, relative prices must be constant except for shifts resulting from technological change; in the geometric index, relative shares must be constant. The constancy of relative shares is not required for the derivation; it results from Domar's added assumption that the aggregate production function (3) is a Cobb-Douglas function. However, with this assumption Domar is able to make a case for an index number that seems to be independent of the notion of an aggregate production function with all of its accompanying implications.

One of the critical assumptions underlying Solow's derivation is the neutrality of the technological change. It must be assumed that technological change does not shift the ratio of the marginal product of capital to the marginal product of labor. While neutrality might seem a relevant first approximation, it is not so easy to accept over long periods of time. After all, why shouldn't technological change shift the isoquant to favor labor or capital? Why should all changes in the share of capital in income be due to relative increases in the capital stock? The degree of neutrality in measured technological change is investigated below.

Domar (1961) notes that the measure of technological change is influenced by the choice of a production function that includes raw materials. Including raw materials leads to a smaller index of technological change. Griliches (1963) suggests that this effect is large in the case of United States agriculture. He argues that the role of intermediate products has increased over time and so the value of the added measure is strongly biased upward.

Another problem of measurement arises in connection with capital. Of all the series required to measure technological change, the capital series is certainly the worst. The underpinnings of data for the capital series are weak. There are even theoretical difficulties concerning what should be included in the capital stock and thus what measure is most appropriate for equation (4). Johansen (1961) has derived a measure of technological change which leaves capital out. This work is described below.

Aggregate Production Functions

Solow's 1957 paper was attacked from both sides of the Atlantic. The diffculty in one form or another was the assumption of an aggregate production function. There are numerous theoretical and practical problems in conceiving of such a function and measuring it. In general, the existence of an aggregate production function would require a homogeneous labor force and a kind of capital jelly that is potentially capable of being combined with labor in any given proportions. In addition, measurement problems arise unless output can be produced by any desired combination of capital or labor.

On another level, one might conceive of aggregating the data of many firms, each of which is operating on a known production function. The circumstances under which the aggregate production function exists have been dealt with in the post war literature (Green [1964]). In general, the individual firm functions must be correctly specified and measured without error (see Chapter 7).

Joan Robinson criticized Solow's implicit assumption of a high elasticity of substitution of capital for labor and of capital for capital. She argued that it was essentially impossible to substitute one piece of capital for another, or to substitute capital for labor. In a more accurate model, the heterogeneous items that make up the capital stock of society would be specified in detail. She contended that as a description of reality, the homogeneous, two factor aggregate production function was sheer nonsense.

Samuelson (1962) has argued that Mrs. Robinson is incorrect; that an aggregate production function with all the necessary neo-classical properties can be derived from heterogeneous capital, fixed coefficient microeconomic production functions. The argument is that every society has a convex region describing its potentialities in the wage-interest plane. The higher are wages, the lower must be the interest rate, *ceteris paribus*. Fixed coefficient, heterogeneous capital functions will give rise to straight lines in this plane. The efficiency frontier of society will be the segments of these lines farthest to the northeast (the dominant segments). A slight bit of geometry shows the resulting frontier to approximate the profile of a function with possibilities of substitution such as the Cobb-Douglas function: the greater the number of possible processes, the closer is the approximation. However, the necessary assumptions are quite stringent and this example has little generality.

Solow (1962b, 1963a) was willing to concede that Mrs. Robinson was correct in principle, but not willing to admit that this objection was sufficient to condemn all macroeconomic research. He set out to derive a measure of the error involved in treating fixed coefficient, heterogeneous capital, microeconomic functions in a Cobb-Douglas macroeconomic model. This work is described in Chapter 9. It should be noted that some further work by Barr (1965) shows the optimistic conclusions to be quite special even within the framework of Solow's Model.

In spite of the encouragement given to its use by Samuelson and Solow, the aggregate production function remains suspect. As described above, Domar reinterpreted the Solow index as a geometric index number rather than a "pure" index of technological change implied by an aggregate production function. Now, as Domar would argue, there is no magic here, and there is still an implicit function in the background. Nevertheless, progress is made to the extent that the index is recognized as an approximation and no indirect conclusions about distribution or improving future production are drawn from empirical investigations.

A number of courageous people have recently formed the opposition and embraced the aggregate production function explicitly. The argument goes that insofar as such a function is used, it is better to derive it explicitly and qualify it explicitly. Otherwise, one cannot know what the function looks like and what properties it has. Even at the risk of being bitten, one had best inspect a horse's teeth prior to purchasing it. Griliches (1963), Brown and Popkin (1962), Brown and deCani (1963), and Arrow, Chenery, Minhas, and Solow (1961) seem to agree.

The Cobb-Douglas Function

The most popular form of aggregate production function has been the linear in logs, or generalized Cobb-Douglas form. Since its introduction in 1928, no single form has enjoyed quite the same popularity. Some of the reasons for this popularity are straightforward: it is simple to explain; it is a plausible form insofar as it displays constant returns to scale, diminishing returns to a factor; and is easily estimated by standard regression techniques.

The form is also particularly easy to handle in connection with questions of aggregation. In the postwar literature it is proved that this form is consistent with geometric aggregation. Domar (1961) uses the function when asking: can technological change indices be aggregated consistently? Domar finds that they can be and he derives the formulas for various cases. For example, two firms producing only consumer goods, two firms producing some consumer goods, some intermediate goods, and so on.

Marvin Frankel (1962) uses the Cobb-Douglas form to measure technological change, but he puts a bit of a twist on it. Frankel is particularly concerned with the small role that capital has been estimated to play in the growth of output per man. As shown in Chapter 9, he manages to transform it to a Harrod-Domar growth model where output is directly proportional to capital increases.

Brown and Popkin (1962) fit the Cobb-Douglas function using aggregate data. They isolate "technological epochs"; periods whose technology is relatively homogeneous and significantly different from surrounding epochs. They are able to estimate the extent of non-neutral technological change as well as to provide a direct measure of neutral technological change.

The Constant Elasticity of Substitution Function

In spite of the popularity of the Cobb-Douglas function, its implicit assumption of a unitary elasticity of substitution has been widely questioned.

Perhaps the most popular assumption has been that of zero elasticity used by Walras, Leontief, Harrod, and Domar, to mention only a few. On the other hand, there may be cases where the elasticity of substitution is greater than unity.

Arrow, Chenery, Minhas, and Solow (1961) have derived a more general production function which allows the elasticity of substitution to be estimated. This constant elasticity of substitution (or CES) function also contains efficiency and distribution parameters so that technological change, both neutral and non-neutral, can be estimated. In applying the CES function to industries in different countries, they find that the elasticity is generally different from unity. They conclude that the Cobb-Douglas function is not likely to be the correct form.

Ferguson (1963) also questions the validity of the aggregate production function. He asks whether the estimated function is really capable of describing the available tradeoffs between capital and labor, as would a production function, or whether its use isn't more limited. Is there an aggregate production function generating these observations? Is the quality of these observations such that this aggregate function can be estimated?

Ferguson suggests that observations of the distribution of national income give rise to an aggregate distribution function rather than a production function. Of course, assuming perfect competition and some specific form of aggregate production function, we are inescapably led from a distribution function to a production function. However, when interpreted strictly, a production function describes the relation between physical inputs and physical outputs. On an aggregate level, such physical statements cannot be made, nor can many of the implications be assumed to hold. The alternative of washing one's hands of the whole business, of naming the estimated relation a "distribution function," and investing its specific properties has some appeal.

The elasticity of substitution is important in the distribution of income. Hicks (1935) pointed out that, when the elasticity of substitution is greater than one, an increase in a factor will increase its share of output. Conversely, an elasticity of substitution less than one will cause the share of an increasing factor to decrease. Brown and deCani (1963) use these observations as descriptions of the properties of the aggregate production function and find an independent way of deriving the CES function.

A third way of deriving the CES function is given by Kamien (1965). The production function implied by a set of log-linear demand equations is their CES function.

The Johansen Approach

One can hardly set out to measure technological change without some knowledge of the available data and the quality of the data sources. Formula

(4) requires series on output, labor, capital, and the share of capital in income. The quality of the series on output and labor is likely to be high, while the quality of the other two is dubious. Of these two, capital's share is less important (Chapter 5) and involves fewer problems, both conceptual and empirical, than the measurement of capital itself. For example, should one measure capital stock (capital available) or the flow of capital services (capital in use)? To what extent does the depreciation series reflect the true depreciation and obsolescence of the capital?[4] For these and other reasons, the capital series leaves much to be desired. Both Massell (1960) and Solow (1957) discussed the quality of their series at length.

Johansen (1961) sets out to derive a measure of technological change which does not use capital data.[5] Starting from the usual Cobb-Douglas formulation, he adds the assumption that producers minimize total costs for a given level of output treating the wage rate and return to capital as fixed. The only additional assumption required is a constant structure of capital costs across industries. He derives formula

$$\frac{a_{it}}{a_{it+1}} = C + \beta \frac{w_{it}}{w_{it+1}} + E_{it} \qquad (7)$$

where a_{it} is the productivity (output per man) in the ith industry at the tth time, w is the proportional increase in wages, C is the average level of technological change across industries, β is the elasticity of output with respect to capital, and E_{it} is the technological change in the ith industry over the time period.

The function can be estimated in either of two ways. If one has series for productivity in the two periods, for the wage increase and for the elasticity of output with respect to capital, technological change can be calculated in a straightforward fashion. Alternatively, Johansen's method is relevant when the relative increase in wages is unknown. In this case one can make the additional assumption that the wage increase in all industries is the same, and proceed to estimate w by ordinary regression techniques. The error term is the estimate of technological change. Chapter 3 presents the application of this measure to United States manufacturing.

The Griliches Approach

Unfortunately, to define technological change as the unexplained portion of the increase in output per man is not very informative. It does not explain what caused the increase in output per man; it doesn't indicate what part of the residual is due to increases in efficiency and what part to increasing returns to scale. There is also the question of the usefulness of a production

---

[4]This problem is taken up in Chapter 10.

[5]Brown (1965) also derives a measure of technological change which makes no use of capital data.

function which is expected to shift regularly. Shouldn't a production function be stable and all increase in output be directly attributable to increases in some factor? In view of these objections, Griliches (1963) sets out to find an alternative measure of technological change which will include a production function with which all increases in productivity might be explained.

An alternative to the general model might be one which would explain that part of the increase in output which is explained neither by increases in capital nor labor. That is, one could take the Solow measure of technological change and attempt to explain it. The advantage of the more general approach is that the problem is dealt with explicitly. Production functions can be constructed with all the relevant variables. Further, it is possible to adjust the independent variables, such as labor, for quality changes. On the other hand, the disadvantages of it are that the more general method depends on the use of an aggregate production function which is not especially realistic. If the aggregate function is really no more than a "distribution function" whose properties must be investigated explicitly, the more general approach will require a good deal more estimation and data. Further, the estimation of such a function is subject to all the usual econometric problems including spurious correlation and multicollinearity. Indeed, adjusting a variable for quality changes is a procedure of questionable validity as it is tantamount to tampering with the data.

What Griliches does is to estimate a production function for the agricultural sector at one period and then substitute in the values of the parameters at some later period to see how much of the increase in output is explained by each factor and whether there is any unexplained increase to be allocated to technological change. The results are discussed in Chapter 4.

Microeconomic Production Functions

Although the macroeconomic production function is a concept of dubious validity, the microeconomic production function has a more secure foundation in economic theory. Heady and Dillon (1961) have estimated microeconomic production functions for different agricultural commodities. They have computed physical production functions that, for example, show the weight increases in hogs when fed any number of possible diets. The function actually shows the tradeoffs between bushels of grain and pounds of pork.

Kurz and Manne (1963) have estimated a function giving the tradeoffs between capital and labor for machine tasks. The data consist of the tasks normally encountered in machining, the machines that can perform these tasks, the number of men required to operate the machine, and the output per day. Given the capital cost of the machines, they attempt to estimate the capital–labor tradeoffs. The estimated function is one of the best production function estimated to date.

There is a difference between the microeconomic technological change concept discussed in this section and the macroeconomic technological change concept discussed above. The former might be estimated by looking at production functions that embody the latest, most advanced machines, then measuring the increase in technological knowledge over the period. The macroeconomic measurements have all been of the *average* level of efficiency between two periods. In this case there was the distinct possibility of negative technological change over a period when a depression threw factors out of work. Thus the macroeconomic measure is perhaps the one most useful for questions of society's welfare since it measures what the economy has actually accomplished.

A Comparison of Methods

These seemingly diverse methods of measuring technological change have much in common. In this section the Solow index, or rather the Solow index as reinterpreted by Domar is used as a standard for comparison. Technological change is measured as the increase in output per man not accounted for by increases in capital per man, where the latter term is defined as the increase in capital per man times the elasticity of output with respect to capital. This geometric index number differs from the Solow index in that it is based on the assumption of constant relative shares. The advantage of this additional assumption is an interpretation of the technological change index which is independent of an aggregate production function: it is simply a geometric index number with constant factor shares as weights. No aggregate production function can be specified without additional assumptions such as perfect competition and the absence of aggregation problems.

Using the arithmetic index, technological change is given as a weighted average of the change in prices, holding inputs constant. That is, it is assumed that relative factor prices are constant except for technological change. Unfortunately, any shift in prices due to changes in tastes or a relative increase in one factor becomes technological change. The geometric index rests on the assumption of constant factor shares in the absence of technological change.

One of the great statistical regularities noted in the early part of this century was the constancy of relative shares (Bowley's law). In the post-World War II period this constancy is less obvious. However, at worst, the amount of shift is small and it has been argued to be nonexistent (Grant [1963]). Since relative prices have been anything but constant, the geometric index seems to better approximate reality than does the arithmetic one.

At first glance a comparison of this index to the Leontief index would seem unreasonable. They are based on very different assumptions and were designed to do different things. However, Domar shows that for one or two industries producing final goods, the two indices will give identical results. Only when the question of the integration of industries arises do the measures differ. When aggregating industries which produce goods for each other as well as final goods, the Leontief index is dependent on the degree of integration. However, the similarity of the two indices seems remarkable in view of their origins.

Another alternative to the geometric index is an aggregate production function of the Cobb-Douglas variety as fitted by Brown and Popkin.[6] They are able to take account of non-neutral technological changes and non-constant returns to scale and thus enhance the measure of technological change. However, all of the objections of aggregate production functions pertain here. The data may not be suitable for estimation and it may not really be a production function that is being estimated after all. Brown and Popkin substitute non-neutrality and returns to scale for an aggregate production function. Depending on the degree of non-neutrality, the Brown-Popkin version might give superior estimates.

The Griliches model has been considered as an example of a macroeconomic production function. Although it is subject to the limitations of aggregate production functions, this measure is an attempt to get at technological change directly, to estimate its causes and effects. The main service of this model is that is brings everything out into the open so that each difficulty may be considered in turn.

The Johansen formulation depends upon unrealistic capital series. Capital series are not necessary as long as series are known for output, labor, and capital's share; the increase in wages substitutes for capital increase. In the special case where the wage increase is unknown, Johansen sets up a regression model that makes use of the assumption that the wage increase across industries is identical. While such an assumption appears to be approximately true in practice, it is still an assumption. Observable data series might have been used instead.

Finally, the microeconomic measures of technological change were considered. They are based on production functions fitted to either value or physical data. The value function is an analogue of the macroeconomic function to which many of the above criticisms lose some of their importance. The physical production function is quite different since it is a measure of the most efficient production possible under the current technical knowledge. As such it is not a description of efficiency in practice as are the others; it is a description of the known technology. This microeconomic measure can be calculated so as to be immune to the above difficulties. But policy concerns are not on the level of the individual process, but rather at more aggregate levels: the product, the firm, the industry, the economy. The pure micro-

[6]The method is more general and might be used with other forms of production function.

economic approach is subject to the difficulty of combining the technological change indices of each process to get the more aggregate index that is of interest.

Bibliography

Section A: the arithmetic index. Abramovitz 1956, 1962; Clemhout 1963; Denison 1962; Denton 1964; Domar 1961, 1962; Domar *et al.* 1964; Fabricant 1959; Kendrick 1958, 1961; Reddeway and Smith 1960; Ruttan and Stout 1958.

Section B: the Leontief index. Domar 1961; Leontief 1953, 1964; Schmookler 1952; Sheshinski 1964.

Section C: the geometric index. Aukrust 1959; Domar 1961; Edwards and Drane 1963; Hogan 1958; Levine 1960; Lundberg 1961; Massell 1960, 1962a, 1962b; Niitamo 1958; Pasinetti 1960; Solow, 1957; Tinbergen 1942.

Section D: aggregate production functions. Green 1964; Griliches and Grunfeld 1960; Houthakker 1955; Massell 1964; Nelson 1964; Peston 1959; Samuelson 1962; Solow 1962a, 1963a; Theil 1954.

Section E: the Cobb-Douglas function. Brown and Popkin 1962; Dhrymes 1963; Domar 1961; Frankel 1962; Valvanis-Vail 1955; Wall 1948.

Section F: the constant elasticity of substitution function. Arrow, *et al.* 1961; Dhrymes and Kurz 1964; Diwan 1964; Ferguson 1963, 1965a, 1965b; Kamien 1965; Kendrick and Sato 1963; Kmenta 1964; Kurz 1963; Marcus 1964; McFadden 1963, 1964; Minhas 1963; Mukerji 1963; Sheshinski 1964; Uzawa 1962; Whitaker 1964.

Section G: the Johansen approach. Johansen 1957, 1960.

Section H: the Griliches approach. Griliches 1963, 1964.

Section I: microeconomic production functions. Heady and Dillon 1961; Komiya 1962; Kurz and Manne 1963; Nordin 1947; Simon 1951; Walters 1963a.

Section J: a comparison of methods. Domar 1961, 1962.

CHAPTER THREE

On the Method of Measurement: I

SECTION A
WHEN IS THE COBB-DOUGLAS FUNCTION NOT A COBB-DOUGLAS FUNCTION?
Arnold Lieberman and Lester Lave

The Hogan-Solow Controversy

Warren Hogan criticized Solow's (1957) technological change model on the grounds that Solow's estimates might not be "... independent of any hypothesis about the exact shape of the production function" (Hogan [1958] p. 411). Hogan maintained that Solow essentially assumed a Cobb-Douglas function even though Solow maintained he had not.

Actually, Solow's estimate of technological change is not dependent upon the assumption of an aggregate production function of the Cobb-Douglas type. His estimating procedure is given in equation

$$\frac{\mathring{A}}{A} = \frac{\mathring{y}}{y} - W_K \frac{\mathring{k}}{k} \tag{1}$$

But, as Hogan observed, if W_K is constant, "... and this seems very close to being the actual situation when the series shown by Solow's Table I is examined," (Hogan, [1958] p. 410) then equation (1) can be integrated to

22

the familiar Cobb-Douglas function. However, is even an essentially constant W_K series sufficient to warrant this integration? What are the effects of small variations in this series?

The Cobb-Douglas function is given in equation

$$Y = AK^{W_K}L^{W_L} \qquad W_L + W_K = 1 \qquad (2)$$

This formulation makes the shares of capital and labor in income (W_K, W_L) as well as output, technological change, capital, and labor (Y, A, K, L) functions of time. If equation (2) is differentiated totally with respect to time and normalized with respect to labor, equation

$$\frac{\mathring{A}}{A} = \frac{\mathring{y}}{y} - W_K \frac{\mathring{k}}{k} - \mathring{W}_L \log\left(\frac{L}{K}\right) \qquad (3)$$

is obtained (where $°$ indicates a derivative with respect to time). Equations (1) and (3) differ only in the final term in the latter: $\mathring{W}_L \log(L/K)$. Hogan's argument then reduces to the contention that an essentially constant W_L series (or W_K series, since $W_K + W_L = 1$) makes this term negligibly small.

This new term might be rewritten as $-(\mathring{W}_L \log L + \mathring{W}_K \log K)$. The economic meaning of the term comes in its interpretation as the change in capital's share in income weighted by the stock of capital plus the change in the share of labor in income weighted by the stock of labor. The technological change index (equation [3]) can be expressed as the percentage change in output per worker corrected for the percentage change in capital per worker (appropriately weighted) and corrected for variation in the relative shares weighted by the stocks of capital and labor.

Equation (3) might be called the Hogan measure. Its importance can be illustrated with respect to Table 2.2. In measuring technological change between periods 2' and 3, the Solow measure gives a technological change index of 1.4 in constant factor shares and of 1.13 in current factor shares. The Hogan index, which assumes a Cobb-Douglas aggregate production function with shifting factor shares, gives an index of 1.10. The value of the correction term is .30.

A more relevant comparison of the Solow and Hogan measures is given in Table 3.1 on page 28. The similarity between the two indices (Column [4] and Column [5]) is evidence that Solow's general linear homogeneous production function can indeed be approximated quite accurately by the Cobb-Douglas function, as Hogan implied, given the particular data that Solow used.

A more thorough investigation of the error term, however, produces some surprising results. Had Solow's labor series been calculated in man-years, instead of man-hours, the error term $\mathring{W}_L \log(L/K)$ would have altered the technological change index from that shown in Column (5) to one declining from 1.00 in 1909 to .938 in 1949.[1]

This strange result is caused by the fact that, unlike the Solow measure or the Cobb-Douglas form with constant factor shares, equation (3) is not independent of the units used to measure the different series. The correction term can be made relatively insignificant when the units of labor and capital are such that the ratio L/K is close to one. Choosing units that cause L/K to differ from one can make the correction term arbitrarily large.

A test, then, for the Cobb-Douglas approximation is the relative significance of the minimized divergence of L/K from 1. Some simple rules for minimizing this divergence are:

1. If W_L appears to be constant (constant growth or decay of labor's share):
    (a) and $L/K = C_0$ (L and K grow proportionately), choose units of L, K such that $C_0 = 1$.
    (b) and $L/K = C(t)$, choose units of L, K such that $C(t_k) = 1$ where t_k is at about the middle of the time series used.
2. If W_L is especially large in any one year compared to its value in all other years, then choose units of L, K such that $L/K = 1$ in the year of the largest $\dot{W}_L$.

Naturally, certain tradeoffs of the advantages in the two rules will occur according to the individual time series.

Conclusions

The existence of the term $\dot{W}_L \log(L/K)$ in equation (3) seems to contradict Hogan's assertion that Solow was essentially using a Cobb-Douglas function simply because the W_K series is fairly constant. That errors in the measurement of W_K have little effect on the measurement of technological change computed by equation (1) is demonstrated in Chapter 7. However, these variations in W_K gain appreciable significance if the underlying production function is assumed to be Cobb-Douglas and appropriate units are chosen for L and K to make L/K differ greatly from 1. A glance at the series used by Solow, however, shows that Hogan was correct in recognizing the approximation of Solow's more general function by the Cobb-Douglas form.

At first glance the conclusion seems a happy one since it tends to justify much of the previous macroeconomic work which assumed aggregate production functions of the Cobb-Douglas form. Of course, the form is rather

---

[1] The man-years series was derived by dividing the Solow series of man-hours by 1600, the approximate number of working hours hours in a year. This measure is not expected to be particularly accurate, it merely illustrates the effect of one transformation.

specialized, but the approximation is so good that it is not worthwhile computing more general forms.

However, the conclusion should not go without question that models based on the most restrictive assumptions yield conclusions which differ little from those based on the most general assumptions. Clearly, there is no point in additional assumptions which do not lead to additional results. However, the economy is not formless; it is a bit too convincing when all models lead to much the same conclusion. One must be suspicious of maps that indicate that all roads lead to Rome: either Rome is indeed the center of the universe or there are at least some misinformed cartographers.

SECTION B

A COMPARISON OF THE JOHANSEN AND SOLOW MEASURES

Lester Lave and Murray Silverman

The early papers on technological change displayed marked concern with the capital series. For example, both Solow (1957) and Massell (1960) adjusted the series for underemployment, and, further, puzzled over the proper definition of capital, quite apart from the measurement problem. Solow was dubious about the significance of the results he obtained, as capital had so small a share in raising productivity. Not so Massell. He concluded that society should devote its resources to technological change rather than to capital formation. Massell's recommendation occasions two questions: (1) Does the Solow measure correctly specify the role of capital in raising productivity? (2) How can one expedite technological change?

Johansen attempted to circumvent the problem when he derived a measure of technological change which did not use capital explicitly. His basic idea was never fully developed but the essentials of the argument are described below.

The Measurement of Capital

Technological change in Solow's model is neutral and disembodied, a kind of better air which changes nothing except the rate of production. Unfortunately this model is so abstract that many questions in capital theory are undefined. For example, one might ask whether the relevant measure is available capital or capital's services. At first Solow (1957) favored capital's services as the appropriate measure, but he has since changed his mind (1962) and now prefers available capital. Similarly there is the question of how the capital stock should be measured (See Brown [1962]). If it is measured in constant prices, all capital embodied technological change will be lumped together with Solow's residual. (See Massell [1962] p. 70.)

As already noted, there have been numerous attempts to build models of capital-embodied technological change and to measure its effect. As Solow (1959) points out,

> Improvements in technology affect output only to the extent that they are carried into practice either by net capital formation or by the replacement of old-fashioned equipment by the latest models . . . .

In general, however, these models are difficult to apply to reality and when gross approximations are made, the results hardly seem to justify the labor in developing them.[2]

The Johansen Model

Assuming that the production function for some industry is of the Cobb-Douglas type and that all inputs can be classified as either capital or labor, then equation

$$Y(t) = A(t)K(t)^{\beta(t)}L(t)^{\alpha(t)}, \tag{1}$$

describes production, where Y is the physical measure of output, K is the capital input, L is the labor input and where α and β are respectively the share of labor and capital in output, all at some time t.

Assuming constant returns to scale, $\alpha(t) + \beta(t) = 1$. The productivity of labor can be expressed as equation

$$P = \frac{Y}{L} = AK^{\beta}L^{\alpha-1} \tag{2}$$

Since $\alpha - 1 = \beta$, the equation can be simplified as in equation

$$P = A\left(\frac{K}{L}\right)^{\beta} \tag{3}$$

In equation (3) all variation in productivity not accounted for by a change in the capital-labor ratio is attributed to technological change. If capital is measured in constant prices, capital embodied technological change will be assigned to the residual. On the other hand, were capital to be measured by its value in the market under perfect competition, capital embodied technological change would be implicit in the price variable and thus changes in A would reflect only disembodied technological change.

Ideally, A would reflect only disembodied technological change if all series (Y, K, L, β) were measured in current prices in a perfectly competitive market. Changes in price would account for changes in the quality of each

[2]See the discussion in Chapter 9.

series and the whole problem of embodied change would be dealt with at its origin. The absence of such a market makes the rest of the derivation potentially interesting.

Equation (3) can be restated in terms of two periods as in equation

$$\frac{P_2}{P_1} = \frac{A_2}{A_1}\left(\frac{K_2}{L_2}\right)^{\beta_2}\left(\frac{L_1}{K_1}\right)^{\beta_1} \tag{4}$$

At this point, an artful substitution allows the elimination of capital. Assuming that firms minimize cost for a given level of output, the first order conditions of the constrained minimization yield equation

$$\frac{WL}{\alpha} = \frac{Kr}{\beta} = \lambda \tag{5}$$

Suppose in addition that relative shares are constant over time, that is, $\beta_1 = \beta_2 = \beta$. Then equation (4) is transformed into equation

$$\frac{P_2}{P_1} = \frac{A_2}{A_1}\left(\frac{W_2}{W_1}\right)^{\beta}\left(\frac{r_1}{r_2}\right)^{\beta} \tag{6}$$

As observed before, the interest rate has been fairly constant over time. Thus, a good argument could be put forth on empirical grounds that equation (6) is essentially equation

$$\frac{P_2}{P_1} = \frac{A_2}{A_1}\left(\frac{W_2}{W_1}\right)^{\beta}. \tag{7}$$

It can also be argued that r is not a determinant quantity unless K is given. Only the return on capital, Kr, is measurable. If r is taken to be constant, any variation in the return on capital will be reflected in the value of capital. Thus equation (7) is the defining equation of the measure of technological change used in this section.

There is another possible interpretation of the ratio of the wages from the two periods. Taking equation (5) at two periods of time and assuming that α, β, and r remain constant, equation

$$\frac{W_2}{W_1} = \frac{k_2}{k_1} \quad \text{where} \quad k_i = \frac{K_i}{L_i} \tag{8}$$

is derived. Thus, the ratio of wages is equal to the ratio of capital per man. Insofar as the labor market is perfectly competitive, that is, wages reflect marginal productivity, the increase in wages over two periods reflects the disembodied technological change, just as the perfect capital measure would have.

Before applying the model, some interesting features of the analysis deserve attention. If capital is readmitted to the derivation, equation (8) could be substituted into equation (7) to get equation

$$\frac{A_2}{A_1} = \frac{P_2}{P_1}\left(\frac{k_1}{k_2}\right)^{\beta} \tag{9}$$

Equations (7) and (9) comprise the *ratio method* of calculating technological change.

An interesting result is obtained by comparing equation (9) with the original Solow (1957) method of measuring the "residual." Consider small time intervals and expand equation (9).

$$\frac{A_2}{A_1} = \frac{A_2 - A_1}{A_1} + 1 = \frac{P_2}{P_1}\left(\frac{k_1}{k_2}\right)^{\beta} = \left(\frac{P_2 - P_1}{P_1} + 1\right)\left(\frac{k_1 - k_2}{k_2} + 1\right)$$

If changes in labor's productivity and capital per man-hour are small over the time interval chosen, then $\Delta P/P_1 \cong \Delta P/P_2$ and $\Delta k/k_1 \cong \Delta k/k_2$ and second order terms such as $(\Delta k)^2$ and $(\Delta k)(\Delta P)$ can be neglected. Expanding, by using the binomial theorem,

$$\frac{\Delta A}{A} + 1 = \left(\frac{\Delta P}{P} + 1\right)\left(1 - \frac{\Delta k}{k}\right)^{\beta}$$

$$= \left(\frac{\Delta P}{P} + 1\right)\left(1 - \frac{\Delta k}{k}\right)^{\beta} + \left(\frac{\Delta k}{k}\right)^2\frac{\beta^2}{2} + \cdots$$

$$= \frac{\Delta P}{P} + 1 - \left(\frac{\Delta k \Delta P}{Pk}\beta\right) - \beta\frac{\Delta k}{k} + \cdots$$

$$= \frac{\Delta P}{P} + 1 - \beta\frac{\Delta k}{k}$$

the final result (equation [10]) is precisely the Solow measure.

$$\frac{\Delta A}{A} = \frac{\Delta P}{P} - \beta\frac{\Delta k}{k} \qquad (10)$$

A comparison of (9) and (10) is given in Table 3.1. The data used come from Solow (1957). The comparison is one between Solow's measure and Johansen's measure using capital rather than wage series. The tabulated results should be strictly comparable.

Table 3.1   A Strict Comparison of the Solow and Johansen Measures

	Equation (10) Solow's Measure	Equation (9) Johansen's Measure (capital figures)
$A(1909)$	1.000	1.000
$A(1927)$	1.235	1.232
$A(1936)$	1.429	1.413
$A(1949)$	1.853	1.856

The remarkable similarity between the two methods evidenced in Table 3.1, in general, should not be expected to obtain. The binomial approximation depends on small shifts in the capital and productivity series. Since the Solow data is annual, this condition holds.

An Application of the Measure

In fitting equation (7), the possibility of errors of measurement should be noted. The equation holds between any two points in time assuming that β is constant. Now, this measure could be applied to annual data and then iterated to get a cumulative index. But such a procedure entails all the errors of measurement problems. Similarly, the measure could be applied to the two end points only, although here there would be too much dependence on two observations.

The best solution seemed to be that followed in Chapter 6, Section C: regressions are computed on the assumption that the data fit exponential curves as in equations (11) and (12).[3] Substituting these into equation (7) and rearranging gives equation (13).

$$w = ae^{bt} \tag{11}$$

$$p = ce^{dt} \tag{12}$$

$$\frac{A_2}{A_1} = \frac{e^{dt_2}}{e^{dt_1}}\left(\frac{e^{bt_1}}{e^{bt_2}}\right)^{\beta} \tag{13}$$

Finally, normalizing yields equation

$$A(t) = e^{(d-\beta b)t} \tag{14}$$

where $A(1) = 1$ and $t_1 = 0$.

The model is applied to the United States economy at the Standard Industrial Classification two-digit level.[4] Wage and productivity estimates come from Kendrick (1961). These series are extrapolations between the census years: 1899, 1909, 1919, 1929, 1937, 1948, 1953. The series of capital's share of output was calculated as one minus labor's share ($\beta = 1 - \alpha$). Labor's share in a given year for some industry is the ratio of compensation of employees to total value added. Although this estimated α displays considerable variation between 1929 and 1953, most of the variation is on a year to year basis and seems to be spurious. For five year averages, labor's share stays remarkably constant over the period. The final estimates used are based on an average over the entire period.

Insofar as β is not really constant in some industry, the assumptions of the model are not realized and the measured technological change is subject to error. This source of error, however, is not likely to be great. The exponential growth assumption seems to fit the data well since the coefficients of determination for the regressions are extremely high. Note also that the

[3]The assumption of exponential growth with respect to the technological change index occurs in Massell (1961).

[4]Technological change at this level was measured by Massell (1961). He used the Solow measure on data from 1950–1956.

results would not be very different if the measure had been applied to the end points instead of to the regression coefficients.

A measure of the share of this disembodied technological change in increased productivity is given in equation

$$\theta = 1 - \left\{ \frac{P_{1953}/A_{1953} - P_{1899}}{P_{1953} - P_{1899}} \right\} \tag{15}$$

The share of technological change varies from 35 per cent to 91 per cent in the sixteen industries considered, indicating a wide variation in the relative importance of capital formation. Contrary to previous results, more than 25 per cent of the increase in productivity may be attributed to capital. This figure is perhaps the highest estimate of the role of capital calculated to date.

One might calculate capital's share in increased productivity as the Solow measure of capital's share plus capital embodied technological change. In Solow's own informal estimate (1959), the latter adds about 50 per cent to the total measure. The above estimates indicate an even larger contribution.

If θ is plotted against $A(1953)$, a rather interesting result is shown in Figure 3.1. Disregarding the three industries with high rates of technological change, these two variables appear to be linearly related. It might be argued that there is a certain amount of inherent technological change in the economy owing to increase in education, working conditions, diets,

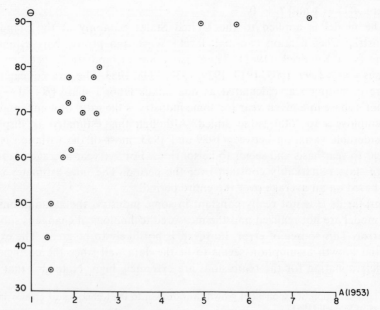

Figure 3-1.   Share of Technological Change in Increased Productivity vs. Index in 1953.

and the like. If this inherent technological change were available to all industries, the line fitted in Figure 3.1 would be expected to have a negative slope: any industry could supplement this inherent technological change with additional capital formation and so cause some induced technological change. These higher capital expenditures and high induced technological change should show up as low values of θ in connection with high values of $A(1953)$.

Yet just the opposite conclusions must be drawn from the figure; in fact, the appropriate straight line has a slight positive slope. Thus it could be argued that capital formation has a negative effect on technological change, but this conclusion is patently ridiculous. Alternatively, it might happen that industries experiencing little technological change increase the amount spent on capital formation, in order to improve their positions. Finally, technological change might be random with respect to capital expenditures, or non-neutral technological change may have been important

Table 3.2   A measure of Technological Change
in Two-Digit Manufacturing Industries

	b	d	R_p^2	R_w^2	β	$\dfrac{P(1953)-P(1899)}{P(1899)}$	$A(1953)$	θ
Food & Kindred	.0407	.0191	.921	.959	.325	91	1.37	42
Tobacco	.0388	.0556	.980	.944	.480	365	7.39	91
Textiles	.0459	.0255	.976	.954	.200	153	2.41	78
Apparel	.0414	.0205	.906	.933	.200	92	1.93	72
Paper	.0464	.0268	.959	.972	.320	139	1.90	62
Printing & Publishing	.0426	.0263	.946	.984	.210	122	2.56	80
Chemicals	.0443	.0361	.933	.968	.435	197	2.49	70
Petroleum & Coal	.053	.0402	.944	.978	.630	193	1.44	35
Rubber Products	.045	.0459	.930	.968	.300	189	5.75	90
Leather Products	.041	.0151	.938	.947	.140	80	1.65	70
Stone, Clay & Glass	.042	.0273	.961	.963	.305	125	2.19	70
Primary Metal	.044	.0216	.936	.963	.260	96	1.73	60
Fabricated Metal	.043	.0258	.971	.964	.260	117	2.20	73
N.E. Machinery	.0426	.0181	.985	.969	.260	95	1.46	50
Electrical Machinery	.0428	.0233	.942	.979	.260	133	1.93	77
Transportation Equipt.	.0476	.0391	.883	.934	.200	134	4.90	90

b is the wage regression coefficient: $w_t = ae^{bt}e^\varepsilon$
d is the productivity regression coefficient: $P_t = Ce^{dt}c^\varepsilon$
R_p^2 is the coefficient of determination for the productivity regression
R_w^2 is the coefficient of determination for the wage regression
β is capital's share in output computed as $1 - \dfrac{\text{Compensation to employee}}{\text{value added}}$
$P(1953) - P(1899)$ is Kendrick's increase in productivity
$A(1953)$ is the estimated technological change index for 1953; $A(1899) = 1$
θ is the percentage share of increased productivity due to the measured technological change.

Summary

This discussion of the comparability of the Solow and Johansen measures of technological change indicates that, when Solow's data are used, the two measures are practically identical. A more general measure is presented which is based on the assumption that wages reflect their marginal productivity, thus taking embodied technological change into account. When this new measure is applied to sixteen two-digit industries the importance of capital to increased productivity is amplified.

CHAPTER FOUR

Some Estimates of Technological Change

Introduction

Almost everyone who has made a contribution to the theory of technological change has made an attempt to measure it. The work has ranged from casual estimates to careful ones. And yet this work is consistent. Even for different measures it remains true that increases in productivity (output per man) have been considerable and thus so has technological change.

Previous investigations are summarized in this chapter under four headings: United States manufacturing, agriculture, services, and foreign technological change indices. These categories hardly comprise all of the work, especially not that directly intended for policy application, for example, Brown and deCani (1963). However, many of these other studies are mentioned in later chapters.

United States Manufacturing

Solow tried to estimate technological change from 1909 to 1949 for the private, nonfarm sector, using equation

$$\frac{\Delta A}{A} = \frac{\Delta y}{y} - W_K \frac{\Delta k}{k} \tag{1}$$

This formula requires series on total output, labor, capital, and capital's share of income. Good quality series are available for the first two variables, but any series for capital is bound to be arbitrary in places. Since Solow was trying to get a series of capital in use (one corrected for utilization), he assumed that capital and labor were unemployed at the same rate during depressions. The adjustment seems to entail an implicit assumption of fixed factor proportions, a strange assumption considering the underlying Cobb-Douglas production function. Finally, the data series for the share of capital in income is based on the judgment that W_K is approximately 35 per cent of value added. The resulting technological change index rose from 1.0 in 1909 to 1.8 in 1949 or at an annual growth rate of 1-1/2 per cent.

In his attempt to separate the growth in productivity which was caused by growth in capital, from that due to technological change, Solow found that the capital increase accounted for approximately 12-1/2 per cent of increased productivity, while technological change accounted for 88 per cent.

Unfortunately, Solow's paper was marred by some arithmetical errors in the calculation of the technological change series (Hogan [1958]; Levine [1960]). Capital's share in increasing productivity should have been 19 per cent, not 12-1/2 per cent. Solow claimed that he started with a general homogeneous production function and then concluded that it was linear from the fact that the sum of the shares of capital and labor was always extremely close to one. This argument is an extremely tenuous one (see Simon and Levy, [1963]) and, upon reconsideration, Solow noted that linearity was more a plausible assumption than a conclusion from the evidence.

At highly aggregated levels, there is little that the economist would call "rigorous theory." Quite beyond the fact that relations are approximate, econometricians would be hard put to specify just what it is these relations are alleged to be approximating. In building a model the usual criterion for accepting assumptions is plausibility within the range the model is to cover. Unfortunately, a wide range of assumptions is consistent with this criterion in macroeconomic models. Some attempts have been made to reject a set of assumptions by showing they are implausible if carried to their logical conclusion. However, *reductio ad absurdum* leaves the field virtually bare; it is as overly restrictive as "plausibility within the observed range" is inadequately weak.

Hogan objected to Solow's use of gross capital as his index of capital. He contended that this assumption implied that capital was a "one hoss shay," that is, it wore out with a final usage leaving no salvage value. A net measure of capital is found to give slightly different but parallel results. Solow argues that Hogan's net series is no better an approximation than his, since Hogan assumes that depreciation is an accurate measure of the loss in productivity.

Solow has a difficult time estimating the share of capital in output. He relied upon some data and many guesses. The resulting series exhibited only slight variation and gave Hogan grounds for arguing that Solow was essentially assuming a Cobb-Douglas function instead of a more general one (see Chapter 3).

Benton Massell (1960) attempted to reestimate Solow's index with improved data so as to avoid many of the criticisms Solow encountered. In an attempt to render the aggregate production function more meaningful, he restricted the investigation to the manufacturing sector. In this way he was hoping to get a more homogeneous set of inputs and outputs.

However, Massell's results were quite similar to Solow's. His technological change index rises from 1.0 in 1919 to 2.9 in 1955. He also argues the plausibility of his series as it exhibits predictable drops in depressions.

For a great many reasons, Solow did not draw the "obvious" conclusion from his findings. Massell seemed encouraged by the fact that his corrections and modifications produced a result so close to Solow's. He argues that the neo-classical emphasis on capital deepening is unimportant; society's resources should be spent on augmenting technological change. Of course, the analysis does not indicate in what ways money should be spent to expedite technological change; but something of such obvious importance must be promoted. Solow's reluctance to draw the conclusion might have come from this observation or from the aggregate nature of the analysis and the poor data series. It is interesting to note that Massell (1961) followed Solow (1960) in deciding later that capital deepening was important.

After further study, Solow (1960) contended that capital's importance was small because his 1957 model did not take its true role into account: technological change might be embodied in new capital. This model can be reduced to a form identical to the 1957 model where now the measure of capital is one of "effective capital." Nelson (1964) has estimated this model for the United States economy over the period 1929 to 1960. Since the difference between effective capital and measured capital depends on the average age of the capital stock, these two measures will not differ in the long run. In fact, over the thirty-one year period the measures are identical although the "embodiment effect" is about 1/6 of measured technological change in the period 1954–60.

Resek (1963) concludes that the manufacturing sector experienced three technological epochs from 1919–1959. The test is one of the relation between the capital–labor ratio and the marginal rate of substitution of capital for labor. The first epoch occurred from 1919–1929 and seems reasonably consistent by his criterion; the second epoch, between 1930 and 1939, is somewhat less consistent; a final epoch, 1940–1959, does not seem to satisfy Resek's definition of an epoch; it displays almost no consistency. Within these epochs, Resek measures the influence on increasing productivity of capital, technological change, and an interaction term. These three play roles of 10.3 per cent, 60.5 per cent, and 29.2 per cent respectively. These shares are quite close to those derived by Solow.

Brown and Popkin (1962) estimate an aggregate Cobb-Douglas function and discover three technological epochs over the 1890–1958 period: 1890–1918, 1919–1937, and 1938–1958. A summary of their results is given in Table 4.1

Table 4.1   Brown-Popkin Estimates of Non-neutral Technological Change

	Capital Coefficient	Labor Coefficient	Returns to Scale
1890–1918	0.49	0.98	1.47
1919–1937	0.60	0.44	1.04
1938–1958	0.53	0.51	1.04

Note their estimate of increasing returns during the first epoch and constant returns after that. Over the last two epochs, 1919–1958, they estimate the contributions to output as due to increases in inputs (labor and capital): 59.6 per cent, and non-neutral technological change: −3.1 per cent. Again, these estimates are close to preceding ones once it is realized that labor as well as capital is measured in the "input increase" category. Redefining the input category to include only capital, in accordance with previous definitions of it, technological change accounts for about 70 per cent of the increase. This paper will receive more careful attention in Chapter 10.

Brown and deCani use the more general CES production function to estimate technological change using these same data. This paper will be treated in Chapter 9.

In developing the CES production function Arrow, Chenery, Minhas, and Solow made use of international data on industries in 19 countries. The data range from reasonable approximations of reality to guesses about it. C. E. Ferguson (1963) set out to reestimate the function with better data. Using data from the United States Census of Manufacturing (1947, 1954, and 1958) at the two-digit level, he estimated the elasticity of substitution between capital and labor, the coefficient b in equation

$$\log v = \log A + b \log w + e \qquad (3)$$

where v is the value added of an industry per worker and w is the wage rate.

The results may be summarized briefly as inconclusive and inconsistent. Half the $R^2 s$ are not significant and the estimated elasticities vary from .54 to 2.5. Furthermore, the elasticities vary from year to year within the same industry. Very few of the results (13 per cent) definitely place b in the 0–1 interval that ACMS found so common. What is worse, for 16 per cent of the industries, the estimated elasticities were significantly greater than unity.

It is dificult to understand how Ferguson got the results he did. It might be that they were a product of the relatively small amount of variation in value added per man-hour in different parts of the country for the same industry. In this case, the results would reflect errors of observation and not much else.

It might be argued that, for changes in the wage rate, the direction of change of labor's share in output is a function of the elasticity of substitution. A high elasticity of substitution indicates that the industry would be able to substitute capital for labor, a low elasticity indicates it would be much more difficult for an industry to make this substitution. Given a wage increase, industries in the former category would substitute capital for labor and labor's share in value added would tend to fall; industries in the latter category would not be able to make such a substitution and so labor's share would tend to rise. This observation can be tested, assuming the cost of capital is equal over the United States, by observing whether the correlation between labor's share and the average wage rate is positive for inelastic industries and negative for elastic ones. Ferguson performs this test and finds the results quite good.

This outcome is not unexpected, particularly when we realize that Ferguson is correlating wages with the ratio of wages to value added per man. Now, for the regression, w/v is set equal to $1/b$. For elastic industries the ratio must be greater than one and vice versa for inelastic industries. Ferguson restricts the range of w/v to be greater than one for elastic industries. If the range of w has not been greatly diminished, the correlation must be negative. Similarly w/v for inelastic industries is significantly less than unity and the same argument would indicate slight positive correlations of the sort found by Ferguson.

Thus, Ferguson's result seems to be a negative one: the function is not an adequate description of the aggregate production function for United States manufacturing over the 1947–1958 period.

Diwan (1964) estimated the CES function for United States manufacturing over the period 1919–1958. As he found an elasticity of substitution significantly less than unity and increasing returns to scale, it is interesting to compare his study to Ferguson's. First, Ferguson employs cross section data while Diwan uses time series data. Second, Ferguson assumed constant returns to scale, while Diwan found increasing returns; and third, the time periods covered were not the same. The differences in results are thus not surprising.

Some of the most appealing results in the measurement of technological change come from disaggregation into sectors such as agriculture. At this level, the aggregate production function seems to have more meaning, is easily interpreted, and can be tested.

United States Agriculture

Chapter 5 is an application of the Solow measure to agriculture. The measure is of particular interest since agriculture offers one of the most restricted and homogeneous sectors so far explored. The technological change index rose from 1 in 1850 to 5.4 in 1958 or an annual growth rate of 1-5/8 per cent. Over the period 1910–1950, the rate of technological change, about 2.5 per cent per year, was almost double the rate Solow found for the private, nonfarm sector, about 1.5 per cent per year. Over the 108 year period, capital accounted for about 1/3 of the rise in productivity while technological change accounted for the other 2/3.

Difficulties in compiling the data series required for the index led to a sensitivity analysis of the Solow measure. Assuming errors of measurement at the beginning of the period, the measure appeared insensitive to errors in the capital series. The share of capital in income series also turned out to be noncritical. The measure is sensitive to errors in both the output series and labor series. Chapter 6 contains further sensitivity tests.

In Chapter 7, the Solow index is calculated for agriculture at four levels of aggregation over the period 1870–1960. Technological change indices are derived for (1) the total agriculture sector, (2) the 10 BAE regions that make up agriculture, (3) the five states in one of the BAE regions, the Corn Belt, and (4) six counties in each of two states in the Corn Belt. The estimates of technological change were consistent at all levels of aggregation and corresponded roughly to the estimates of Chapter 5.

Griliches (1963) investigated technological change for the period 1947–49 to 1960. He fit an aggregate cross section production function for the initial period 1947–49 and then substituted 1960 inputs into the formula to derive the 1960 output that would have been produced with 1947–49 inputs and technology. Griliches finds high increasing returns to scale (1.36) with individual coefficients of labor = .45, capital = .62, and intermediate products = .29. This method is described in detail in Chapter 2.

He adjusts the factor inputs for quality changes not reflected in the official indices. These corrections are one-sided, since no account is taken of quality changes in outputs. There is some difficulty in the conclusion of increasing returns. Griliches (1957) showed that empirical production functions would tend to show increasing returns. Depending on which of the corrections one accepts, the technological change index over the period is between 1.48 (constant returns to scale, no quality adjustments) and .94 (increasing returns to scale and all quality adjustments.). Given all of

Griliches' corrections, it seems that technological change over this eleven year period was negative.

It is interesting to note that Griliches also calculates the arithmetic indices of technological change implied by his data. These run from 1.42 to 1.18. The pairwise comparison of geometric and arithmetic indices indicates a close correspondence (148–142; 132–130; 125–129; 94–118).

In investigating rates of technological change for five countries in the postwar period, Domar and a group of collaboratore (1964) produced indices for the large United States sectors. The annual rates of growth over the period 1948–1960 using an arithmetic index is the same, 2.6 per cent for both agriculture and manufacturing. Domar's indices are within the range of Griliches' arithmetic estimates, that is, between 1.5 per cent to 3.5 per cent.

Services

Phoebus Dhrymes (1963) sets himself a formidable task in attempting to measure technological change in the United States service sector and to compare it with technological change in the manufacturing sector. The quality of the data leaves much to be desired. However, such an investigation is important since there has been substantial conjecture that productivity in manufacturing has grown much more rapidly than in services. In view of the growing relative importance of the service sector, such a comparison is useful in the prediction of future trends in real wages.

Dhrymes begins with the assumption that production is governed by a Cobb-Douglas function whose constant term rises exponentially with time as an indication of technological change and whose error term is assumed to be normally distributed with mean zero, zero covariance, and homoscedastic. Since the form of the regression implies that the equations for factor prices will include an error term, Dhrymes has derived a two-step procedure for estimation. First he derives unbiased estimates of the factor shares. Then he uses a least squares minimization to derive an unbiased estimate of the geometric rate of productivity growth.

In applying his method to United States manufacturing and services industries, Dhrymes runs into innumerable data problems. The relative shares are calculated by approximating labor's share and then subtracting it from 1 to derive capital's share. The labor figures are calculated from The Department of Commerce series on the full-time employee equivalent, while capital in manufacturing is from The Department of Commerce series for end of the year real capital stock. The capital series for service industries is a "heroically concocted amalgam" (Dhrymes [1963, p. 66]). Starting with the implied capital stock for Leontief's 1947 input-output table, he calculates the stock in successive years by adding net capital formation (defined as the

Department of Commerce figures for expenditure on new plant and equipment minus depreciation). Little need be said about the capital series except that it is ingenious and it is to be hoped that Dhrymes results are not sensitive to it.

In estimating his coefficients, Dhrymes calculates capital's share as .2890 for manufacturing and .3422 for service industries. The higher capital share for service industries is a bit suprising but Dhrymes gives no explanation. In calculating technological change for the two sectors, he finds that the service group tends to have a slow, unspectacular, but steady increase over the period 1945 to 1958. Technological change in the manufacturing sector, however, shows considerable volatility, falling sharply in the 1945–47 period and then rising cyclically to 1958. Dhrymes concludes that there is no statistical difference between the rates of productivity growth in the two sectors. However, it should be noted that 1945 was a boom year for manufacturing while 1958 was a recession year. Since the postwar period has been characterized by a manufacturing sector subject to most of the boom and bust of the business cycle, this peak to trough period had much more effect on manufacturing than services. It is clear that the overall trend for technological change in manufacturing is slightly higher than for the service industries, even though it is not significantly higher. Dhrymes' conclusions seem to be an artifact of the period he chose to investigate.

Foreign Technological Change

Johansen (1961) applies his method to the British manufacturing data collected by Salter (1960). He estimates technological change as the difference between the log of productivity increase and of wage increase times the share of capital in income

$$\frac{a_{ij}}{a_{ij+1}} = A + B\frac{w_{ik}}{w_{ij+1}} + E \tag{4}$$

Johansen assumes that wage increases are constant across the industries considered over the period 1924–1950. Wage increase is then the coefficient of the share of capital income and technological change is the residual. He finds technological change to have totaled 20 per cent over the period or an average of .7 per cent per year. Capital is responsible for 57 per cent of the increase in output per man while technological change is responsible for 32 per cent, leaving 12 per cent for the interaction between the two. Johansen also splits up the industries on the basis of productivity increase and runs the regression again. Not surprisingly, these new groups are shown to have large differences in productivity.

Some of the limitations of Johansen's method are his assumptions that the wage structure is constant and that each producer minimizes cost for a given level of output. The one is a strong statement about relative wages while the other is a strong statement about optimizing behavior. Salter's data indicate little relation between productivity and wage increase, and so the data exhibit a more or less constant wage structure. However, the lack of a relation between wages and productivity suggests that either laborers are not being paid their marginal product, or that producers are not minimizing cost.

Just what is being measured in the productivity and technological change figures that have come out in recent years? As long as the figures are for long periods of time and show considerable difference between any two sectors, there is little cause for alarm. For example, in Chapter 5 results are presented that technological change is nearly twice as rapid in agriculture as in manufacturing over the 1909–1949 period. But, for shorter time periods and smaller differences, the situation is not so simple.

Brakel (1962) sets out to attack the problem of which figures are most directly related to national welfare. In 1956 the Organization for European Economic Cooperation issued a report on productivity in Western Europe. The OEEC figure is an obvious one: gross national product divided by population. A better measure for welfare purposes would be net national product or perhaps disposable income divided by population. But the corrections involved in getting NNP or DI are arbitrary in view of the available data. GNP/P seems a reasonable first approximation of the productivity of an economy or of the potential income per person.

Brakel begins with the question of what is being measured and what should be measured. His first correction concerns the use of exchange rates for translating the various GNP's into a single currency. While exchange rates offer a first approximation of the value of one currency in terms of another, a closer look reveals many difficulties in this approach. For example, the tax structure of each nation will influence exchange rates depending, for instance, on whether income or commodity taxes are employed, whether taxes on export goods are refunded, the relative monopoly powers of different countries, and so on. Brakel makes rough correction for the above difficulties and finds that the productivity figures lose their extreme differences.

Further, Brakel questions the denominator of the ratio. After all, productivity is generally taken to mean output per worker. Output per man is more of a term to measure welfare than productivity. If a nation chooses to take some of its income in leisure for women, children, and the aged, productivity is not lowered. Finally, Brakel shows the growth in output and productivity in Western Europe.

The elasticity of substitution between factors has occupied an important place in economic theory since Hicks (1932) showed it to be an important factor in wage determination. There have been few attempts to estimate the elasticity of substitution for several reasons. The quality of available data has not been all that it might be and most empirical work on production functions has made use of the Cobb-Douglas form which has an elasticity of substitution of one.

Arrow, Chenery, Minhas, and Solow (1961) were among the first to attempt a careful investigation of the elasticity of substitution. They argued that estimates were not likely to be good unless large variations in wages and capital-labor ratios could be observed. To get these large differences, they used cross section data from industries in 19 countries as observed some time in the 1950's. They fit equation

$$\log \frac{V}{L} = \log A + b \log W + E \tag{5}$$

where the log of value-added per worker is regressed on the log of wages. The coefficient of wages, b, is an estimate of the elasticity of substitution. For a linear homogeneous production function of two factors, the elasticity of substitution of one factor for another is equal to the elasticity of the average production of a factor with respect to its marginal product.

The results of fitting (5) show that the elasticity of substitution is significantly different from 1 at the 90 per cent level of confidence in 14 out of 24 industries. They conclude the Cobb-Douglas form would be a misspecification in these 14 industries and should give misleading results.

The authors go on to derive a more general function that will allow the elasticity of substitution to be varied. This function is given in equation

$$\frac{V}{L} = \gamma [K^{-\rho} + (1 - \delta)L^{-\rho}]^{-\frac{1}{\rho}} \tag{6}$$

The three most popular functions, the fixed coefficients, unitary elasticity, and infinite elasticity functions are all special cases of this more general function. The parameters can be given interpretations as follows. The elasticity of substitution is, $\sigma = 1/(1 + \rho) = b$; ρ is the substitution parameter. The constant term γ is an efficiency parameter and can be used to measure neutral technological change. The distribution of income between labor and capital is determined by δ, the distribution parameter.

ACMS assume constant returns to scale in the paper, although they recognize the assumption and construct a test that could prove or disprove it. They also worry about whether their constructed function is really a production function or merely a description of the distribution of income. They conclude that this is a hypothesis that can be tested, although their test is merely a restating of the test for constant returns to scale and does not answer Ferguson's (1963) later objections.

Under the assumption of neutral technological change, the CES function can be used to estimate changes in both the efficiency parameter and the elasticity of substitution parameter σ. Furthermore, the CES function is relevant to variations of commodity prices between countries.

In view of the evidence, the hypothesis that all three parameters are the same across countries should be rejected. Instead, the elasticity of substitution and one other parameter remain constant. Furthermore, the efficiency parameter seems to be constant across industries within a given country. Thus, ρ and δ seem to remain fixed across countries while γ, the efficiency parameter, seems to be constant for all industries within a country but to vary between countries.

In a comparison between Japan and the United States, a substantial difference between basic commodities and finished goods is indicated. In the former, the elasticity of substitution seems to be greater than unity while in the latter it is less. Since factor proportions seem to be sensitive to changes in factor prices, much of the earlier work in international trade theory which involved the contrary assumption is suspect. Thus, the question of the gains from international trade is reopened.

As noted in the section on technological change in United States manufacturing, Ferguson did not find elasticities of substitution significantly less than one. Sheshinsky (1964) runs some further tests and finds the results are even more surprising. One consistency check can be made by using the equivalent of equation (5) for capital instead of for labor. The estimated elasticity of substitution should stay the same if the assumptions are satisfied.

Sheshinsky runs this test on both United States data from Census of Manufacturing and on the ACMS data. In both cases the elasticity of substitution in the second equation is significantly different from that of the first equation. Thus, there seems virtually no consistent evidence to substantiate the conclusion that the elasticity of substitution is less than one.

The Israeli economy has been investigated by Gaathon (1960) and later by Sheshinsky (1964). A comparison of different methods of estimating technological change over the period 1952–61 is given in Table 4.2.

Table 4.2   Annual Rate of Technological Change in Israel

	Manufacturing		Total Economy
Arithmetic Index (Gaathon)	1952–55	4.7%	6.2%
	1955–59	4.8%	2.9%
Geometric Index (Sheshinsky)	1952–61	4.3%	2.8%
Solow Index (Sheshinsky)	1952–61	3.5%	1.13%

Note that the Solow index gives figures that are far below those of the other two measures, the arithmetic index and geometric index. The results also seem to indicate that labor is being paid more than its marginal product to the detriment of capital over this period.

Edwards and Drane (1963) have estimated technological change for Australian manufacturing from 1947–48 to 1959–60. They concluded that technological change over this twelve year period was between .08 and .14, an annual growth rate of about 1-1/8 per cent. They also found that capital only contributed 30 per cent of this increase in productivity. Their work was questioned by Neville (1964), but they both agreed that the rate of technological change in Australian manufacturing was substantially lower than that in United States manufacturing.

The most careful investigation of technological change across countries in the post-World War II period was undertaken by a group at MIT under the direction of Evsey Domar (1964). They looked at the sectors and the total economies of the United States, Canada, the United Kingdom, Germany, and Japan. The method used is very close to that of Kendrick, that is, the index of productivity is computed from an arithmetic index. The innovation they introduce is that of ignoring all years except those at the beginning and the end of the data series. They then calculate the geometric rate of growth that would have brought about this increase and use this annual rate as the basis of their calculations.

Their first conclusion is that Germany and Japan are far out in front of the other three nations so far as growth is concerned. The United States and Canada follow with about half the growth rate of the leaders and finally the United Kingdom with a rate slightly greater than half that of the United States. Indeed, the output of the United Kingdom has grown little, its capital has increased little, and it has experienced little technological change.

The authors warn that their figures are likely to be biased since they made no correction for under-utilization.

Agriculture is worth following through Tables 4.3 and 4.4. The growth of agriculture's value added is not very striking in any of the countries. However, the labor and capital in agriculture has fallen rapidly in all of the countries. Thus, the growth in productivity (output per worker) is substantial in all countries. The calculated increase in technological change is quite marked. It is apparent that agriculture has gone through a revolution in the postwar period since the ratio of annual-growth rates is many times that for the whole economy. Thus, technological change has affected agriculture so as to keep output rising while inputs fell substantially.

There is an interesting contrast between the countries in Table 4.4. The figures for the United States, Germany, and Japan fall in the range .4 to .5 while those of Canada and the United Kingdom are .25 to .3. In other words, nearly half the growth in the top three countries results from technological change while it accounts for only 1/4 to 3/10 of the growth in the remaining two. Domar, *et al.*, introduce the term "technological stagnation" for this phenomenon. Further, they assert that the United States might have had the greatest growth rate but for the postwar recessions. Of course an alternative interpretation is possible: if technological change is exogenous to the economy and its growth never varies much, then a booming United States economy would have used more inputs (at least capital inputs), increased total output, and so decreased the ratio. However, the former explanation is intuitively more reasonable.

Domar reports a correlation between productivity and technological change (output per man and the residual). He is a bit alarmed to find the coefficient is .83. Such a high correlation might be the basis of an argument that there is no use going to all the extra trouble to calculate a technological change index as a productivity index will do as well. The result is certainly not surprising in view of the way Domar has interpreted Solow's measure (a relatively close substitute): he maintains that it represents changes in output per man corrected for changes in capital per man. For the Solow measure, the capital correction term is small and cannot have much of an effect.

Finally, Domar found little relation between net investment and technological change. The relation between changes in output and technological change was positive, but not strong, indicating that these two interact.

Table 4.3   Annual Percentage Rates of Growth
of Value Added Arithmetic Residual

	U.S. 1948 –60	Canada 1949 –60	U.K. 1949 –59	Germany 1950 –59	Japan 1951 –59
The Economy	n.a.	1.2	0.6	3.6	3.7
Private economy	1.4	n.a.	0.7	n.a.	3.8
Private nonfarm economy	n.a.	n.a.	n.a.	n.a.	3.9
Sectors					
Agriculture	2.6	2.0	}2.0ᵃ	}4.3	}1.2
Forestry, fishing, trapping	n.a.	0.7			
Mining, quarrying, oil wells	n.a.	0.9	0.3		−0.6
Manufacturing	2.6	1.4	0.7ᵃ		4.1
Construction	n.a.	0.6	0.2ᵇ	}3.4	2.2
Public utilities	}3.4	2.0	1.9ᶜ		}4.5
Transportation and communication		1.5	1.8	}1.5	
Wholesale and retail trade	n.a.	−0.6	−1.0ᵇ		−0.5
Finance, insurance, real estate	}n.a.	0.6	}0.6	}1.4	4.1
Other services		}−0.8			
Government	n.a.		−2.8		6.7

ᵃ1950–1959
ᵇ1953–1959
ᶜ1950–1958

Table 4.4 Ratios Between Annual Rates of Growth of Residual
and Output in Percentages

	U.S. 1948 -60	Canada 1949 -60	U.K. 1949 -59	Germany 1950 -59	Japan 1951 -59
The Economy	n.a.	30	25	50	44
Private economy	47	n.a.	30	n.a.	46
Private nonfarm economy	n.a.	n.a.	n.a.	n.a.	40
Sectors					
Agriculture	289	118	}95[a]	}154	}36
Fishing, forestry, trapping	n.a.	23			
Mining, quarrying, oil wells	n.a.	11	*		−29
Manufacturing	65	38	21[a]	}39	38
Construction	n.a.	16	10[b]		19
Public utilities	}94	20	37[c]		}50
Transportation and communication		39	100	}24	
Wholesale and retail trade	n.a.	−15	−38[b]		−8
Finance, insurance, real estate	}n.a.	12	}35	}25	}40
Other services		}−21			
Government	n.a.		−560		65

*Negative rate of growth of output
[a] 1950–1959
[b] 1953–1959
[c] 1950–1958

Bibliography

Section B: United States manufacturing. Abramovitz 1956; Arrow *et al.* 1961; Barzel 1963; Brown and de Cani 1962, 1963a; Brown and Popkin 1962; Denison 1962; Enos 1958; Fabricant 1959; Frankel 1962; Fuchs 1962; Hildebrand and Liu 1965; Intriligator 1965; Iulo 1961; Kendrick 1958, 1961; Komiya 1962; Ling 1964; Massell 1960, 1961, 1962b; Nerlove 1963; Schmookler 1952; Solow 1957; Valvanis-Vail 1955; Wall 1948.

Section C: United States agriculture. Barton and Loomis 1961; Bray and Watkins 1964; Chandler 1962; Griliches 1963, 1964; Gruen 1961; Meiburg 1962; Rasmussen 1962; Ruttan 1956, 1960; Ruttan and Stout 1958, 1960; Tolley and Smidt 1964; Tostlebe 1957; Towne and Rasmussen 1960.

Section D: United States services. Dhrymes 1963; Fuchs 1964.

Section E: foreign technological change. Arrow *et al.* 1961; Aukrust 1959; Brakel 1962; Clark 1958; Cole, Holland, and Posner 1960, 1961; Domar *et al.* 1964; Edwards and Drane 1963, 1964; Gaathon 1960; Gasser-Stager 1964; Lundberg 1961; Minhas 1963; Neville 1964; Nicholson and Gupta 1960; Niitamo 1958; Railway Productivity data 1962; Reddeway and Smith 1960; Rothbart 1946; Salter 1960; Tsuru 1962.

CHAPTER FIVE

Empirical Estimates of Technological Change in United States Agriculture. 1850-1958

Introduction

Increases in real income per man-hour are a function of both relative increases in capital and the more efficient utilization of resources. The notion that higher levels of real income are generated by increasing the capital stock—the higher the level of capital, the higher the marginal revenue product of a worker and so the higher his real wages—is stressed in classical economic theory. But real wages might also be increased by an upward shift of the production function stemming from research that leads to better resource combinations, new techniques, etc. This is technological change. Much of the current interest in technological change centers around its relative importance as a determinant of higher real wages.

The results of previous empirical studies provide a basis for investigating the process of growth and adjustment by comparing the rate of technological change in different sectors of the economy, for example, the agricultural and

[Note]   Charles A. Lave helped in formulating the ideas in this chapter; criticism was generously provided by John R. Meyer, Evsey D. Domar, William Letwin, and Elizabeth Burdash. Any remaining errors are those of the author.

SOURCE: This chapter is reprinted with minor changes from the *Journal of Farm Economics*, XLIV, No. 4, November, 1962, by permission.

manufacturing sectors. These results are extended to nineteenth-century agriculture in this chapter. The problem of separating capital increase from technological change is considered and the growth of efficiency in agriculture is compared to that in manufacturing for the period 1909–1949.

Some Difficulties in Measurement

Qualitatively, technological change is simply the shifting of a production function. That is, assuming that factors of production are unchanged and that commodities are always produced in the same proportion (so-called "balanced growth"), technological change takes place when inputs yield proportionally more output. The quantitative measure of technological change would then be the ratio of the increase in output to the previous output. If $A(t)$ is the technological change function and Y_1 is output at time t (as a vector of physical quantities), the measure would be given by formula

$$\frac{\Delta A(t)}{A(t)} = \frac{Y_1 - Y_0}{Y_0} \qquad (1)$$

Note that if $Y_1 = Y_0$ (that is, no technological change has taken place), $A(t)$ remains at 1. This measure is "pure" in the sense that inputs are unchanged and, since both terms of the ratio are in physical units, no index number problems exist.

But the world is not so obliging; the factors of production vary both in magnitude and proportion. Outputs rarely increase in strict proportion and so, this purest measure of technological change is not possible. Thus, rates of exchange (prices) must be introduced to compare the ratio of the total cost of inputs with the revenue from outputs in the two periods.

Furthermore, the quality of both inputs and outputs changes over time. There are even philosophical difficulties in constructing a price series for plows, for example, from the wooden mammoth pulled by six oxen to break the prairie to its multipurpose descendant that requires far less power to operate. The two plows cannot simply be equated on the assumption that a plow is a plow. But it makes no more sense to construct indices showing their relative qualities based on price series of wheat or labor.

Finally, technological change does not take place in an instant; consumer tastes (and the productive uses of outputs) change. It might happen that the outputs of one period have no value in the other. These are extreme examples, but 1850 sunflower stalks (used for firewood on the prairie) and 1950 soybeans provide an illustration. Price indices do not mitigate this difficulty.

A First Approximation: Increased Productivity per Man-Hour

Increases in the output-labor ratio are comprised of capital increases and technological change. With a constant capital-labor ratio, technological change and the output-labor ratio (output per man-hour) are equivalent.

Consider Figure 5.1, which shows output as a function of capital with labor held constant. Starting with an initial production function, F_0, the economy is operating at (K_1, Y_1) or point 1 in the diagram. At a later time period, the economy is operating at point 3 or (K_3, Y_3). The movement from 1 to 3 is a result of the capital increase $(K_3 - K_1)$ and of the shift of the production function $(F_1 - F_0)$. (This shift is approximated in this section by the vertical distance $[Y_3 - Y_1]$). Although it ignores many of the problems inherent in the analysis, this simplified description of the economy may still help to distinguish the components of growth in per capita real income.

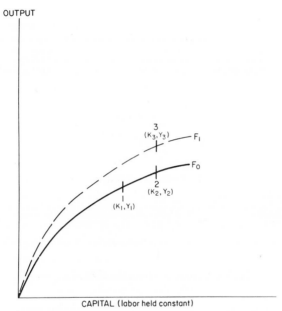

Figure 5-1.   Differentiation Between Capital Increases and Technological Change in the Growth of Real Per Capita Income.

During the period 1850–1958, agricultural output greatly increased while the labor force first rose and then declined sharply. A recent NBER monograph by Tostlebe (1957) gives output per man-year figures from 1870 to 1950. A corresponding series (1850–1910) is given by Towne and Rasmussen (1960) which agrees quite well with the Tostlebe series. The 1958 figure is quoted by Chandler (1962). A summary of these figures is given in Table 5.1 with more detailed information presented in Table 5.2.

The increase in output per man-year is quite substantial. This increase is even more impressive considering that the modern farmer takes much of his higher income in leisure. Thus, if the measure were revised to one of increases per man-hour, it would be higher than calculated here. This modification will be incorporated later.

Capital per man-year for the period is also given in Table 5.2. This statistic

Table 5.1 Growth in Output Per Man-Year and in Capital Per Man-Year

Levels in Specified Years		Growth During Specified Period		
Year	Amount (in 1910–14 dollars)	Period	% Increase Over Period	% Growth*
Real Output Per Man-Year				
1850	3,321	1850–1950	414	1 3/4
1870	3,860	1870–1950	357	1 7/8
1920	6,525	1870–1920	74	1 1/8
1950	17,054	1920–1950	161	3 1/4
		1950–1958	53	4 1/2
Real Capital Per Man-Year				
1850	2,784	1850–1950	179	1
1870	2,884	1870–1950	169	1 1/4
1920	4,353	1870–1920	51	7/8
1950	7,775	1920–1950	78	1 7/8
		1950–1958	51	4 1/4

*Compound annual rate of growth that would have brought about the increase.

rises, although not so rapidly as Y/L. If the second series were divided by the first, $K/L \div L/Y = K/Y$, the capital-output ratio is derived. Assuming no rapidly increasing returns to scale, the fall of the capital-output ratio by 45 per cent during this one hundred year period requires that there have been both technological change and capital increases; that is, there have been both movements along the production function and shifts of it.

Capital's Role in Increased Productivity

In order to account for the effect of capital increase, a further revision must be made in the measure. For a second approximation of technological change, some percentage of the capital increase must be deducted from the increase in output per man-year. What should this percentage be? Perhaps the most obvious answer is the ratio of capital's income to total income. If the factors of production were paid their marginal product, this share would measure the contribution of capital. Now, if the production function is also assumed to be linear and homogeneous, this is precisely the amount that should be subtracted to account for movements along the production function.

In the previous section $\dfrac{y_3 - y_1}{y_1}$ was used to approximate $\dfrac{F_1 - F_0}{F_0}$. (While labor was held constant, the argument is generalized by stating output and capital in terms of labor: $y = Y/L$, $k = K/L$.) The above argument can be made geometrically by noting that the overestimate is $\dfrac{y_2 - y_1}{y_1}$ or the increase in capital times the share of capital in income (the equality is strictly true only for indefinitely small movements): (that is, $\Delta k W_k$). Thus,

Table 5.2 Application of the Solow Model to Agriculture

Year	Employ-ment in Agricul-ture (thou-sands)* (1)	Capital in Agricul-ture in 1910–14 dollars (millions)* (2)	Agricul-tural Gross Product 1910–14 dollars (millions)* (3)	Share of Capital in Output* (4)	$\Delta A/A$ from Formula 2* (5)	% of Tech. Change Previous Decade (6)	Tech. Change Function $A(t)$* (7)
			Assuming All Labor at Market Wage				
1850	4,902	13,650	1,628	0.000			1.00000
1860	6,208	18,743	2,317	.000	0.1237	1 1/8	1.12375
1870	6,850	19,758	2,713	.298	.0566	1/2	1.18732
1880	8,585	27,819	4,028	.303	.1476	3/8	1.36252
1890	9,938	33,707	4,992	.224	.0584	1/2	1.44213
1900	10,912	40,307	6,187	.271	.1065	1	1.59488
1910	11,592	45,367	6,708	.395	.0013	1/8	1.59700
1920	11,449	49,842	7,471	.436	.0809	3/4	1.72620
1930	10,472	49,160	8,660	.567	.2280	2 1/8	2.11970
1940	9,163	48,472	9,632	.516	.2010	1 7/8	2.54580
1950	6,906	53,693	11,778	.504	.3846	3 1/8	3.50482
1958				0.226	0.4204	4 1/2	5.03177
			Assuming a 5% Interest Rate				
1850				0.419			1.00000
1860				.404	0.0891	5/6	1.08732
1870				.364	.0439	5/12	1.13689
1880				.346	.1408	1 1/4	1.29693
1890				.338	.0547	1/2	1.36707
1900				.326	.0991	1	1.50247
1910				.338	.0014	0	1.50455
1920				.334	.0899	3/4	1.63980
1930				.284	.2431	2 1/4	2.03838
1940				.253	.2363	2 1/8	2.52105
1950				.228	.5106	4 1/8	3.80689
1958				0.226	0.4204	4 1/2	5.40734
			Assuming an 8% Interest Rate				
1850				0.671			1.00000
1860				.647	0.0671	8/12	1.06813
1870				.582	.0336	3/8	1.10405
1880				.553	.1147	1 1/8	1.23066
1890				.540	.0452	5/12	1.28624
1900				.521	.0814	3/4	1.39097
1910				.541	−.0102	− 1/8	1.37680
1920				.534	.0672	3/4	1.46945
1930				.454	.2286	2	1.80534
1940				.404	.2157	2	2.19468
1950				.365	.4429	3 3/4	3.16671
1958				0.226	0.4204	4 1/2	4.49802

[1]1850 and 1860 from Towne and Rasmussen (1960, p. 269): 1870–1950 from Tostlebe (1957, p. 46).

[2]1850 and 1860 from *Hist. Stat.* (1960, p. 278) deflated by Warren-Pearson index p. 115; 1870–1950 from Tostlebe (1957, p. 66).

[3]1850–1910 from Towne and Rasmussen (1960, p. 266); 1910–1950 from Tostlebe (1957, p. 101).

[4]Calculated respectively as one minus labor's share in output, assuming all labor was paid the market wage, as a 5% return on all capital, including land, and as an 8% return on all capital, including land.

[5]1950–58 calculated from Chandler (1962).

[6]Calculated from col. (5) with 1850 = 1.

$$\frac{y_2 - y_1}{y_1} = \frac{\Delta k}{k_1} \frac{k_2}{Y_2} \left[\frac{dy}{dk} \right]_{k_2}$$

$$\frac{\Delta A}{A} = \frac{(y_3 - y_1)}{y_1} - \frac{(y_2 - y_1)}{y_1}$$

$$= \frac{(y_3 - y_1)}{y_1} - \frac{W_k \Delta k}{k_1}$$

or (2) $\quad \dfrac{\Delta y}{y} - W_k \dfrac{\Delta k}{k} = \dfrac{\Delta A}{A}$.

Formula (2) was derived by Solow (1957) in quite a different fashion. Beginning with a general production function of capital, labor, and time, he assumed neutral technical change and a linear homogeneous production function.

This formula yields an amazingly simple method of estimating technological change. The only remaining difficulty involves finding suitable data to estimate the parameters. There is considerable difficulty in getting any complete data for agriculture before 1910 or 1920 and even where the data are available, their suitability for use in formula (2) is questionable.

The data. The principal source of data is the previously mentioned NBER book by Tostlebe. The total employed agricultural labor force (1870–1950), the gross product originating in agriculture (1919–1950), and the capital stock in agriculture (1870–1950) series come from this excellent study. Employed labor force (1850–1860) and gross product figures (1850–1910) come from the Towne and Rasmussen paper. The capital figures for 1850 and 1860 appear in current dollars in *Historical Statistics* (1960) and so have been deflated by the Warren-Pearson price index and spliced into the Tostlebe series at 1870.

Not one of these series is used without reservations. They are constructed from limited data and represent a great many educated guesses. All the series in dollars are deflated by price indices and so are subject to additional weaknesses. Furthermore, the fundamental objection remains that what is required is a measure of capital services, a flow, not total capital, a stock. (No adjustment was made for unemployed capital.)

The series of capital's share in income presented a problem since no published series seemed satisfactory. It was possible to calculate labor's share in total product by multiplying the total labor force by the market wage given by Budd (1960). Capital's share in income is then calculated as $1 - W_L$. This series can be regarded as a lower bound for W_k, at least for the first part of the period, since labor takes up such a high percentage of income. Toward the end of the period, when family labor is not so important, and there is income that should be regarded as proprietor's income (a return over the market wage), the series no longer provides a lower bound.

Railway bonds yielded about an 8 per cent return in the mid to late nineteenth century. The yield gradually fell and then rose to about 5 per cent in 1950. With this alternative open to the farmer, it might be assumed that all of the capital in agriculture earned, or should have earned, an 8 per cent return. The second way of calculating capital's share in income merely involves finding an 8 per cent return on the capital in agriculture and dividing this by the total income. Note that this estimate is clearly an upper bound for the period. Later interest rates fell appreciably and so, at least from 1900 onward, the series is too high. Thus, this second measure provides an upper bound for W_k.

The figure given by Chandler for capital's share in income for 1950 is 22.6 per cent; an estimate far below that of either of the above two series. Thus, both these series seem generally too high which means that the measure of technological change is biased downward. If the farmer were to enjoy a 5 per cent return on farm capital, W_k would agree more closely with Chandler's figure (although the adjustment is still too conservative). Thus, a third series is calculated under the assumption that agricultural capital (including land) earned a 5 per cent return.

Technological change adjusted for capital increases. The data and the derived indices of technological change are shown in Table 5.2. The calculation has been made on a gross rather than a net basis which, as Domar (1961) has shown, introduces a bias. The extent of the bias can be judged from a comparable calculation for manufacturing whose gross measure was only slightly higher (4.1 per cent) than the net measure. The bias is explained by an implicit "one hoss shay" assumption made by the gross measure.

Thus the average rate of technological change over the century is in the range $1\frac{1}{8}$ to $1\frac{3}{4}$ per cent. It is necessary to correct for the reduction in man-hours worked per week. Making the full correction involves the assumption that an 1850 farm laborer, given modern equipment, would have the same productivity as a 1950 worker; that is, a man-hour is a man-hour whether it was worked in 1850 or 1950.[1] If the average work week declined from 72 hours to 48 hours (33 per cent over the 108 years), $A(t)$ would have increased at rates between $1\frac{3}{4}$ and $2\frac{1}{4}$ per cent. The assumption is the one characteristically made in the application of Solow's measure to the private, nonfarm sector and so the adjustment will be made for comparison with technological change in the latter sector.

The share of capital in increased productivity. Having Table 5.2, it is easy to calculate the relative parts played by capital and technological change in raising output per man-year. Over the century 1850–1950, output per man-year increased by 414 per cent; technological change accounted for 60 to 73 per cent and capital 27 to 40 per cent of this increase.

In empirical studies similar to this one capital has also been assigned a

---

[1]This assumption is in contradiction to Denison's (1960) findings.

relatively minor role. Domar (1961) has shown this conclusion to be guaranteed by a stable capital-output ratio. In fact, with a constant ratio W_k, the share of capital in income is the contribution of capital. Capital must have grown faster than output if the contribution of capital is to exceed W_k; that is, the capital-output ratio must have risen. Over the century covered by these data, k/Y fell from 8.38 to 4.55, indicating capital must have contributed less than W_k. A multiplicity of arguments besides Domar's indicate that the "obvious" conclusions from capital's relative unimportance in the rise of output per worker should be drawn with caution. However, using the Solow measure, agriculture in this period offers an example *par excellence* of the relative unimportance of capital.

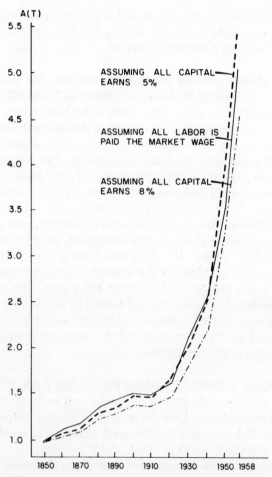

Figure 5-2. Technological Change in Agriculture.

A Sensitivity Analysis of the Solow Model

The technological change index is shifted when $A(t)$ is estimated by decade instead of by year. That all factors are being used as efficiently as technological knowledge permits is an implicit assumption of Solow. This assumption is not valid when the data cover time periods of only one year. However, when decade estimates are made, such as those given here, the assumption is more appropriate. On the other hand, the share of capital in income will have changed over the period and so this approximation will become less accurate. Calculating the magnitude of this difference by comparing decennial estimates using Solow's data with his annual estimates gives an error of .606 per cent per decade. Thus, all that seems clear is that it makes little difference whether the period taken is a year or a decade.

It would have been easier to calculate $A(t)$ in one jump, neglecting even the decennial breakdown. For the 108 year period this would have yielded values for $A(t)$ of 5.41, 5.84, and 5.94 or errors of 16.8, 13.7, and 8.9 per cent respectively. The comparable error for Solow for his forty-year period is 7.4 per cent indicating the variation is probably linear with time.

These one step figures for $A(t)$ can be used to derive the errors underlying varying assumptions about inaccuracy in the data. An error in the capital series would be most likely to occur in the first years of the series. Under the assumption of a 10 per cent error in measuring capital in 1850, $A(t)$ would be in error less than 2.9 per cent. If there were an error in the gross product series, it would most likely have occurred at the beginning of the period. Again, assuming a 10 per cent error in 1850, $A(t)$ would be in error 14.7 per cent indicating that the model is sensitive to errors in the gross product series. However, this series contains fewer "educated guesses" and is much more likely to be correct; it is not likely to lead to a major source of error. An error might have occurred in the employed workers series. Here a 10 per cent error in 1850 would lead to an error of less than 11.2 per cent in the estimation of $A(t)$.

The sensitivity of the index to changes in the share of capital in income can be judged directly since calculations are shown using three quite different series. The figures range from 00.0 to 67.1 in 1850 and from 25.3 to 50.4 in 1950. These very substantial changes in W_k did not affect $A(t)$ to the extent that might have been expected. The estimated range of $A(t)$ is 3.17 to 3.81, or a range of 16.8 per cent over the century. One can only conclude that the Solow index is relatively insensitive to changes in W_k.

In a study of this sort where the data cover more than a century, the likelihood of error in some of the figures is a certainty. The only alternative open in this case involves computing the likelihood of certain errors and their effect on the conclusions. Since some of the errors in the above discussion probably offset each other, the estimate for $A(t)$ is not likely to differ more than 15 to 20 per cent from the figure that would result from completely accurate data (whatever they might be) using the Solow approach.

Technological Change: Agriculture vs. The Private, Nonfarm Sector

It is possible to compare the measurements of technological change previously derived for the private, nonfarm sector with those here derived for agriculture. Solow's estimates are reported in Table 5.3.

The "first approximation index" of technological change increased 244 per cent [$A(t) = 3.44$] over the period 1909–49 (assuming the work week dropped from 60 to 48 hours or 25 per cent). This implies a growth rate of just over 3.25 per cent per year. The calculation based on Solow's work, (using assumptions similar to those used in his study of the private, nonfarm sector)

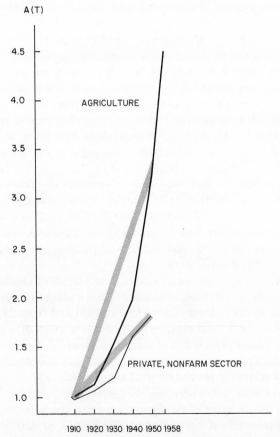

Figure 5-3. Technological Change: Agriculture vs. the Private, Nonfarm Sector.

yielded a growth rate of $2\frac{3}{8}$ to $2\frac{7}{8}$ per cent [$A(t) = 2.55$ to 3.16] for agriculture. Comparison of the figures leads to this conclusion: technological change in agriculture has been twice as rapid as in the private nonfarm sector.

While the share of national income originating in agriculture in 1950 was only 7 per cent (*Historical Statistics*, 1960), it was an order of magnitude higher in 1850. In fact for most of the period covered by these data, agriculture has been of predominant importance merely in terms of the above crude measure. Departing from this index to a concept of the sort used by Rostow (1960), technological change in agriculture has contributed to the growth of the American economy through the release of workers to industry, the provision of a cheap and abundant food supply, and through an increase in agricultural output.

Table 5.3 Technical Change in the Private, Nonfarm Sector

Year	Tech. Change Function $A(t)$	% Growth
1909	1.000	
1910	.983	
1920	1.069	7/12
1930	1.197	1 1/8
1940	1.590	2 3/4
1949	1.809	1 3/4
1909–1949 average		1 1/2

Bibliography

Abramovitz 1956; Barnett 1961; Bidwell and Falconer 1925; Budd 1960; Chandler 1962; Denison 1960; Domar 1961; Griliches 1958; *Historical Statistics* 1960; Hogan 1958; Johansen 1961; Kendrick 1961; Massell 1960; Rostow 1960; Ruttan 1960; Ruttan and Stout 1958; Solow 1957, 1960; Tostlebe 1957; Towne and Rasmussen 1960.

CHAPTER SIX

On the Method of Measurement: II

SECTION C
ERRORS OF MEASUREMENT IN THE SOLOW MEASURE
Lester Lave and Fred Rueter

The measure of technological change derived by Solow (1957) was criticized on many grounds. Even accepting such notions as the aggregate production function, the economy is not always in full adjustment, and the required data series were only loosely approximated by available data. These objections are realized in occasional dips in the technological change index which might be argued to invalidate the whole analysis. Insofar as the measure is one of technological know how, dips indicate that knowledge is lost, an implausible implication.

Errors in measuring output will bias the measure of technological change downward under certain conditions as shown in Chapter 7. This question will be reexamined in an attempt to get more general answers. The importance of a general answer can hardly be overstated. All the data series are measured with error and many are only vague approximations of the required series. The general sensitivity of the Solow measure to error of measurement was examined in the previous chapter. Now the question of bias will be taken up.

Errors of Measurement in One Period

Starting from some initial point, consider the technological change index in period three equation

$$A(3) = A(2)\left\{\frac{Y_3}{Y_2} - W_{K,2}\left(\frac{K_3}{K_2} - 1\right) - W_{L,2}\left(\frac{L_3}{L_2} - 1\right)\right\} \tag{1}$$

where

$$A(2) = \frac{Y_2}{Y_1} - W_{K,1}\left(\frac{K_2}{K_1} - 1\right) - W_{L,1}\left(\frac{L_2}{L_1} - 1\right)$$

This index is normalized by getting $A(1) = 1$. Errors of measurement in the output series take the form of equation,

$$\hat{Y}_2 = \alpha Y_2 \tag{2}$$

where $\hat{Y}$ is the observed output, Y is true output, and α is a measure of the error (see Theil [1957] for an alternative treatment of error). If $\hat{A}(3)$ is the observed technological index for period three, the error in measuring technological change is given in equation

$$A(3) - \hat{A}(3) = \left(\alpha + \frac{1}{\alpha} - 2\right)n \tag{3}$$

where n is some constant, depending on the growth rates of the variables. In order to get some idea of its magnitude, output is assumed to increase at 3 per cent per year, capital at 2 per cent, labor at 1 per cent; the share of capital in output is .3. These figures are roughly the experience of the United States economy since 1900. The value of n, .01339, is given in Table 6.1.

Table 6.1   Errors of Measurement in One Period

Let $\hat{Y} = \alpha Y$. Then $A(3) - \hat{A}(3) = \left(\alpha + \dfrac{1}{\alpha} - 2\right)$	(.01339)	
$\hat{K} = \alpha K$	$\left(\alpha + \dfrac{1}{\alpha} - 2\right)$	(.40484)
$\hat{L} = \alpha L$	$\left(\alpha + \dfrac{1}{\alpha} - 2\right)$	(1.219)
$\hat{W}_K = \alpha W_K$	$(\alpha - 1)$	(.00610)
$\hat{W}_L = \alpha W_L$	$(\alpha - 1)$	(.007120)

What is the effect on $A(3)$ when Y is overestimated rather than underestimated? Is the error ever minimized? These two questions can be answered by taking the derivative of Equation (3) with respect to α to get equation

$$\frac{d\{A(3) - \hat{A}(3)\}}{d\alpha} = 1 - \frac{1}{\alpha^2} \tag{4}$$

Setting this derivative to zero, there is only one extreme point and that at $\alpha = 1$. To test whether this point is a maximum or minimum, equation

$$\frac{d\{A(3) - \hat{A}(3)\}^2}{d^2\alpha} = \frac{2}{\alpha^3} \tag{5}$$

is derived by taking the derivative of Equation (4) with respect to α. At $\alpha = 1$, Equation (5) is positive, implying that the error function attains a minimum at that point.

Thus, for errors on the measurement of Y in period two, $A(3) - \hat{A}(3)$ is at a minimum when $\alpha = 1$. From here it is easy to see that the error can never be negative, which in turn implies that $A(3) \geq \hat{A}(3)$. Any error in the middle of a time series, whether overestimating or underestimating output, will bias the final cumulative index of technological change downward.

This investigation is easily generalized to errors of measurement in the series for capital and for labor. These two have errors that take the same form as that of output. Letting α again be the measure of the error and n be some function of the growth rates, the results are summarized in Table 6.1. As just stated, the error is quadratic, indicating that an error will bias the cumulative measure of technological change downward.

For errors in measuring W_K, the share of capital in output, the error term takes a slightly different form. The error is linear, as shown in equation

$$A(3) - \hat{A}(3) = (\alpha - 1)n \tag{6}$$

Thus, $\hat{W}_K < W_K$ will cause a positive error or $A(3) < \hat{A}(3)$. The cumulative index can have either an upward or downward bias.

Errors of Measurement in Two Periods

The analysis can be extended to cover errors of measurement in more than one period. The first step involves computing $A(4)$ as given in equation

$$A(4) = A(3)\left\{\frac{Y_4}{Y_3} - W_{K,3}\left(\frac{K_4}{K_3} - 1\right) - W_{L,3}\left(\frac{L_4}{L_3} - 1\right)\right\} \tag{7}$$

The errors of measurement are assumed to take place in periods two and three, Equation (8).

$$\hat{Y}_2 = \alpha Y_2 \qquad \hat{Y}_3 = \beta Y_3 \tag{8}$$

The error in the fourth period is given in equation

$$A(4) - \hat{A}(4) = \left(3 - \alpha - \frac{\beta}{\alpha} - \frac{1}{\beta}\right)n_1 + \left(\frac{1}{\alpha} + \frac{\alpha}{\beta} + \beta - 3\right)n_2 \tag{9}$$

where n_1 and n_2 are constants depending on the growth rates of the various series. Equation (9) is minimized at $\alpha = \beta = 1$.

The analysis is summarized in Table 6.2. As before, errors in output, capital, and labor give rise to error terms of the same form. Errors in the share of capital and labor in output give rise to roughly linear error terms.

Table 6.2   Errors of Measurement in Two Consecutive Periods

Let $\hat{Y}_2 = \alpha Y_2$

and $\hat{Y}_3 = \beta Y_3$

Then $A(4) - \hat{A}(4) = \left(3 - \alpha - \dfrac{\beta}{\alpha} - \dfrac{1}{\beta}\right)(.000174) + \left(\dfrac{1}{\alpha} + \dfrac{\alpha}{\beta} + \beta - 3\right)(.0138)$

Let $\hat{K}_2 = \alpha K_2$

and $\hat{K}_3 = \beta K_3$

Then $A(4) - \hat{A}(4) = \left(3 - \alpha - \dfrac{\beta}{\alpha} - \dfrac{1}{\beta}\right)(-.535) + \left(\dfrac{1}{\alpha} + \dfrac{\alpha}{\beta} + \beta - 3\right)(-.124)$

Let $\hat{L}_2 = \alpha L_2$

and $\hat{L}_3 = \beta L_3$

Then $A(4) - \hat{A}(4) = \left(3 - \alpha - \dfrac{\beta}{\alpha} - \dfrac{1}{\beta}\right)(-2.101) + \left(\dfrac{1}{\alpha} + \dfrac{\alpha}{\beta} + \beta - 3\right)(-.862)$

Let $\hat{W}_{K,1} = \alpha W_{K,1}$

$\hat{W}_{K,2} = \beta W_{K,2}$

Then $A(4) - \hat{A}(4) = (\beta + \alpha - 2)(.00624) + (1 - \alpha\beta)(.00004)$

Let $\hat{W}_{L,1} = \alpha W_{L,1}$

$\hat{W}_{L,2} = \beta W_{L,2}$

Then $A(4) - \hat{A}(4) = (\beta + \alpha - 2)(.00729) + (1 - \alpha\beta)(.00005)$

The Interaction between Successive Errors

What is the effect of the interaction between these errors in periods two and three? An error in measuring output in the second period will give rise to an error in the fourth period as given in equation

$$A(4) - \hat{A}(4) = \left(\alpha - \frac{1}{\alpha} - 2\right)n \quad \text{for} \quad \hat{Y}_2 = \alpha Y_2 \tag{10}$$

Similarly, an error in the third period will give rise to an error in the fourth period given in equation

$$A(4) - \hat{A}(4) = \left(\beta - \frac{1}{\beta} - 2\right)n \quad \text{for} \quad \hat{Y}_3 = \beta Y_3 \tag{11}$$

If both these errors were to occur together, the bias in the measure of technological change would be given in equation

$$A(4) - \hat{A}(4) = B_{4,2} + B_{4,3} - \frac{B_{4,2} B_{4,3}}{A(4)} \quad \text{for} \quad \hat{Y}_2 = \alpha Y_2; \ \hat{Y}_3 = \beta Y_3 \quad (12)$$

where $B_{4,i}$ indicates the bias in the fourth period caused by an error in the ith period. In the cases of output, capital, and labor, these bias terms are given in equation

$$A(4) - \hat{A}(4) = \left(\alpha + \frac{1}{\alpha} - 2\right)n + \left(\beta + \frac{1}{\beta} - 2\right)n$$
$$- \frac{[\alpha + (1/\alpha) - 2][\beta + (1/\beta) - 2]n^2}{1.052} \quad (13)$$

For the share of capital and labor in output, these terms take the form of equation

$$A(4) - \hat{A}(4) = (\alpha - 1)n + (\beta - 1)n - \frac{(\alpha - 1)(\beta - 1)n^2}{1.052} \quad (14)$$

The constant n again depends on the growth rates of the various series and is given in Table 6.3.

Table 6.3 Value of Constant Term
for Two Successive Errors

Series	n
Y	0.0136
K	0.411
L	1.240
W_K	0.00620
W_L	0.00724

When the consecutive errors of two periods are broken down as in Formulas (13) and (14), the individual effects may be separated. The third term, which measures the interaction of the effects of the two errors, is an order of magnitude smaller than the first two terms. With α approximately 1.1, this term will be much smaller than the previous two terms. Only if the observed point were twice that of the true point, $\alpha = 2$, would the third term be even half the size of the previous two in Equation (13). The relative importance of the third term in Equation (14) is substantially reduced by the presence of n^2. As a first approximation, the error of two consecutive errors is the sum of the two errors.

Since an error is always greater than or equal to zero (for Y, K, and L), errors can never be offsetting. Any error in a subsequent period can only add to the downward bias of the cumulative technological change index. For errors in W_K and W_L, compensating errors are possible.

Tables 6.1 and 6.3 can be used to estimate the sensitivity of the Solow index to errors in the various series. For given percentage errors, the cumulative technological change index is most sensitive to labor, and the sensitivity declines for capital, output, and then W_L and W_K. Labor is the only one of these series to which the index can be said to be very sensitive. A sensitivity analysis is reported in Chapter 5 based on errors in the first of two observations. The index is most sensitive to output, then labor, and finally capital.

Some Empirical Results

An illustration of the effects of errors of measurement came up in connection with the work of Chapter 11 on the Appalachian region. Technological change was measured for 342 counties over the period 1870–1960. Over this interval, the census changed its definitions many times and almost no single series was strictly comparable over the ninety years.

The choice of whether to measure the series in constant or some other kind of dollars has not been answered satisfactorily. The usual method is to use constant prices as is done in Chapter 11. It is an implicit assumption of the measure that the economy is in long-run equilibrium. It is a heroic assumption that the economy is always in equilibrium with respect to current prices, but it is something more than that to suppose the economy is in long-run adjustment with respect to 1910–14 prices. Samuelson (1962, p. 201) goes against orthodoxy:

> While I come to defend Solow, not to criticize him, this shows he might better have used a current-weighted index number of capital (measured in terms of *numeraire* units) rather than the available fixed-weight indexes that purport to measure relevant real capital.

Finally, there are the problems associated with booms and depressions. If the highest efficiency points of the Second World War and the Korean War were taken as the base for efficient utilization of resources, almost all the time under consideration would have resources half-utilized. Striking a balance between high-efficiency booms and deepest depressions, the high and low utilization might be interpreted as errors of measurement. Since Solow (1957) and Massell (1960) corrected for underutilization of capital in the Depression, they should have corrected for overutilization in the 1940's and early 1950's.

Thus, three disruptive elements are present in the series used to measure technological change: (a) errors of measurement in the series; (b) non-homogeneity of the series over time; (c) errors stemming from the economy's not always being in long-run equilibrium. All three of these elements serve to bias the measure of technological change downward, and all three can be treated as errors of measurement in the context of the present analysis.

The problem is of paramount importance for the Appalachian counties. With 1870 as unity, the cumulative technological change index $A(1960)$ went negative in about 95 per cent of the 342 counties. That is, $A(1960)$ went negative in all but about 17 of 342 counties. The $A(1960)$ for the aggregate Appalachian region is $-.07$. This result occurred even though output per man more than quadrupled over the period.

Another way of viewing the problem involves examining the frequency function of the decennial measures of technological change. This function is given in Figure 6.1. Note that the range goes from -39.96 to $+.98$. A figure of -40 indicates a disaster of some sort: flood, drought, or insect damage. It indicates that total output fell virtually to zero. It should be noted that any $\Delta A/A$ less than -1 turns the accumulated technological change index negative. Finally, it should be noted that the mean of these $\Delta A/A$ is -0.31. Clearly these figures are nonsense.

The problems with the various data series are that severe deviations occur and the series display a great deal of variation over time. One way to handle the difficulty involves smoothing the series in some way. As long as any deviation from normal can serve only to bias the technological change index downward, smoothing is necessary to get meaningful figures.

Perhaps the most logical assumption for the Appalachian counties is exponential growth. Output per man and capital per man seem to grow geometrically over time. Thus, the proper model seemed to be that of equation

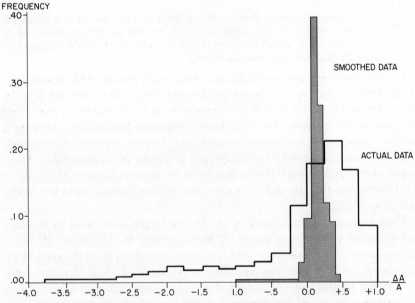

Figure 6-1. Comparison of Technological Change from Actual and Smoothed Data.

$$\log \left(\widehat{\frac{Y}{L}}\right)_t = a + b \log \left(\frac{Y}{L}\right)_t + \varepsilon_t \qquad (15)$$

where, for example, Y/L grows exponentially with time and there is an error term. Time is measured in blocks of ten years and there are a total of ten observations. One difficulty is that the model relies on the assumption that the mean of the error term is zero. It might be argued that the mean error is negative, indicating that underutilization is the most common phenomenon. The constant term can, however, be seen to serve as a measure of the mean error. As long as it is negative, the mean error is underutilization. But the sign of the error will have no effect on the growth coefficient. The model is likely to display heterscedastisity, but no adjustment is made.

The method employed does have one unfortunate property: simple exponential growth is assumed. If the series were to start growing at one rate and end growing at quite a different and higher one, the regression coefficient would underestimate growth. This problem does seem to occur.

When these regressions were fitted to the data series for each county, the results were quite reasonable. The coefficients of determination were all significant and averaged approximately .6. The results of the series on output per man and capital per man were then put into the Solow measure, where the regression coefficient was used as a direct estimate of the increase in Y/L and K/L. W_K was still estimated as $K/(20\,Y)$.

These smoothed results were much more reasonable than the previous ones. They are described in detail in Chapter 11. The frequency function for $\Delta A/A$ is given in Figure 6.1. The range is -1.00 to $+.49$ and the mean is .17. The $A(1960)$ for Appalachia is 4.26 as compared to $-.07$ for the unsmoothed figures.

A Detailed Comparison with Twelve Counties

Some estimates of technological change produced by the smoothing method are quite high, and all are higher than the nonsmoothed estimates. A question that immediately occurs is the extent to which smoothing may have produced an upward bias. From an examination of errors of measurement, it was apparent that any deviation from exponential growth produces a downward bias. To the extent that the smoothed figures eliminate all such deviations, they eliminate bias. The estimates of increase in the various series might be biased, however, and so give rise to biased results.

In order to answer these questions and get greater insight into the measures, the 12 counties considered in Chapter 7 will be examined more closely. These 12 counties displayed quite reasonable rates of growth of technological change over the same period. The measures of the various series are almost identical to the measures used for the Appalachian counties. The regressions used to smooth the Y/L and K/L series give results comparable to the Appalachian counties insofar as the measures of goodness of fit were concerned.

The $A(1960)$ for both the unsmoothed and smoothed results are presented in Table 6.4. The results are quite uniform insofar as the smoothed measure is always smaller than the actual figure. A glance at the residuals shows the reason for this result: the spectacular growth from 1940 to 1960 is underestimated in all twelve regressions. This underestimate of the 1940–1960 period also occurs in the regressions for the Appalachian counties. This fact would seem to suggest that the smoothed results provide an underestimate of the actual level of technological change in 1960.

Table 6.4   Comparison of Actual and Smoothed Series

	1	2	3	4	5	6
Indiana Counties:						
Actual	6.64	7.79	3.40	4.96	5.46	6.06
Smoothed	5.17	5.36	2.92	3.21	3.50	3.84
Iowa Counties:						
Actual	5.92	5.10	4.72	3.71	3.02	2.74
Smoothed	3.20	3.15	2.57	2.35	2.16	1.40

Summary

Errors of measurement are extended to include not only conventional errors of measurement, but also nonhomogeneity of the data series and the possibility that the economy isn't always in full adjustment. The effects of these errors are examined in a model where they occur in the middle of a series. The cumulative technological change index is found to be most sensitive to errors in the labor series, with other series ranking capital, output, W_L, and W_K, respectively. In investigating the effect of two errors in a row, the errors are found to be approximately additive.

These errors of measurement were examined in the context of the county data for Appalachia. The data series presented such wide swings that the cumulative indices wore nonsensical in 95 per cent of the counties. The data were adjusted for errors by fitting them to an exponential regression. When the results were fitted into the technological change measure, the cumulative indices were quite reasonable.

A more detailed examination was undertaken for the twelve Corn Belt counties of Chapter 7. In all cases, the smoothed cumulative indices were lower than the actual ones. This underestimate resulted from the failure of the regression to account for the spectacular rise from 1940–60. Since the Appalachian regressions showed the same characteristic, there is some evidence that technological change was underestimated.

SECTION D
MEASURING CHANGE IN AGRICULTURE: THE CASE FOR INTERMEDIATE PRODUCTS
Lester Lave and Arnold Lieberman

Introduction

In interpreting the estimates of technological change in the agricultural sector, Chapter 5 along with most of the work on technological change implicitly assumes the correct measure of output is value-added. Domar (1961) has pointed out that technological change indices will differ, depending on whether the measure of output is a gross or value-added measure.

Assuming a Cobb-Douglas form, the gross output function is given in equation

$$y = AK^{W_K}L^{W_L}M^{1-W_K-W_L} \qquad (16)$$

This form can be transformed into a value-added function by dividing by intermediate products equation

$$y' = AK^{W_K}L^{W_L} \qquad W_K + W_L < 1 \qquad (17)$$

Such a transformation is, however, not equivalent to the regular value-added form since the sum of coefficients is not unity as in equation

$$\bar{y} = A'K^{W'_K}L^{W'_L} \qquad W'_K + W'_L = 1 \qquad (18)$$

The A's that come from Equations (16) and (18) will be different in general. As long as M is increasing faster than L and $K(W_K$ and W_L constant), Equation (18) will give higher estimates of technological change than Equation (16).

A slightly different but related argument is concerned with quality changes in the inputs to agriculture over time. As long as the relevant measure is considered to be the change in efficiency in agriculture over time, any quality changes in both inputs and outputs must be accounted for. To a certain extent, these changes are reflected in price changes.

Since the production function of Chapter 5 was a value-added one and since no real attempt was made to adjust for quality changes, the measure of technological change is a hodge-podge consisting of elements of efficiency increase in manufacturing, education, and so on. The correction is likely to be important since, as Meiburg (1962) argues, the greatest increases in productivity have come precisely at the time when the share of intermediate products was increasing most rapidly. Table 6.5 presents data to illustrate such an argument.

Although net-farm inputs increased only 29 per cent during this period, farm productivity increased over 60 per cent as shown in Table 6.5. At the same time, intermediate products from outside agriculture increased over 280 per cent. These figures lend strength to the possible importance of intermediate products. It is important to go on to develop a gross output measure of technological change for agriculture.

Table 6.5

	Nonfarm Inputs (A)	Net-farm Inputs (B)	Gross Output (C)	Productivity (D)
1910	1.678×10^9	45.358×10^9	8.366×10^9	0.178
1915	1.874	47.961	10.018	.201
1920	2.105	49.853	9.576	.184
1925	2.732	46.108	11.391	.233
1930	3.114	49.171	11.774	.225
1935	2.634	44.039	11.772	.252
1940	3.854	48.581	13.477	.257
1945	5.263	51.019	15.733	.279
1950	5.940	53.700	17.718	.297
1953	6.382	58.244	18.159	0.280

source: Columns (A) and (C). (Tostlebe [1957]; Atkinson and Jones [1954].) Tostlebe's decennial figures for net output were divided into gross output and intermediate products according to the proportion given by Jones and Atkinson for that particular year. The decennial figures were then extended to yearly data by simple extrapolation.

Column (B). Tostlebe's series of capital was combined directly with his series of labor given in man-hours to produce a series of total agricultural inputs of production. This assumes a constant labor wage of $1 an hour to apply throughout the series, but since wages have risen and not fallen during the duration of the time series, the net effect of the assumption is to understate rather than exaggerate the conclusions.

Column (D). Productivity is considered simply as gross output/total input, where gross output is given in column (C) and total input is the addition of columns (A) and (B).

Of course, it must be recognized that other sectors of the economy have received the benefit of quality changes in agriculture and that the tendency to use intermediate products from outside every sector has increased over time. Thus, a relevant question is the measure of technological change in manufacturing when a gross measure of output is used.

The Measures of Gross and Net Technological Change

The Solow derivation is easily extended to the case where output is gross and intermediate products are included in the production function, Equation

Table 6.6

	Gross Y (billion dollars) (A)	M (billion dollars) (B)	L (millions of people) (C)	K (billion dollars) (D)	W_K (E)	W_M (F)	W_L (G)	$A(t)_{1b}$ (H)	$A(t)_{2b}$ (I)
1910	8.366	1.658	11.592	45.367	0.271	0.198	0.531	1.000	1.000
1911	8.162	1.689	11.673	45.571	.279	.207	.514	0.959	0.967
1912	9.296	1.787	11.750	46.451	.250	.192	.558	1.102	1.081
1913	8.570	1.835	11.574	46.959	.274	.214	.512	0.996	0.996
1914	9.036	1.853	11.814	47.858	.265	.205	.530	1.041	1.031
1915	10.018	1.874	11.472	47.950	.239	.187	.574	1.207	1.160
1916	9.257	2.011	11.297	48.869	.264	.217	.519	1.080	1.059
1917	9.633	1.962	11.530	49.032	.255	.204	.542	1.125	1.095
1918	9.528	2.227	11.596	48.840	.256	.234	.510	1.068	1.051
1919	9.792	2.200	11.260	49.301	.252	.225	.524	1.133	1.097
1920	9.576	2.105	11.449	49.842	.260	.220	.520	1.098	1.071
1921	9.534	2.403	10.525	48.203	.253	.252	.495	1.125	1.089
1922	10.162	2.438	10.877	47.548	.234	.240	.426	1.192	1.140
1923	10.642	2.426	10.911	47.628	.224	.228	.548	1.264	1.193
1924	10.722	2.763	10.944	46.680	.218	.258	.525	1.228	1.168
1925	11.391	2.732	11.132	46.097	.202	.240	.558	1.321	1.236
1926	11.507	2.940	11.163	46.849	.204	.256	.541	1.300	1.220
1927	12.316	3.086	10.649	47.215	.192	.251	.558	1.453	1.323
1928	11.983	3.134	10.758	47.554	.198	.262	.540	1.379	1.273
1929	12.364	3.129	10.635	47.527	.192	.253	.555	1.453	1.323
1930	11.774	3.114	10.472	49.160	.209	.264	.527	1.370	1.263
1931	12.928	2.990	10.678	47.275	.183	.231	.586	1.558	1.394
1932	12.453	2.948	10.274	44.749	.180	.237	.584	1.553	1.392
1933	12.105	2.898	10.251	43.477	.180	.239	.581	1.515	1.368
1934	12.215	2.587	9.168	42.971	.210	.253	.536	1.375	1.265
1935	11.772	2.634	9.526	44.030	.187	.224	.589	1.590	1.114
1936	10.892	3.008	9.203	44.845	.206	.276	.518	1.403	1.282
1937	12.736	2.955	9.935	46.291	.182	.232	.586	1.625	1.432
1938	13.099	3.191	9.237	47.384	.181	.244	.576	1.741	1.504
1939	13.453	3.572	9.217	47.462	.177	.266	.557	1.735	1.500
1940	13.477	3.854	9.163	48.572	.180	.286	.534	1.695	1.472
1941	14.586	4.207	8.993	49.307	.169	.288	.543	1.852	1.567
1942	16.180	4.707	9.197	50.100	.155	.291	.554	2.004	1.659
1943	15.605	4.855	9.102	50.226	.161	.311	.528	1.893	1.593
1944	15.751	4.890	8.933	49.987	.159	.310	.531	1.944	1.622
1945	15.733	5.263	8.393	51.011	.162	.331	.503	1.968	1.628
1946	16.318	5.318	8.003	53.533	.164	.338	.498	2.097	1.690
1947	15.899	5.613	7.616	56.699	.178	.353	.469	2.060	1.660
1948	17.211	5.591	7.377	60.750	.166	.325	.499	2.363	1.807
1949	16.954	5.611	7.140	63.901	.188	.331	.481	2.348	1.790
1950	17.718	5.940	6.909	53.693	.152	.335	.513	2.578	1.922
1951	17.377	6.186	6.985	56.221	.162	.356	.482	2.408	1.835
1952	17.811	6.583	6.682	57.983	.370	.468	.080	2.521	1.880
1953	18.159	6.382	6.371	58.238	0.160	0.351	0.488	2.723	1.971

Column (A) = extrapolation from Column (C) Table 6.5.
Column (B) = extrapolation from Column (A) Table 6.7.
Column (C) = extrapolation from Tostlebe's Decennial Labor Series.
Column (D) = extrapolation from Tostlebe's Decennial Capital Series.
Column (E) = $.05(K/Y)$ 5 per cent return.
Column (F) = (intermediate products/y).
Column (G) = $1 - (E) - (F)$.
Column (H) = from Equation (5), Chapter 2.
Column (I) = from Equation (19').

(18). Taking time derivatives and rearranging gives Equation (19) and Equation (19′) where capital, output, and intermediate products are divided by labor.

$$\frac{\dot{A}}{A} = \frac{\dot{Y}}{Y} - W_L\frac{\dot{L}}{L} - W_K\frac{\dot{K}}{K} - W_M\frac{\dot{M}}{M} \tag{19}$$

$$\frac{\dot{A}}{A} = \frac{\dot{y}}{y} - W_K\frac{\dot{k}}{k} - W_M\frac{\dot{m}}{m} \tag{19′}$$

Equation (19′) differs from the value-added measure of technological change only by the last term: W_M $(\dot{m}/m)$. Both indices of technological change are presented in Table 6.6. As expected, the results are quite different.

Decennial versus Annual Estimates

As argued in Chapter 5, there is a difference between measuring technological change annually and decennially. The difference for the Solow data was, however, estimated at only .606 per cent per decade. Since the data in Table 6.6 are annual, another estimate of this difference is possible. Table 6.7 summarizes the figures. Note that the difference between the 1953 figures is only .77 per cent for both the value-added and gross output measures. Thus, the earlier conclusion is confirmed and there is little difference between using annual and decennial figures.

Table 6.7   Comparison of Annual and Decennial Measures of Change*

	Annual Computation		Decennial Computation	
	Value Added	Gross	Value Added	Gross
$A(1910)$	1.00	1.00	1.00	1.00
$A(1953)$	2.72	1.97	2.70	1.96

*Deflated by price indices.

Conclusion

Domar noted that measuring output in gross terms would give a measure of technological change which differed from the conventional one where output was in value-added terms. The Solow measure of technological change was derived for the gross value measure of output. Both measures were computed for agriculture from 1910 to 1953. The 1953 measures of technological change for the gross and net measures are 1.97 and 2.72 respectively.

CHAPTER SEVEN

Technological Change in U.S. Agriculture:
The Aggregation Problem*

The Aggregation Problem

A number of studies have utilized aggregate data to measure technological change. Examples include the private, nonfarm sector (Hogan [1958], Kendrick [1961], Solow [1957]), the manufacturing sector (Abramovitz [1956], Massell [1960]) and the agricultural sector (Chandler [1962], Chapter 5, Ruttan and Stout [1958]). While the use of highly aggregated data is widespread, no assessment has been attempted of the effect aggregation has on the measure.

The postwar literature on aggregation has been concerned with the relation between macroeconomic and microeconomic production functions under linear and geometric aggregation (see the symposium in *Econometrica*, Vol. 14, 1946); (Houthakker [1955], Theil [1954]). These formulations have been based on prohibitive assumptions: exact specification of the production functions, all firms operating at efficient points of identical functions, no

*This paper was supported, in part, by the Ford Foundation which takes no responsibility for the views expressed. While sharing none of the errors, Hendrik Houthakker, Charles Lave, Wallace Falcon, Zvi Griliches, Richard Heflebower, Simon Kuznets, Ruth Westheimer, and Arthur Carlson contributed to this paper.
SOURCE: This chapter is reprinted with minor changes from the *Journal of Farm Economics*, XLVI, February, 1964 by permission.

errors of measurement, and no market imperfections or heterogeneous factors. The effect of relaxing these assumptions even slightly has not been determined.[1] A more pragmatic test of the aggregation problem is attempted here.

Has the aggregate nature of the previous studies of technological change determined their conclusions? This question can be broken into two parts: (1) Is the level of the technological change index biased by the aggregation? and (2) Does the aggregation mask important and informative variations in the indices? Implicit questions here concern possible differences in the time profiles and levels of technological change in different crops.

These questions are approached by computing an 1870–1960 index of technological change at four levels of aggregation: (1) 12 counties in Indiana and Iowa, (2) the five states of the Corn Belt, (3) the 10 USDA regions composing the agricultural sector, and (4) the entire United States agricultural sector.

The Measurement of Technological Change

Technological change is defined as a shift of the production function, a change in the efficiency of the use of resources. On a crude level, it might be measured by the rate of output increase holding labor constant. The increase in output per man (in 1910–14 prices) for the period 1870–1960, for the regions dealt with in this chapter, is presented in Table 7.1. The increase is substantial in every case.

The Mountain states stand out even in comparison to the generally high rate of increase. This increase implies a high rate of technological change in livestock production, the principal product. Other than technological change, the output increase might be explained by the realization of increasing returns to scale through the increasing size of ranches and by the use of irrigated land (reflected in the capital measure only as "improved acres").

There are no stagnant regions although capital increases are varied[2]. This relative uniformity might be used to argue that farm labor really is mobile —that it was labor movement which evened out the increases of output.

Capital increases must also be taken into account. Table 7.1 contains figures for the increase in capital per man in 1910–14 prices for the period 1870–1960. Comparing output and capital over the period, the former has increased twice as rapidly as the latter.

In order to take account of capital increase in the calculation of techno-

[1]For a partial result see Houthakker (1955)..
[2]The data for the states of the Corn Belt and counties in Indiana and Iowa are not comparable to the data for the 10 USDA regions although they form a consistent group, see Appendix.

logical change, the effect of capital on output must be specified. Solow's approach is used; we assume the production function is linearly homogeneous and that technological change is neutral. Equation

$$\frac{\Delta A}{A} = \frac{\Delta y}{y} - W_k \frac{\Delta k}{k} \qquad (1)$$

Table 7.1 Increases in Output per Man and Capital per Man, 1870–1960

Region	Increase Output Per Man	Increase Capital Per Man
	(Per cent)	
U.S.	9.49	4.11
Corn Belt	9.27	3.26
Northeast	6.89	1.48
Appalachians	6.74	3.44
Southeast	11.88	6.27
Lake states	11.39	5.82
Delta states	10.64	7.03
Great Plains	12.22	6.72
Texas-Oklahoma	12.79	5.63
Mountain	22.05	11.81
Pacific	5.58	.21
Illinois	6.67	2.78
Indiana	7.78	2.90
Iowa	6.10	2.49
Missouri	6.75	3.38
Ohio	6.74	2.73
Indiana counties		
Carroll	11.15	3.67
Clinton	11.54	5.07
Morgan	4.23	2.70
Rush	6.94	3.47
St. Joseph	9.08	2.96
Wabash	9.91	4.60
Iowa counties		
Benton	7.85	2.87
Blackhawk	6.46	2.11
Clinton	5.41	2.13
Johnson	4.17	2.01
Marion	4.00	2.90
Winneshick	2.83	1.66

Output increase is calculated as $\dfrac{Y\ 1960/L\ 1960}{Y\ 1870/L\ 1870} - 1$.

Capital increase is calculated similarly.

SOURCE: The data are derived in the Appendix.

gives the increase in the technological change index, $A(t)$, based on changes in output and capital per man, y, k, and the share of capital in income, W_k.

To the extent that these assumptions are not met, caution must be used in calling $A(t)$ "the technological change index" rather than "the residual of increase in output per man not explained by the increase in capital per man" (Domar [1961]). An objection raised by Griliches is that the single most important element in this production function is the class of intermediate goods such as fertilizer or seed, since output is measured in gross terms. An alternative formulation based on the assumption that output is a linear homogeneous function of three factors might include intermediate products. This formulation would entail the addition of another term to the right-hand side of Equation (1), namely:

$$-W_m \frac{\Delta M}{M}$$

The new index of technological change might be substantially smaller than the $A(t)$ defined by Equation (1). That is, intermediate products might explain a large part of the residual. An argument can be presented that

$$-W_m \frac{\Delta M}{M}$$

is a legitimate part of technological change, given the growth of other sectors (although such an assumption is hardly legitimate for policy purposes). However, technological change is measured as a residual, and since the object of analysis is to explain such a residual, Griliches' suggestion represents a future line of research. Because of other objections, from increasing returns to scale for the production function to the imperfect market for labor, the exact meaning of $A(t)$ is obscured. The results following should be viewed in the light of these qualifications.

Technological Change: Regional Estimates

Equation (1) has been applied to the United States agricultural sector at various stages of aggregation with results summarized below.[3] Table 7.2 presents technological change in the agricultural sector over the period 1870–1960. Figures for all agriculture and for the 10 USDA regions that divide the United States, roughly on the basis of crop similarity, are given.[4]

---

[3]Labor is measured in man-years and to the extent that a man-year of labor is smaller in 1960 than it was in 1870, $A(t)$ is underestimated. Correcting for the reduction in the work week would make up for this bias. An assumed reduction from 72 hours to 48 hours worked per week would multiply $A(1960)$ by $1/(1 - .33)$ or by 3/2.

[4]Comparison of the 1930–60 increase in $A(t)$ with that derived by Ruttan and Stout (1958) using an arithmetic index shows the Solow measure to give a substantially higher estimate.

Occasional declines in the technological change index within the regions should be noted, although the aggregate index rises continuously. A number of factors contribute to the decline of the Great Plains index from 1930–1949. The droughts of the mid-1930's are evidenced, particularly in livestock production. Exports dwindled in the 1930's and almost reached their nadir in 1939. Finally, 1939 was a year with substantial crop supports.

In a number of regions (the Corn Belt, the Appalachians, the Southeast, and the Delta states) the technological change index was constant or fell in the 1910–1920 period. Temporary market aberrations from the First

Table 7.2 Technological Change Index for the 10
USDA Regions and the Agricultural Sector, 1870–1960

	T.C. Index for Region in Year:						
	1870	1880	1890	1900	1910	1920	1930
U.S.	1	1.21	1.31	1.48	1.49	1.67	2.20
Corn Belt	1	1.30	1.32	1.62	1.73	1.68	2.22
Northeast	1	1.14	1.21	1.26	1.13	1.57	1.84
Appalachians	1	1.24	1.23	1.50	1.51	1.51	2.16
Southeast	1	1.23	1.60	1.41	1.57	1.17	2.28
Lake states	1	1.33	1.32	1.48	1.44	1.81	2.01
Delta states	1	1.16	1.32	1.15	.98	.89	1.50
Great Plains	1	1.10	1.53	2.12	2.39	2.79	2.99
Texas-Oklahoma	1	1.08	1.53	1.93	1.73	2.41	2.66
Mountain	1	1.05	1.11	1.87	1.75	2.06	2.60
Pacific	1	1.24	1.39	1.45	1.37	1.96	2.42
	1940	1950	1960				
U.S.	2.71	4.13	7.58				
Corn Belt	2.88	4.07	6.70				
Northeast	2.56	3.85	6.62				
Appalachians	2.64	3.90	5.89				
Southeast	3.04	4.35	12.35				
Lake states	2.42	3.55	7.56				
Delta states	1.91	2.79	8.48				
Great Plains	2.44	3.76	6.28				
Texas-Oklahoma	3.10	6.51	10.19				
Mountain	3.30	4.56	8.35				
Pacific	3.26	3.99	7.45				

SOURCE: Technological change index $A(t)$ calculated from

$$\frac{\Delta A}{A} = \frac{\Delta y}{y} - W_k \frac{\Delta k}{k}$$

where A(1870) = 1 and

$$A(t + 1) = A(t)\left(1 + \frac{\Delta A}{A}\right)$$

Derivation of the data is explained in the Appendix.

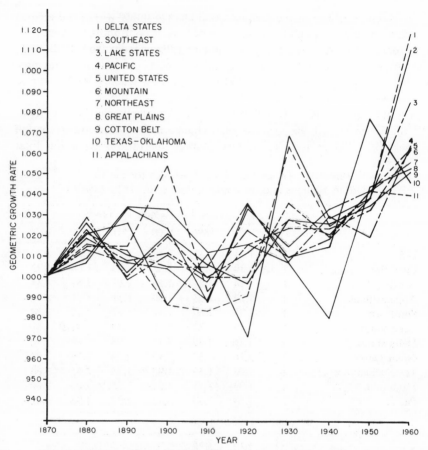

Figure 7-1 (a). Geometric Growth of Technological Change. (Note: The purpose of this figure is to show how closely together the change rates for different samples move. The author dose not intend the reader to follow the line for any particular sample.)

World War might have caused this. The index of the Delta states suffered a long series of declines, beginning in 1890 and extending through 1920. The decline was so severe that the 1920 index is .11 below the 1870 initial value and .43 off the 1890 high. However, by 1960, $A(t)$ for this region was third highest.

Technological change for the Corn Belt is presented in Table 7.3. There are two series for this region: the first, which is comparable to the measures of the previous Table, is given in column 1, while the second, the aggregation of the five states of the Corn Belt, is given in column 2. Technological change is shown for twelve counties in Indiana and Iowa in Tables 7.4 and 7.5. These figures are comparable to the state figures of Table 7.3.

A discussion of these data and their derivation is given in the Appendix. The geometric growth rate of technological change for each region in each

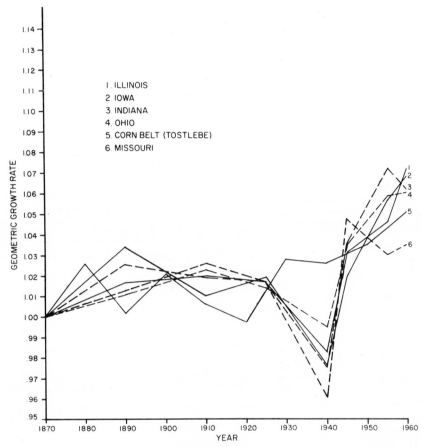

Figure 7-1 (b).

Table 7.3 Technological Change Index for the
Five Corn Belt States and their Aggregate Index, 1870–1960

Corn Belt (Tostlebe)		Corn Belt (Aggregate)		Corrected				
				Ill.	Ind.	Iowa	Mo.	Ohio
T. C. Index for Region in Year:								
1870	1		1	1	1	1	1	1
1880	1.30							
1890	1.33		1.51	1.41	1.30	1.94	1.64	1.25
1900	1.71							
1910	1.78		2.18	2.11	2.17	2.35	2.39	1.94
1920	1.74	1925	2.34	2.34	2.37	2.69	2.64	2.06
1930	2.22	1940	1.78	1.80	1.62	1.86	1.46	1.85
1940	2.88	1945	1.99	1.97	1.92	1.94	1.85	2.14
1950	4.07	1955	2.82	2.52	3.30	2.62	2.30	3.50
1960	6.70	1960	4.38	3.85	4.85	4.09	4.22	4.87

SOURCE: See Table 7.2.

Table 7.4   Technological Change Index for Six
Indiana Counties, 1870–1960

	Carroll	Clinton	Morgan	Rush	St. Jos.	Wabash
	T. C. Index for Region in Year:					
1870	1	1	1	1	1	1
1890	1.524	1.346	.929	.803	1.866	2.117
1910	2.073	2.672	1.202	1.864	2.103	2.574
1925	2.782	3.548	2.043	2.926	1.945	3.138
1940	2.776	3.299	1.069	1.165	1.607	1.541
1945	2.501	2.963	1.166	1.594	1.613	2.266
1955	5.162	6.160	3.089	2.795	4.002	4.066
1960	6.639	7.792	3.398	4.956	5.463	6.062

SOURCE: See Table 7.2.

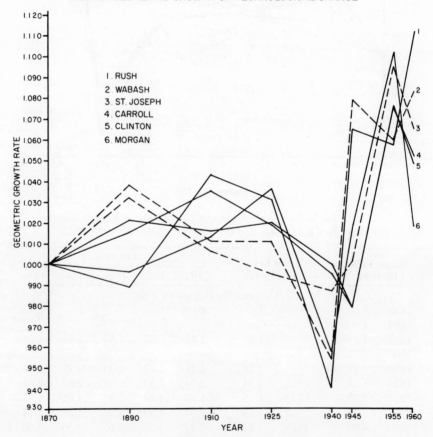

INDIANA : GEOMETRIC GROWTH OF TECHNOLOGICAL CHANGE

1 . RUSH
2 . WABASH
3 . ST. JOSEPH
4 . CARROLL
5 . CLINTON
6 . MORGAN

Figure 7-1 (c).

Table 7.5 Technological Change Index for
Six Iowa Counties, 1870–1960

	Benton	Blackhawk	Clinton	Johnson	Marion	Winneshick
	T. C. Index for Region in Year:					
1870	1	1	1	1	1	1
1890	2.242	1.973	1.701	1.532	1.509	1.314
1910	2.363	2.308	2.032	1.895	1.962	1.578
1925	2.895	2.691	2.453	2.373	3.298	2.613
1940	2.180	1.744	1.374	1.300	1.412	1.009
1945	2.502	1.925	1.396	1.580	1.195	1.355
1955	3.811	4.426	3.374	3.018	2.552	2.150
1960	5.915	5.099	4.717	3.911	3.024	2.741

SOURCE: See Table 7.2.

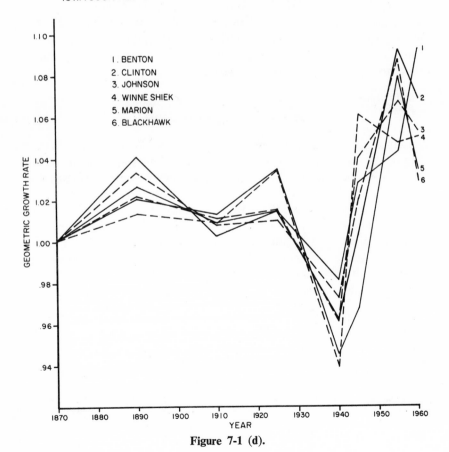

Figure 7-1 (d).

time period is shown in Figure 7.1. The general decline in the 1925–40 period might be similar to that in the Great Plains region or it might be caused by the lingering effects of the agricultural depression. Notice that regions seem highly correlated in their time profiles, a rather unexpected conclusion.

Capital's Share in Increased Productivity

Using Solow's measure, it may be observed that, if both capital and output grow at the same rate, the share of capital in income, W_k, will measure the contribution of capital to increased output per man.[5] Thus, W_k might seem to have a marked influence on the share of capital in increased productivity.

But W_k does not bear nearly so heavily on measured technological change as the observation might indicate. Over the period, capital per man increased less than half as fast as output per man, as shown in Table 7.1. Therefore, with W_k less than 1 (increases in capital raise output less than proportionally) the share of capital in increased output must be less than one-half. But even more can be said since all available estimates of W_k put it firmly below one-half (see Table 7.12). Thus, given the assumption that technological change is neutral, an upper bound of 25 per cent for the contribution of capital to increased output seems reasonable.[6]

Measuring the Aggregation Problem

Disaggregation may be expected, a priori, to increase variation. The additional variation obtains from uncontrolled factors in the analysis which become more prominent as the averaging is reduced. Some of this additional variation is relevant, such as disaggregation into two regions specializing in different crops. In this case the index for each region is essentially a measure of the technological change in its special crop. Disaggregation into regions experiencing different weather conditions can also be relevant if regions which experienced normal weather conditions are isolated. However, this disaggregation may increase the importance of factors irrelevant to the analysis such as cross sectional variation in labor quality.

[5]Starting with Equation (1), output and capital are assumed to increase at the same rate to get equation

$$\frac{\Delta A}{A} = \left(1 - W_k\right)\frac{\Delta y}{y} \quad \text{if} \quad \frac{\Delta y}{y} = \frac{\Delta k}{k} \tag{2}$$

Here the share of technological change in increased output is $(1 - W_k)$ while that of capital is W_k.

[6]Domar (1961) and Solow (1960) have warned against taking such a figure too seriously because of the assumption of neutral technological change. However, Phelps (1962) casts doubt on the importance of the "new view."

The extent of disaggregation should be determined by the level of spurious variation. When this "noise" begins to obscure the results, disaggregation ceases to be useful (Griliches and Grunfeld [1960]). This difficulty can be minimized if long time periods are employed since spurious variation is unlikely to persist over a number of years. The length of the period under consideration gives some assurance as to the accuracy of the county estimates.

One test of the influence of disaggregation might involve examining the variation at each stage to see if wide differences are being obscured. The arithmetic means and standard deviations of each set of disaggregate regions considered are presented in Table 7.6. For comparison, the index for the aggregate area is also presented. The unweighted mean of each set of disaggregate regions is quite close to the index of their aggregate area (See Domar's conclusions about optimal aggregation [1961]). Thus, the first objection to aggregation, that it might introduce a bias in the level of the measure, is not an important one. A glance at the table shows the variation around the mean to be considerable. This result might obtain for a variety of reasons, such as inaccurate observations or abnormal weather.

Table 7.6   Comparison of Aggregate and Disaggregate
Technological Change Indices

	Mean of 1960 Regional Indices	Standard Deviation of Regional Indices		1960 Index of Aggregate Region
	Disaggregate Regions:			
10 USDA regions	8.025	1.975	U. S. index	7.58
5 Corn Belt states	4.376	.464	C. B. index	4.381
6 Indiana counties	5.718	.510	Ind. index	4.852
6 Iowa counties	4.235	.389	Iowa index	4.089

SOURCE: Tables 7.2–5. The mean is the simple arithmetic mean of the 1960 estimate of the technological change index.

A test for significance of differences that takes account of spurious variation is an analysis of variance. A two way classification is employed to test equality of both regional and year means. In performing this test the assumption is made that the index of technological change grew geometrically within each period. The data used in the test were the geometric rates of growth over the nine decennial periods under consideration (see Figure 7.1).

Before this test may be performed, the assumption of normality upon which it is based must be verified. To examine the distribution of the geometric rates of growth within each region over time a chi square goodness of fit test was employed. Results of the test are summarized in Table 7.7.

In no case can the hypothesis of normality be rejected. Bartlett's test for homogeneity of variance across regions was also performed with results summarized in Table 7.7.

In Table 7.8 the results of the two-way classification analysis of variance are presented. In all cases the F values for between region (column) variation,

Table 7.7   Tests on Geometric Growth Rates
of Technological Change

	χ^2 Test for Non-normality Within Regions			
	Number of Observations	χ^2	df	Critical χ^2 for $\alpha = .05$
10 USDA regions	90	6.81	5	11.07
Corn Belt	35	1.417	1	3.84
Indiana counties	42	3.79	3	7.81
Iowa counties	42	0.99	1	3.84
	Bartlett's χ^2 Test for Equality of Variance Between Regions			
		χ^2	df	Critical χ^2 for $\alpha = .05$
10 USDA regions		8.3	8	16.9
Corn Belt		0.9	6	12.6
Indiana counties		3.7	6	12.6
Iowa counties		0.3	6	12.6

holding the variation between years constant, are not significant. Thus, in view of the variation between years, regions were highly similar in their growth rates of technological change. The tests also indicate in all cases that the F values for between year (row) variation, holding the variation between regions constant, were highly significant. Thus, in view of the variation between regions, the geometric growth rates of technological change were varied in different periods. A consequence of the first conclusion is

Table 7.8   Two-way Analysis of Variance:
Variation in Geometric Growth of T.C. between Regions and Between Years

	F Value Between Regions (Holding Years Variation Constant)	F Value Between Years (Holding Regional Variation Constant)	df v_2/v_1	Critical F for $\alpha = .01$
10 USDA regions	<1	16.4	8/72	5.00
Corn Belt	<1	42.6	6/24	7.31
Indiana counties	<1	10.3	8/32	5.20
Iowa counties	<1	18.3	8/32	5.20

that the aggregation of various regions into an aggregate one did not do great damage to the underlying figures. Both of these conclusions could have been guessed from examination of Figure 7.1. The regional indices in each section of the figure are highly collinear while the variation between years seems to overshadow between region variations.

The results of the analysis of variance seem so conclusive that even the slight departure from normality that might be present in the data would not affect their significance. The F test is a hardy one since departures from normality tend to have small effects.

Conclusion

When using Solow's method of measuring technological change, aggregation of data does not appear to be a problem, at least not in going from the county level to the total agricultural sector. The foregoing analysis does not apply to the problems of (a) disaggregating to the farm level or (b) fitting a multifactor aggregate production function of the Griliches (1963) variety to measure technological change.

Qualifications

The variation in the calculated rate of technological change for the regions composing an aggregate area has been measured. If the variation is not significant, the aggregation should not obscure the data assuming that the aggregation per se introduces no bias.

However, the results must be qualitied in the absence of perfect competition. A downward bias in the aggregate labor measure as suggested by Kendrick (1961) is one possible error. If there is a shift toward higher wages, the aggregate rise in productivity will be less than the productivity increases in individual areas. Kendrick deals with the problem by weighting labor by the industry wage. In order for the problem to be important in these data, labor must have shifted in search of higher wages with wage differentials quite large in 1870. Neither of these possibilities seems important, although there is an argument to the effect that the homogeneity of productivity increase across regions is some evidence for the mobility of factors. To the extent that this argument is important, Kendrick's adjustment would have value.

The preparation of the data may partially account for the absence of an aggregation problem. However, the analysis utilizes state and county data taken directly from the census where built-in uniformity would seem minimal. Since the state and county figures agree with the conclusion, such a possible objection loses importance.

Other problems associated with aggregation center around the estimate of W_k and the use of only two factors of production. While these difficulties are discussed elsewhere in this paper, it might be noted that breaking up the residual would tend to emphasize the differences between regions to the extent that the unexplained portion of the residual is not homogeneous. Thus, intermediate products might be much more important for one crop than another. Taking account of these difficulties might increase variation between regions and possibly alter the conclusions.

Finally the aggregation of farms into counties should be considered. Such aggregation might mask considerable variation and prove unjustified by the test employed in this paper. When several hundred farms have been aggregated into a county, the differences steming from cross sectional variation in managers and labor and in the efficiency of different farms are likely to be considerably diminished. However, when policy is at issue, this last disaggregation is of little interest since agriculture can hardly be dealt with farm by farm.

Appendix : Derivation of the Data

Labor estimates. Estimates of labor came primarily from Tostlebe [1957]. These tables give labor by the USDA regions and the entire United States for the period 1870–1950. Extending the estimates to 1960 involved using census figures comparable, according to the census, with the 1950 estimates of Tostlebe.

Estimates for the Corn Belt states were prepared in a fashion comparable to Tostlebe's figures. These procedures could not be utilized at the county level since there was no county breakdown over the first part of the period. For 1870–1925 labor was assumed to be spread uniformly across the farms of the state. Thus, the ratio of total labor to the number of farms was computed for the state and then multiplied by the number of farms in each county to obtain county labor estimates.

The labor estimates for the 1940–60 period were prepared with the aid of the agricultural census for the appropriate year. The census counted all workers as of the date of enumeration. However, the census definition of total labor as family plus hired labor resulted in figures significantly higher than the state estimates, which were derived from the population census as described above. To obtain consistency, the extent of the state bias was calculated; county figures were adjusted by assuming that the bias was evenly spread across the state.

Output estimates. Tostlebe's estimates of output for the United States and USDA regions provided the basis of the figures used. These output indices as well as the ones derived for states and counties can be characterized as measuring the output of farms. (The estimates are basically those of Strauss-Bean for 1860–1919 and the USDA for 1909–1949.) The indices include estimates of deflated cash receipts and the value of home consumption. Tostlebe excludes government payments and rental value of farm dwellings from the USDA index. To the extent that factors were included that were paid for by the government, there is an underestimate of production in the later years and a downward bias in the estimate of technological change.

The gross nature of the measure presents some difficulties with respect to intermediate products. Neither the oats raised for horses nor gasoline, seed and fertilizer are counted. Such a procedure may seem consistent and unbiased; however, there is speculation that the share of these intermediate goods has been increasing over time. The earlier discussion would lead to the conclusion that such increase in an excluded variable increases the estimate of $A(t)$.

Extending the output estimates to 1960 involved deflating cash receipts from marketing by the USDA price index. This 1960 figure does not include an estimate for home consumption and so is subject to a substantial downward bias.

State estimates of output were prepared by multiplying the quantities produced (listed in the census) by their 1910–14 prices as calculated from series in *Historical Statistics* (1960); for the 1910 estimate the census value of cash receipts and estimated value of home consumption was used. For the early years there is double counting since some of the crops were animal feed. Such double counting entails an overestimate of output in the early years and thus an underestimate of the increase in output and therefore of technological change.

For the 1940–60 period a slight variation in procedure was used. Deflation indices were calculated on the basis of implicit prices (quality sold divided into value of commodities sold) deflated to 1910–14 prices. The percentage share of a commodity in one of six categories was calculated and used to derive the deflation index for the total category. These indices were used to convert current values of commodities sold into 1910–14 prices (see Table 7.9). These state deflation categories were retained for use in deflating the county output figures.

Consistency in the state deflations was checked by comparing the output for the Corn Belt as given in Tostlebe with that calculated by adding the five state outputs. The added figure is lower in 1870 and higher in 1960 indicating that output per man has increased less with the estimate used than it would have increased using figures strictly comparable to those of Tostlebe. The differences are due to Tostlebe's attempt to eliminate double counting and his inclusion of the value of home consumption.

The county estimates of output were derived in the same fashion as the

Table 7.9 Deflation Indices for Output, 1910–1914 = 100

	U. S.*	Ill.	Ind.	Iowa	Mo.	Ohio
1940						
(1) field crop	84	80.8	81.1	81	82.2	86.1
(2) vegetables	122	122	122	122	122	122
(3) fruits and hort.	81	81	81	81	81	81
(4) dairy prod.	120	120	120	120	120	120
(5) poultry	98	101	102	88.8	80.1	111
(6) other livestock	108	133	121	139	120	111
1945						
(1) field crop	166	173.6	177.1	158.8	169.1	180
(2) vegetables	236	236	236	236	236	236
(3) fruits and hort.	233	233	233	233	233	233
(4) dairy prod.	222	222	222	222	222	222
(5) poultry	177	171	177	171	167	185
(6) other livestock	190	228	216	264	213	193
1955						
(1) field crop	232	204	201	182	227	201
(2) vegetables	216	216	216	216	216	216
(3) fruits and hort.	209	209	209	209	209	209
(4) dairy prod.	246	246	246	246	246	246
(5) poultry	178	135	163	132	148	181
(6) other livestock	283	269	266	272	267	278
1960						
(1) field crop	202	177.4	175.6	158.4	197.3	175.6
(2) vegetables	235	235	235	235	235	235
(3) fruits and hort.	212	212	212	212	212	212
(4) dairy prod.	257	257	257	257	257	257
(5) poultry	143	109	131	106	119	145.5
(5) other livestock	313	297	294	301	295	308

	1870	1890†	1925	1940	1945	1955‡	1960
Implements	136	93.5	150	159	195	312	381

SOURCE: *U.S. Indices from USDA (1961), *Agricultural Prices*.
†1870–1945 values from Tostlebe (1957) calculated from Tables 7.7 and 7.9.
‡USDA (1961), *Agricultural Prices*, "Deflation Indices for Machinery."

state estimates for the period 1870–1925. For the last twenty years, county figures were deflated from the census figures of the current value of output sold by the calculated state deflation figures within each category. This change was instituted to account for the increasing number and importance of specialty crops not easily subject to price-quantity deflation.

An exception to these procedures was noted in 1925 when the census did not list the value of livestock sold. USDA figures on total livestock production in 1909 and 1924 were used to measure the increase in output. A calculated increase of 13.6 per cent was applied to the 1910 census figure for "other livestock sold alive or slaughtered" to derive the 1925 estimate.

Capital estimates. Capital estimates are based on Tostlebe's figures giving capital by regions 1870–1950. Extending the series to 1960 was straightforward for the United States, but capital was not broken into regional estimates. Thus, the assumption was made that capital in each sector increased by the same percentage as it did in the United States. Both state and county 1960 capital figures were calculated similarly.

In deriving state and county capital estimates for 1870–1950, the value of implements and machinery was given in each census until the 1950's. This value was deflated by the series implicit in Tostlebe's current and constant price data from 1870–1945 and by the USDA machinery indices, thereafter. The value of livestock on hand was estimated by the same method outlined for estimating output. After these components were added, it became apparent that certain series were missing. Crop inventories, implements, and machinery in 1955 and 1960, and the value of buildings from 1940 on were not available. For lack of more information the share of these missing components was calculated from the USDA Balance Sheet of Agriculture (1961) figures giving the percentage of total capital occupied by the missing categories (see Table 7.10).

Land prices present the most important problem in state and county figures since land remained overwhelmingly important in total capital over the period. Tostlebe estimated land prices in the ratio 3:1 (in favor of improved over unimproved acres) based on a small sample of land sales. He modified the ratio to 3:2 for the Great Plains and Illinois and Iowa.

Table 7.10 Physical Assets of Agriculture
Billions of 1947–49 Dollars

	Land	Livestock	Machinery	Crops stored	Household furnishings	Total
1940	33.6	5.1	3.1	2.7	4.3	48.8
1945	34.4	5.6	3.1	3.2	4.4	50.7
1955	37.3	5.1	7.6	3.6	6.6	60.2
1960	38.2	5.3	7.3	3.8	7.2	61.8

SOURCE: *Balance Sheet of Agriculture* (1961). For 1940 and 1945 state and county figures were available for land, livestock, and machinery; figures for crops stored and household furnishings were not available. For 1955 and 1960 state and county figures were available for land and livestock; figures for machinery, crops stored, and household furnishings were not available. Thus, the observed figures for capital in the years was adjusted by multiplying it by the figures below to derive total capital.

1940	1.165	= total/(land + livestk. + mach.)
1945	1.175	
1955	1.42	= total/(land + livestk.)
1960	1.42	

The cost of improving land would seem constant within a given type of terrain and so not the ratio, but the difference in price, should be constant. Using this assumption, the land clearing costs in 1910–14 prices are required. However, research in this area is not far advanced and, of a number of arbitrary values tried, $40 per acre seemed most reasonable since it roughly agreed with Tostlebe's estimates (see Table 7.11). The estimated $40 an acre is intended to reflect quality differentials in the land to be cleared.

Table 7.11   Value of Improved and Unimproved Land

	Ill.	Ind.	Iowa	Mo.	Ohio
(1) Improved $/acre	$119.50	$67.90	$87.80	$53.35	$61.45
(2) Unimproved $/acre	$79.50	$27.90	$47.80	$13.35	$21.45
(3) Ratio improved/unimproved	1.195	2.43	1.83	4.00	2.86
(4) Tostlebe ratio improved/un-improved	1.5	3	1.5	3	3
(5) Tostlebe improved $/acre				$56.00	$63.27
(6) Tostelbe unimproved $/acre				$18.00	$21.27

SOURCE: (1) and (2) value of land calculated from 1910 census assuming that improved land is worth $40 an acre more than unimproved land. (3) the ratio of the value of improved to unimproved land. (4) the ratio as assumed by Tostlebe (1957). (5) and (6) the value of land given in Tostlebe (1957) as the basis of his assumed value ratios.

The actual values for these land prices were derived using the 1910 census figures for improved and unimproved acres and the value of all land. A simple linear equation was solved for each state and the resulting prices assumed to hold for the counties within that state.[7]

The preparation of the capital series may lead to biased results. The capital stock is being measured, rather than the flow of capital services, the relevant measure. The approximation is at best a tenuous one, and in the case of farmland it may be worthless. The land in farms stayed approximately constant over the period although the percentage of improved acres increased markedly. If the unimproved land were of no productive value, this considerable share would be represented in capital without contributing to output. The considerable part that land plays in capital indicates that capital would have been overestimated at the beginning of the period and so rose more than indicated.

The share of capital in income. An in a previous study (Chapter 5), the data series causing the greatest difficulty was the share of capital in income.

---

[7]The linear equation is given in Formula (3) where P is (3) $P_1 Q_1 + P_u Q_u = V$ the price of land subscripted for either improved or unimproved acres, Q is the quantity of each type of land, properly subscripted, and V is the total value of all land. Since Formula (3) is one equation with two unknowns, it was assumed that $P_i - 40 = P_u$ to derive Formula (4).

$$P_i Q_i + (P_i - 40)Q_u = V \qquad (4)$$

Evidence presented in the previous study indicated that the most satisfactory measure involved the assumption that all capital earned a 5 per cent return. This measure amounts to assuming that W_k is 1/20 the capital-output ratio. Expressed in this way it can be seen that a spuriously low observation of output would bias the index of technological change downward.

The calculated estimates of capital's share in income as compared to the estimates of three other researchers are given in Table 7.12. It is apparent that, so far as the figures of Griliches, and Ruttan and Stout are concerned, the values are too small. An underestimate of W_k leads to a higher measured $A(t)$ for the latter years. However, as previously noted, the technological change index is not sensitive to errors in this series.

Table 7.12   Estimates of Capital's Share in Income

Johnson*		Ruttan and Stout†					
U. S.		U. S.	NE	NC	S	M	P
1910 .48							
1925 .427	1925–28	.354	.298	.420	.284	.332	.355
1940 .307	1938–40	.283	.262	.326	.248	.270	.256
1945 .195							
	1954–57	.319	.279	.340	.309	.354	.268

Griliches‡		K/20y				
U. S.		U. S.	Corn Belt	NE	APP	SE
	1910	.348	.459	.322	.264	.167
	1920	.366	.492	.245	.280	.246
	1930	.350	.382	.208	.200	.132
	1940	.283	.316	.166	.182	.123
1949 .45	1950	.203	.275	.142	.170	.141
	1960	.213	.263	.138	.209	.112

SOURCES: *Johnson (1948), Table II, p. 729.
†Ruttan and Stout (1960), Table 3A, p. 62.
‡Griliches (1963), Table 2, p. 11 a.

Bibliography

Abramovitz 1956, Arrow, Chenery, Minhas and Solow 1961, Barnett 1961, Bidwell and Falconer 1925, Budd 1960, Chandler 1962, Denison 1960, Domar 1961, 1962, Griliches 1958, 1963, Griliches and Grunfeld 1960, *Historical Statistics* 1960, Hogan 1958, Houthakker 1955, Johnson 1948, Johansen 1961, Kendrick 1961, Massell 1960, Phelps 1962, Primack 1962, Rasmussen 1962, Robinson 1962, Rostow 1960, Ruttan 1960, Ruttan and Stout 1958, 1960, Samuelson 1962, Solow 1957, 1960, 1962, Tostlebe 1957, Theil 1954, Towne and Rasmussen 1960, USDA 1961a, 1961b.

CHAPTER EIGHT

The Aggregation Problem : Some Further Results

Lester Lave and Fred Rueter

A first look at the aggregation problem was offered by Chapter 7. Two questions were examined: (1) Was there a bias in aggregating? (2) Was significant variation covered by aggregation? A series of tests showed both answers to be negative, although the first question was approached only by an informal comparison of the unweighted mean of the regions with the technological change estimate of the aggregate.

The aggregation problem takes on a broader definition when applied to the level of the entire economy. A third proposition can be added to the two above: (3) is there significant interaction between different sectors of the economy?[1] In measuring technological change for two-digit manufacturing industries as was done in Chapter 3 and in Massell (1961), the output of one industry is the input of another; resources are shared. What part of measured technological change is specific to each industry?

Aggregate technological change might be viewed as the sum of technological change in each industry plus the efficiency increase resulting from the movement of factors to more efficient industries. The efficiency of the economy rises when a man takes a job in a new industry which gives him

---

[1]Meade (1961) and Gordon (1961) have looked at neutrality in a two sector model under changing relative prices.

a higher wage, when capital is invested in an industry giving it a higher rate of return.

Massell (1961) measures technological change at the two-digit industry level and then divides aggregate technological change into intraindustry technological change and efficiency increases owing to movements of labor and capital. His results are shown in Table 8.1.

Table 8.1   Technological Change: Intraindustry and Interindustry

Year	Intraindustry Technological Change	Interindustry Shifts owing to Labor Shifts	Interindustry Shifts owing to Capital Shifts
1950	.023	.0012	.0032
1951	.021	.0027	.0078
1952	.002	.0016	.0114
1953	.007	.0005	.0140
1954	.036	.0004	.0034
1955	.020	.0006	.0085
1956	.024	.0011	.0042
mean	.019	.0012	.0075

SOURCE: Massell (1961).

Massell concludes that there is significant interindustry technological change. However, there are difficulties in his data. The only measure of output that can make sense in this investigation is value added. These data were not available to Massell and so his output figures are Federal Reserve indices of industrial production weighted by value added in 1954. There are also problems with the other series, capital in particular. Beginning with the Department of Commerce series for total book value of capital in manufacturing, Massell divides this capital among the various industries according to the Treasury data on each industry's share of book-value capital. Finally, the capital stock is adjusted for idle capacity by assuming capital is unemployed in the same ratio as labor. In view of these data difficulties, the conclusions must be qualified.

The first two questions concerning aggregation can be answered at a level where the data offer fewer problems. Domar (1961) has shown the relation between the aggregated technological change index of a sector and the index of the aggregate sector under two assumptions: (1) the form of the production function is Cobb-Douglas; (2) no firm uses the output of another firm in this sector as an input. His algebra shows

> ... the rate of growth of the residual for the whole sector equals the sum of the A's of the component industries, each A weighted by the ratio of the

value of the output of the industry to the value of the final product of the sector (in the base period) (Domar [1961, p 49]).

This result is translated into Equation (1)

$$A = \sum_{i=1}^{n} \gamma_i A_i \qquad (1)$$

where γ_i is the ratio of the output of firm i to the total output of the sector; A_i is the measure of technological change for the ith firm as calculated by the geometric index; and A is the measure of technological change for the whole sector.

Strictly speaking, the measure is not related to the measure of Chapter 7 since (1) the measure of W_k used in calculating technological change was neither consistent with a Cobb-Douglas function nor with the geometric index and (2) farms do use some of the output of other farms as their inputs. It was the conclusion of Chapters 3 and 7 that the Cobb-Douglas function is a good approximation to the general function used in the geometric index and that the measure of W_k is not important in the analysis. It is also probable that the error from farms using the outputs of other farms as inputs is not likely to be large. We assume that Equation (1) is likely to be a good predictor of Equation (2),

$$\hat{A} = \sum_{i=1}^{n} \gamma_i A_i + u_i \qquad (2)$$

the true equation, where u is an error term resulting from these objections.

Method

The data of Chapter 7 were fitted into Equation (2) at three levels of aggregation: the entire agricultural sector, the ten BAE regions, and the five states that make up the Corn Belt. Weights have been computed for each of the years in which a measurement of technological change was made and each of these sets of weights has been applied to data from 1870 through 1960. In addition, we have also computed a moving weighted average, in which the values of the technological change index in a given region in a given year are weighted by the appropriate factor for that region in that year. Thus, a sequence of static weighted averages of the following form has been constructed:

$$\hat{A}_t = \frac{\sum\limits_{i=1}^{n} Y_i A_{it}}{\sum\limits_{i=1}^{n} Y_i} \qquad (3)$$

where $\hat{A}_t$ = the value of the technological change index in the aggregate sector in time period t, using Domar's aggregation method

Table 8.2   United States Regional Weights

Sector	1870	1880	1890	1900	1910
			Year		
Corn Belt	.306	.319	.276	.279	.260
Northeast	.259	.199	.170	.132	.103
Appalachians	.143	.126	.108	.113	.110
Southeast	.081	.078	.087	.068	.083
Lake states	.079	.096	.092	.094	.090
Delta states	.068	.068	.073	.060	.054
Great Plains	.015	.041	.084	.105	.127
Texas-Oklahoma	.020	.030	.045	.072	.081
Mountain	.005	.008	.015	.029	.039
Pacific	.024	.035	.049	.048	.053
	1920	1930	1940	1950	1960
Corn Belt	.208	.218	.237	.228	.224
Northeast	.106	.099	.112	.092	.091
Appalachians	.103	.101	.110	.103	.076
Southeast	.071	.067	.065	.061	.077
Lake states	.094	.095	.103	.101	.095
Delta states	.055	.058	.055	.050	.057
Great Plains	.119	.120	.082	.097	.103
Texas-Oklahoma	.116	.095	.081	.104	.082
Mountain	.053	.058	.060	.066	.071
Pacific	.075	.089	.095	.098	.125

Y_i = the value of the output final to region i in the appropriate period

A_{it} = the value of the technological change index in region i of the aggregate sector in time period t derived by Solow's method

n = the number of regions

and one moving average of the form has been constructed:

$$\hat{A}_t = \frac{\sum\limits_{i=1}^{n} Y_{it} A_{it}}{\sum\limits_{i=1}^{n} Y_{it}} \qquad (4)$$

where Y_{it} = the value of the output final to region i of the aggregate sector in time period t

Each of these measures has been compared both to the aggregate index of the total sector and to the unweighted average of the indices of the various regions which comprise the sector. The criterion of goodness of fit is defined as follows:

$$\text{Variance}_t = \sum_{i=1}^{n} \frac{(A_t - A_{it})^2}{n} = \text{the variance of the various} \qquad (5)$$

technological change indices from the actual aggregate index in period t as calculated directly by Solow's method. The denominator of this equation is n rather than $(n-1)$ since A_t is determined independently of A_{it} and, hence, no degrees of freedom have been lost due to estimation.

$$\text{Residual } t,k = (A_t - \hat{A}_{t,k})^2 = \text{the squared difference between} \qquad (6)$$

the actual aggregate index and the estimated aggregate index derived using weighting method k.

Thus,

$$r_k^2 = 1 - \sum_{t=1}^{T} \frac{\text{residual}_{t,k}}{\text{variance}_t} \qquad 1 - \sum_{t=1}^{T} \frac{(A_t - \hat{A}_{t,k})^2}{\sum_{i=1}^{n} \frac{(A_t - A_{it})^2}{n}} \qquad (7)$$

where T is the number of periods under consideration. The statistical properties of r_k^2 have not been fully explored and so it is used only as a means of comparing the relative goodness of fit of these various aggregate measures. A high, or low, value of r_k^2 does not imply a good or bad fit, but merely indicates a relatively better, or worse, fit than that indicated by an intermediate value of r_k^2.

Results

Ten BAE regions versus the agricultural sector. Domar's weights, computed for each of the ten BAE regions for each decade between 1870 and 1960, are presented in Table 8.2. The technological change indices calculated using these weights, and the unweighted average and aggregate indices with which they are to be compared, are presented in Table 8.3. In nine of eleven instances weighted averages which incorporate Domar's method are markedly superior to the unweighted average. The two exceptions occur when using the weights of periods which have experienced rather extreme economic dislocations—recovery from the first World War in 1920 and the Great Depression in 1930. Surprisingly, however, many of the static weighted averages produce more precise results than the measures generated using moving weights. This result becomes clearer after exploring the geometric index. For any period after the first few periods, the index takes the form:

$$A(t) = \left(1 + \frac{\Delta A_1}{A(1)}\right)\left(1 + \frac{\Delta A_2}{A(2)}\right) \cdots \left(1 + \frac{\Delta A_{t-1}}{A(t-1)}\right) \qquad (8)$$

Consequently, the index is not particularly sensitive to recent changes in the residual unless these changes are extremely large in magnitude. For this same reason, it is not surprising to discover that neither the initial nor the final year, but, rather, one of the intervening years, provides the best weights for aggregation. In fact, several of the intermediate years provide superior measures to those obtained in both 1870 and 1960, the ones that

Table 8.3   Technological Change Index:
United States—Regional Aggregation

Year	Aggregate	Average	1870	1880	1890	1900	1910
				Measure			
1880	1.21	1.187	1.229	1.229	1.215	1.217	1.211
1890	1.31	1.356	1.311	1.326	1.341	1.350	1.361
1900	1.48	1.576	1.460	1.500	1.524	1.571	1.603
1910	1.49	1.560	1.459	1.506	1.544	1.584	1.630
1920	1.67	1.785	1.589	1.641	1.697	1.770	1.805
1930	2.20	2.268	2.080	2.128	2.183	2.238	2.279
1940	2.71	2.755	2.684	2.691	2.796	2.722	2.742
1950	4.13	4.133	3.891	3.931	4.007	4.365	4.209
1960	7.58	7.987	7.351	7.349	7.517	7.459	7.577
r_k^2	...	(.4403)	(.7062)	(.7918)	(.8520)	(.6512)	(.4893)

1920	1930	1940	1950	1960	Moving Average	
1.196	1.205	1.212	1.205	1.208	1.229	
1.363	1.383	1.345	1.352	1.359	1.326	
1.612	1.604	1.578	1.606	1.597	1.524	
1.618	1.614	1.578	1.606	1.603	1.584	
1.842	1.854	1.718	1.833	1.823	1.805	
2.296	2.296	2.254	2.289	2.294	2.296	
2.760	2.749	2.826	2.790	2.802	2.749	
4.196	4.256	4.340	4.181	4.139	4.340	
7.680	7.722	7.892	7.684	7.720	7.634	
(.4002)	(.3259)	(.5111)	(.4777)	(.4688)	(.6240)	

intuitively would be expected to produce the most precise basis for aggregation. There appears to be no way to determine a priori the optimal weights. Yet, since almost all the measures using Domar's weighting scheme are markedly superior to the unweighted average, selection of any one optimal set of weights appears less important than use of the weighting system itself, provided that the weights of a relatively stable period are chosen.

Five Corn Belt states versus the Corn Belt. The results obtained on the next lower level of aggregation, using the weights presented in Table 8.4, are strikingly similar to, yet slightly less conclusive than, those previously presented. As illustrated in Table 8.5, Domar's weighting method is superior to an unweighted average in six of nine instances. At this level, however, the exceptions are more difficult to explain. The bad fit obtained using the 1945 weights is attributable to the wartime conditions existing during that period, but the other two inferior series cannot be explained by purely economic phenomena. The 1960 deficiencies become less significant when it is realized that, owing to lack of available data, the 1960 values of

Table 8.4   Corn Belt Weights

State	Year							
	1870	1890	1910	1925	1940	1945	1955	1960
Illinois	.306	.257	.250	.266	.260	.259	.261	.267
Indiana	.154	.126	.146	.139	.136	.150	.159	.144
Iowa	.174	.290	.256	.271	.300	.289	.312	.320
Missouri	.132	.169	.183	.150	.148	.151	.122	.143
Ohio	.235	.158	.165	.173	.157	.151	.146	.126

capital, labor, and output have been obtained by projecting the trend of these series through 1955. From Table 8.3, a similar effect seems to occur on the national level when the 1960 weights are used, but the effect is not so great as to make Domar's series worse than an unweighted average. A

Table 8.5   Corn Belt: State Aggregation

Year	Aggregate	Average	Measure				
			1870	1890	1910	1925	1940
1890	1.51	1.508	1.479	1.564	1.546	1.544	1.564
1910	2.18	2.192	2.162	2.208	2.203	2.194	2.208
1925	2.46	2.420	2.381	2.438	2.443	2.434	2.452
1940	1.78	1.718	1.753	1.745	1.734	1.747	1.752
1955	1.99	1.964	1.984	1.961	1.962	1.965	1.965
1960	4.381	4.376	4.337	4.268	4.336	4.282	4.276
r_k^2	...	(.7430)	(.7922)	(.7085)	(.7560)	(.8296)	(.7867)

1945	1955	1960	Moving Average
1.559	1.563	1.576	1.479
2.216	2.205	2.213	2.208
2.450	2.451	2.465	2.443
1.748	1.756	1.750	1.747
2.781	2.791	2.757	2.781
4.276	4.276	4.225	4.276
(.7109)	(.7581)	(.6152)	(.8059)

reasonable explanation for the weakness of the 1890 series appears to be that errors have occurred in the measurement of the output series at the state level.

Once again, the static weights derived from an intermediate period have proved superior to both moving weights and the static weights of both the initial and the final year. Significantly, the r_k^2 are uniformly higher on this level of aggregation than on the preceding level—with the exception of 1890. This result becomes more understandable when it is realized that the five states being aggregated are relatively homogeneous in both level of output, as illustrated by the weights in Table 8.4, and in their respective levels of technology. Hence, the individual state indices do not diverge very widely from the aggregate, and selection of an optimal method of weighting becomes less vital. Thus, adopting Domar's weighting method appears just as reasonable at this level of aggregation as it was at the national level, although more caution is advisable in choosing the base period.

Conclusions

Domar's method is valid and useful in aggregating technological change indices even when the assumptions are not strictly satisfied. It is important, however, to avoid periods of economic instability when selecting the base period; the weights must be characteristic of the entire series of indices.

Bibliography

Massell 1961, 1964; Peston 1959; Green 1964; Griliches and Grunfeld 1960; Houthakker 1955; Nelson 1964; Samuelson 1962; Theil 1954, 1957.

PART TWO

Technological Change and Economic Theory

CHAPTER NINE

Technological Change in Macroeconomic Models

Introduction

With the demonstration of the importance of technological change in increasing output per worker in the mid 1950's, macroeconomic models began to include an additional variable. Technological change played a role in determining the way the capital stock should be measured, the amount of investment needed for growth, the best way to use new investment, and the way the national income of society is distributed among various factors. These areas are subdivided into three headings: models concerned with capital, growth, and distribution.

Capital Models

Solow's 1957 model appears plausible and gives results that are not easily shaken, at least not within a reasonable range. The sensitivity analysis of Chapter 5 showed that errors of measurement within plausible ranges would hardly change the conclusion. Yet the deeper implications of the formulation violate neoclassical ideas. The principal factor raising output per man is exogenous to the model and no factor within the control of the model raises efficiency to a significant extent. Certainly the model gives a misleading, if not incorrect, picture when the primary focus is on policy. Deepening the capital stock has only marginal effects; the value of net investment is almost negligible, at least as compared with what would happen in the absence of any net investment. The model implies that the economy would grow almost as quickly if we simply waited, not bothering to undertake any net capital formation, and indeed, not worrying about gross capital formation. As a description of history, the model might be entirely adequate. In the presence of high net investments, of high expenditures on education and basic research, of high expenditures for technological change, perhaps the marginal contribution of net capital formation is low. It is certainly not clear, however, that the model is really one where only a marginal change would occur if net capital formation were reduced substantially. As a guide for policy, the model only raises questions.

If the model is to satisfy policy needs, modifications are needed. One assumption of the model that seems questionable is that all capital and labor share equally in the technological change. Although men can learn to perform their tasks more efficiently, capital is brittle; once molded into a particular machine type, it is rarely changeable. Thus, one might construct a model where only new capital embodies technological change. (Robinson [1952], Johansen [1959], Salter [1960], Solow [1960], Kaldor and Mirlees [1962], Phelps [1963].)

Solow (1960) builds such a model, assuming that technological change is still neutral, by allowing capital to embody the latest technology when it is built; the efficiency of a machine is fixed throughout its life. Technology advances exponentially at rate λ. Thus the capital stock is a weighted function of past investment $I(v)$ given by Equation (1).

$$J_{(t)} = e^{-\delta t} \int_{-\infty}^{t} e^{(\lambda \alpha^{-1} + \delta)v} I(v)\, dv \qquad (1)$$

J is a measure of the "effective" capital stock at time t. $I(v)$ is investment at time v in the past; thus, effective capital is a weighted sum (or integral) of past investment. Then output at time t is a Cobb-Douglas function of labor, effective capital, and unembodied technological change, Equation (2).

$$Y_t = B_0 e^{\mu t} (J_t)^{\alpha} (L_t)^{1-\alpha} \qquad (2)$$

To emphasize obsolescence rather than depreciation, capital is assumed to be subject to a constant force of mortality δ. For example, glasses in a cafeteria have an average life of $1/\delta$ and the life left in any particular glass is independent of its age. Thus, there will always be capital goods which are obsolete.

Solow uses Equation (2) to get an estimate of technological change for United States nongovernment production from 1919–53. The results are more in the nature of an experiment than a careful study. The estimated value of technological growth: λ is .025, substantially larger than the estimated value of .015 from his 1957 model. The explanation for this difference is straightforward: since only new capital benefits from technology, when the average age of the capital stook falls the rate of technology must advance faster to produce a given increase in output per man.

The significance of the model is evident in the increased role given to capital. The contribution of capital to increased output per man rises between 50 per cent and 100 per cent under the new view (from .12 to .19 or .24). The basic contribution of technological change, the residual, is still overwhelming. But the increase in capital's contribution is impressive, and Solow has succeeded in formulating a model which gives a somewhat large role to capital.

Solow's "new view" of technological change is taken up by Phelps (1962) in an effort to see just how it differs from the old view. It is clear that the new view holds promise for capital in the short run, but the mathematics of the long run make further investigation necessary.

The first result is that Equation (2) is a general form that can provide a place for both the old and new views. The old view is represented by $\mu > 0$, $\lambda = 0$. With $\lambda = 0$ the capital stock becomes the aggregate of past investment minus capital lost to the force of mortality. The new view is represented by $\mu = 0$, $\lambda > 0$. In this case, $\mu = 0$ insures that technological change is introduced only through new capital. When both parameters are positive, a composite of the two views emerges.

The measure of output can be differentiated with respect to time to provide estimates of the two technological change parameters, μ and λ. The resulting differential equation also provides a decription of the growth path of output under different conditions.

Although the two models are quite different in the short run, it is the long run that interests Phelps. His analysis shows (1) that the limiting long-run growth rate is independent of the type of technological progress assumed, (2) in this long-run equilibrium the elasticity of growth with respect to the investment ratio depends only on the capital elasticity of output and is independent of the type of technological progress, (3) the equilibrium mean age of the capital stock is independent of the investment ratio, (4) various sorts of short-term changes, such as increases in the labor force, will give rise to different estimates under the two views.

Matthew (1964) shows that the third conclusion, mean age of the capital stock independent of the saving's ratio, depends critically on the elasticity of substitution of capital for labor. If this elasticity is unity, Phelps is quite correct. On the other hand, Arrow, et al. conclude that the elasticity is generally less than one. When factors are not easily substitutable, an increase in the investment ratio will lower the equilibrium age of the capital stock.

As noted in Chapter 2, Solow's 1957 model came under attack as an aggregate production function. Joan Robinson (1962) contended that a picture of the world would show many different kinds of capital, that there were few possibilities of substitution of either capital for capital or capital for labor. Samuelson (1962) thereupon produced a model where each capital good was distinct, where no capital good could be modified so as to do something it had not originally done, where each piece of capital had a fixed amount of labor required; in short, a model very much like that described by Mrs. Robinson. From this model, Samuelson derived a production frontier that could hardly be differentiated from the frontier of a J. B. Clark-Ramsey-Solow aggregate production function.

There were, however, some restrictive conditions on the Samuelson model that hamper possible attempts at generalization. Solow (1962, 1963b) set out to find the extent to which results differed when an aggregate production function was applied to many small fixed coefficient, heterogeneous capital production functions. He attempts to measure the magnitude of the error involved in treating the complex function as if it were a simple one.

The model has capital, the basis of the controversy, embodied in machines that cannot be modified once they have been built. Each machine produces one unit of output and requires the services of λ men. Although the choice of units has each machine produce one unit of consumer goods, there is no restriction in the model, only in the choice of units. The assumptions of a single consumer good and a homogeneous labor force are weighty and not easily brushed aside.

Although no machine may be modified after it is built, a machine may be built so as to substitute capital for labor. The cost of a machine of type λ is $C(\lambda_i) = C_0 \lambda^{-\gamma}$, where γ is some positive constant. Machines are assumed to be built by labor alone and last N periods before falling apart with no scrap value. Thus, the technology is a simple one and the capital-labor substitution relation reasonable.

This model is quite similar to the 1959 model which attempted to allocate more of the increase in productivity to capital. The notion of technological change being embodied in the newest capital is present. In fact, the difference seems to come from Solow having realized that the earlier model was more general than he had supposed. There is little cost in going from an aggregate Cobb-Douglas relation with effective capital to an aggregate fixed coefficient production relation. The difference in the treatment of capital life, "one hoss shay" as against constant force of mortality, is not important in the two models. The constant force of mortality was assumed so as to make obsolescence the primary feature of the first model. In the second model, capital should become obsolete before it falls apart, at least when the model is operating in an interesting fashion.

Since the model focuses on technology and capital measurement, Solow does not hesitate to fill in additional factors needed to produce a growth model that he can simulate. Investment is exogenously determined so as to make sure there are always more jobs than there are men to fill them. Some machines always become obsolete before they fall apart. The wage rate and demand for labor are thus determined by the machines in existence at any time. The higher the wage, the higher must be the capital input into a machine in order to make it profitable to operate. On the other hand, the lower the wage, the more machines will be profitable to operate and so the greater will be the demand for labor. The fixed coefficient nature of the model insures that there are always areas of indeterminacy of the wage rate.

A critical assumption is introduced about the nature of expectations. When a new machine is to be built, there is a need to know the most profitable λ. In the neoclassical tradition, Solow's machine builders maximize the present discounted value of the machine. To carry out the operation, the builder must know the future stream of interest rates over the life of the machine as well as the future stream of wages. In order to simplify the analysis, Solow assumes that expectations are constant; that is, investors believe that current wages and interest will prevail over the life of the machine. The assumption is something less than plausible in the model; Solow determines investment so that wages are constantly rising.

Solow (1964) goes on to investigate a number of properties of the model. In the second paper, he simulates this model so as to get some idea of how it behaves in the short run. In this simulation, there are rising wages and more capital-intensive machines. As capital per man rises continually, the interest rate must fall and eventually it becomes negative. This peculiar result is a direct consequence of static expectations since machines become obsolete before they have returned their capital value.

The model can be forced into a long-run equilibrium, under the proper conditions. Insisting that the interest rate and wages are always positive, Solow shows that the model converges to a state described by a Cobb-Douglas function.

The questions for the simulation are (a) if a production function is estimated from data generated by the model, are the short-run results good estimates of the long-run elasticities; (b) does the estimated relation serve as a good description of the distribution of income and return on investment?

Paraphrasing Solow, the results can be described in capsule form as follows:

(a) There is a tendency for the model to give indications of increasing returns to scale where none exist.[1]

(b) When the Cobb-Douglas form is restricted to give constant returns, the short-run estimates provide excellent indications of the long-run relations.

(c) Even models that permit no capital-labor substitution in the short

[1]Cf. Griliches (1963) as described in Chapter 2.

run can be estimated by functions which do, since the character of long run substitutability is revealed in short-run data.

(d) For production function analysis, a measure of capital stock in labor-time equivalent prices may be a more appropriate measure than one in constant prices.

(e) Smooth approximating production functions applied to discrete technologies may give excellent, though smoothed, interpolations of such important quantities as the rate of return to social savings.

Bar (1965) has shown that these conclusions depend strongly on the initial conditions and model. Bar's attempts to make these more compatable with the world or with economic theory tend to upset the above results.

Growth Models

Models with technological change embodied in new capital appeal to intuition, just as deriving new production functions appeals to the creative instinct. Bergstrom (1962) works with the former while attempting to do the latter in order to produce a model explaining cyclical growth. His work is a generalization of work by Phillips (1961).

He begins with six assumptions:

(1) Technological change is embodied in new capital.

(2) Capital goods and consumer goods are identical insofar as one can measure the capital produced at the expense of one unit of consumption goods.

(3) The full capacity output-capital ratio is constant.

(4) There is neutral technological change at an exponential rate.

(5) Capital is subject to a constant force of mortality.

(6) Capital is utilized in the most efficient way.

In addition, he is interested in a model that gives rise to a constant saving-income ratio when income is growing at a constant rate and where there is a steady state of exponential growth with the quality of labor constant.

The production function is given in Equation (3)

$$Y = \nu K - (\nu + \delta)K\left\{1 - \frac{\delta e^{\rho t}L}{(\rho + \delta)K}\right\}^{(\rho+\delta)/\delta} \tag{3}$$

and is subject to the restriction, Equation (4).

$$L \leqq \frac{\rho + \delta}{\delta}e^{-\rho t}K \tag{4}$$

ρ is the rate of neutral technological change, ν is the maximum output of a unit of capital, δ is the constant force of mortality, and Y, L, and K are defined as usual. The function is linear homogeneous, and exhibits diminishing returns to a single factor. Bergstrom embeds the function in a growth model and examines the steady state and stability properties.

The Constant Elasticity of Substitution (CES) function is a general form that includes Cobb-Douglas and fixed coefficient production functions as special cases. It does so by generalizing one of the properties they share; the constant elasticity of substitution between factors. The form is useful as a production function in static contexts, especially for microeconomic data.

The functions each possess another dimension which has made them popular; indeed, their general popularity seems to have little to do with their CES property. The Cobb-Douglas form has been particularly useful in explaining constant factor shares under changing factor proportions. It is also a form particularly plausible and well adapted to the measurement of neutral technological change. The fixed coefficient function derives its greatest popularity from simple growth models where output is simply a function of capital with labor assumed to be accommodating.

Frankel (1962) managed to synthesize these properties in a general form that made use of both the growth properties of the Harrod-Domar form and the distribution and technological change properties of the Cobb-Douglas. He was attempting to allocate more of the responsibility for productivity increase to capital and at the same time to provide a better explanation of neutral technological change. One important assumption is that all quality changes in the factors are reflected in their prices.

The general production function for the aggregate economy is written as Equation (5).

$$Y = AHK^{\alpha}L^{1-\alpha} \tag{5}$$

Note that this form is identical to previous attempts to measure technological change if $H = e^{\lambda t}$, where λ = rate of technological change. Frankel, however, takes H to be a function of the capital-labor ratio, $H = (K/L)^{\gamma}$. Now if $\gamma = 1 - \alpha$, the aggregate production function reduces to Equation (6),

$$Y = AK \tag{6}$$

a Harrod-Domar model. On the other hand, this general function stays a Cobb-Douglas form for the individual firm since H is the aggregate capital-labor ratio and is invariant to actions of an individual firm. Thus, the production function for a single firm might be written as in Equation (7)

$$Y_i = A_i H K_i^{\alpha} L_i^{1-\alpha} \tag{7}$$

or, substituting for H, as Equation (7a).

$$Y_i = A_i \left(\frac{K}{L}\right)^{1-\alpha} K_i^{\alpha} L_i^{1-\alpha} \tag{7a}$$

This sleight-of-hand does nothing to injure the previous measurements of technological change. It merely specifies that increases in the capital-output ratio, rather than time, get allocated productivity increases. The idea is based on a fallacy of composition: when all firms raise their capital-labor ratios, they receive a gain much greater than anyone anticipated.

Consider the case when $\gamma \neq 1 - \alpha$; the function is now a mixed Cobb-Douglas, Harrod-Domar model. Here again, capital will exert a much larger influence than if $H = e^{\lambda t}$. A still more general case would be $H = K^\gamma / L^\gamma$. Much the same conclusions follow as long as the function exhibits almost constant returns to scale.

Frankel fits a simple Cobb-Douglas form to United States data over the period 1899–1933. Arbitrarily taking the share of capital to be .35, he derives the following function, Equation (8).

$$Y = .32 \left(\frac{K}{L}\right)^{.636} K^{.35} L^{.65} \tag{8}$$

He fitted the function again, this time allowing differences in the coefficients of capital and labor to get Equation (9).

$$Y = 0.9 \frac{K^{.41}}{L^{.10}} K^{.35} L^{.65} \tag{9}$$

When H is a function of the capital-labor ratio, the rate of savings in society tends to take on new importance. For example, a savings rate of 4.7 per cent would produce the measured technological change of 1.5 per cent per year. High savings rates tend to produce high rates of productivity increase that only gradually fall to the long-term rate of growth. On the other hand, low savings rates, such as 5 per cent, give rise to productivity increases which are below normal and only gradually rise to meet the long-term rate. Policy recommendations from this model would be toward much higher rates of savings and incentive payments to increase the capital stock. These conclusions are in marked contrast to those derived from the model where $H = e^{\lambda t}$.

The crux of Frankel's approach lies in his assumption that all productivity is embodied in the aggregate capital-labor ratio. Since capital per man has risen proportionally to time, the increase in this ratio "accounts" for all the unexplained growth in productivity. Since there seems little theoretical reason for such an assumption, Frankel's ingenuity must be taken with a grain of salt.

Distribution Models

The distribution of income between the various factors of production is intimately bound up with technological change. Perhaps the most obvious connnection is that, under technological change, the marginal product of each worker and each dollar of capital increases. A second effect is that the technological change may be non-neutral and thus change the relative marginal products of factors. Under this second condition, the marginal product of one factor (labor) might rise rapidly while that of the second factor (capital) decreased or stayed constant.

On a macroeconomic level, technological change can affect the total payments to the factors. Have the total payments to labor increased over time? If there has been neutral technological change, the marginal product of each worker has risen, and so (assuming the number of workers has stayed constant or risen) the total payments to labor will increase. Similarly, the total payments to capital will increase. Assuming a linear homogeneous production function, any increase in output due to technological change will be completely allocated over labor and capital.

Statements about change in relative factor shares are necessarily more complex than those concerning absolute shares. Under a linear homogeneous production function, the relative shares (each factor's total payment divided by national income) will sum to one. Under this condition, the relative share of capital will also be the elasticity of output with respect to capital. Has this elasticity gone up or down over time? If capital accumulates, labor being held constant, in the absence of technological change, then capital's share would be expected to decrease. The relative share of labor is important in answering the charge that technological change is going to bankrupt the worker. As long as the relative share of labor does not fall, increases in output due to technological change will benefit him that much more.

One of the great empirical conclusions from the late 1920's was the constancy of relative shares (Bowley's law). Either because production was governed by an aggregate Cobb-Douglas function (which guarantees constant shares) or simply because the economy was so massive that movements were necessarily slow, relative shares were constant in the late nineteenth and early twentieth centuries. It seemed that constant relative shares would be the great law of the United States economy. However, Irving Kravis (1959), D. Gale Johnson (1954) and Robert Solow (1958) have questioned this constancy and produced estimates to show that labor's share rose from about 55 per cent of national income in 1900–09 to about 67 per cent in 1949–57.

Arthur Grant (1963) contends that there were constant shares over the period and that any variation is just accounting fiction. He carefully examines the series from 1899 to 1929, recomputing estimates, making corrections, and attempting to account for the more obvious errors in the measurement of national income. He concludes the constancy of relative shares over this thirty-year period. Weintraub (1958) has done a similar analysis with like conclusions for the 1929–57 period. Perhaps the correct interpretation of these results is that the data cannot be used to prove deviation from constant shares.

Kendrick and Sato (1963) draw on recent work by the National Bureau of Economic Research (NBER) to describe the important trends in the United States economy from 1919 to 1960. Capital has grown relative to labor, that is, the capital-labor ratio has increased, and so one might expect to find the return to capital has fallen. Kendrick and Sato find no tendency for the return to capital to fall over the period. When they look at relative shares, however, they find that the share of labor in income has risen from 72 per cent to about 78 per cent. Over the period, the total return to capital has risen, although the share of capital in income has fallen.

They argue that all the benefits of technological change have gone to labor since both the total return and the share of labor have risen. However, by the above paragraph, the share of labor would have been expected to rise even with neutral technological change since the capital-labor ratio has risen There is no evidence here for non-neutral technological change as the authors seem to imply.

The figures are used to calculate an arithmetic index of technological change over the period. Kendrick and Sato find that the efficiency index grew at a rate of 2.1 per cent per year over the period.

Since the share of capital has changed, the elasticity of substitution of capital for labor must be different from unity. They estimate this elasticity to be substantially below one. In fact, it is much lower than the estimates of Arrow, et al. (1961) or Ferguson (1963), about .6. They go on to derive an aggregate production function with an explicit parameter for the elasticity of substitution.

One way of approaching the distribution question on the aggregate level is through the elasticity of substitution of capital for labor. If this elasticity is unity, relative shares must be constant. If it is less than one, the more rapidly increasing factor will lose relatively, and vice versa if elasticity of substitution is greater than one. Since capital has increased relative to labor in the United States economy, an elasticity less than one implies that labor's share is rising, even under neutral technological change.

Ferguson (1963) estimates the elasticity of substitution for two- and three-digit industries on a cross-section basis from the 1947, 1954, and 1958 *Census of Manufacturing*. His estimated elasticities vary from .54 to 2.5. Few of them are significantly less than one. As argued in Chapter 3, however, the results are questionable.

Brown and deCani (1963) examine technological change with respect to neutrality and non-neutrality from the point of view of the distribution of income. They begin with three propositions about relative shares:

1. A factor-saving innovation will, *ceteris paribus*, lower the share of that factor.
2. If the supply of one factor increases more rapidly than the other, the elasticity of substitution will affect relative shares in the following way:
   (a) if $\sigma < 1$, the plentiful factor will lose relative share,
   (b) if $\sigma = 1$, the shares will stay constant,
   (c) if $\sigma > 1$, the plentiful factor's share will rise.
3. An increase in the elasticity of substitution will lower the share of the scarce factor.

Brown and deCani use these propositions to derive a general constant elasticity of substitution production function and thus give a derivation independent of that of Arrow, *et al.* This more general production function enables them to reestimate the Brown-Popkin (1962) results under the assumption that the elasticity of substitution can be different from one. Some of their results are presented in the following tables. They used the same epochs as Brown-Popkin.

Table 9.1   Elasticity of Substitution, 1890–1958

		Log of Labor Intensity Parameter	Short-run Elasticity of Substitution	Long Run	Rigidity of K
Epoch:	1	1890–1918	−0.89	0.35	0.55	0.38
	2	1919–37	−7.17	0.08	0.31	0.75
	3	1938–58	−2.93	0.11	0.47	0.76

A first conclusion is that the elasticity of substitution, both short run and long run, is significantly less than unity. Thus, other results should be different from those of Brown-Popkin. As before, they find that the second epoch was much less labor intensive than the first, but that the third tended to restore some of the previous balance. The elasticity of substitution drops substantially between the first and second epochs and only rises a bit in going into the third. Finally, capital becomes increasingly rigid over the period.

Finally, Brown and deCani investigate the factors causing change in the share of labor in total product. The table below lists five factors:

Table 9.2   Partial Derivative of Log of Labor's Share of Income with Respect to

		Elasticity of Substitution	Rigidity of Capital	Log of Labor Intensity	Log of Current Factor Prices	Log of Lagged Factor Prices
Epoch:	1	−0.48	−0.03	0.22	−0.66	0.38
	2	−2.01	−0.08	0.02	−0.92	0.75
	3	−1.03	−0.20	0.03	−0.89	0.76

Between epochs, the principal factor affecting changes in labor's share of income is the change in the elasticity of substitution. Within epochs, however, changes in relative factor prices have the most effect, with the change in lagged factor prices being almost as important. Changes in the rigidity of capital and in labor intensity have little effect.

Having specialized their measurements of technological change to deal with questions of the distribution of income, Brown and deCani (1963) present another specialization to examine changes in employment. Again their data are Kendrick's private, nonfarm data from 1890 to 1958. They begin with the assumption of a CES function and the division into technological epochs that were derived by Brown and Popkin. Last time they investigated the partial derivative of labor's share of income with respect to the parameters of the CES function, now they take the partial derivatives of employment with respect to these same variables.

The CES function is more difficult to estimate than the Cobb-Douglas form, as one would expect, since it is a more general form. The estimating techniques have not been widely explored with respect to significance tests and the assumption of competition seems more strained in these circumstances.[1] In order to estimate the CES function, they go through a two-stage procedure of deriving some of the estimates by one equation and then substituting these into a second equation and again applying regression analysis. These methods are not well understood and there are strong possibilities of bias.

Brown and deCani use their previous results to derive additional estimates of neutral technological change, returns to scale and the change in employment related to a simple time trend. These estimates are shown in Table 9.3. The principal result here is the high increasing returns to scale (much larger than estimated by Brown-Popkin) except for the last period. However, they note that the estimates are only indirect ones and would be more appropriately derived in explicit form.

Table 9.3 Neutral Technological Change and Returns to Scale

	Neutral Technological Change	Returns to Scale	Coefficient of Regression of Log t on Log N
1890–1917	0.791	1.704	0.109
1918–37	1.986	1.564	−0.041
1938–52	0.820	0.803	−0.187

Finally, they present a measure of the contribution to the change in the log of employment by the various factors in their analysis. These relations are shown in Table 9.4.

Table 9.4 Change in Employment due to Percentage Changes in

	Log Output	Log Relative Prices	Neutral Technological Change	Non-neutral Technological Change
Epoch 1–2	0.074	−0.119	0.883	0.876
Epoch 2–3	0.409	0.003	−0.095	−0.132

[1] Some recent work has made some progress on these questions. In particular see Kmenta (1964) and McFadden (1964).

Bibliography

Section B: capital models. Amano 1964; Barr 1965; Brems 1959, 1963; Brown 1962; Cairncross 1955; Chakravarty 1964; Champernowne 1958; Eisner 1956; Finley 1963; Frankel 1955; Fuchs 1962; Gordon 1956, 1961; Heertje 1963; Hicks 1932, 1960; Howrey 1965; Intrilligator 1965; Johansen 1957; Kaldor 1961; Kennedy 1961; Kindleberger 1961; Lerner 1965; Lutz and Hague 1961; Massell 1962b; Matthews 1964; McCarthy 1965; Phelps 1962, 1963, 1964; Robinson 1952, 1956, 1962, 1964; Rosenberg 1963; Samuelson 1959, 1961, 1962; Solow 1960, 1962a, 1962b, 1963a, 1963c; Stigler 1963; Swan 1956.

Section C: growth models. Arrow 1962; Asimakopulos 1963; Asimakopulos and Weldon 1963; Banerji 1956; Bergstrom 1962; Bierwag 1964: Black 1962; Brozen 1957; Burton 1956; Cragg 1963; Denison 1962; Drandanakis 1963; Eltis 1963; Fellner 1958; Hahn and Matthews 1964; Hamberg 1959; Harrod 1939, 1957; Hodjera 1963; Inada 1964; Johansen 1960; Jorgenson 1961; Kaldor 1957; Kendrick and Sato 1963; La Tourette 1964; Massell 1962c; Mirrlees and Kaldor 1962; Morishima 1964; Phillips 1961; Riese 1964; Solow 1956; Sraffa 1960; Stoleru 1965; Tweeten and Tyner 1964; Uzawa 1961, 1965; Williams 1964; Zweig 1936.

Section D: distribution models. Bronfenbrenner 1960; Brown 1965; Brown and de Cani 1963a, 1963b; Budd 1960; Finley 1960; Ferguson and Pfouts 1962; Gallaway 1964; Grant 1963; Helmut 1963; Johnson 1954; Kennedy 1964; Kravis 1959; Krelle 1961, 1964; Machlup 1934; Marcus 1964; Morrissett 1953; Newman and Read 1961; Pitchford 1960; Robinson 1938; Ruttan and Stout 1960; Solow 1958, 1963b; Weintraub 1958.

CHAPTER TEN

Some Studies of Technological Change

A large part of the research on technological change has been focused on its applications for other areas of economics, rather than on attempts to define and measure it. Chapter 9 contained two examples: the inclusion of technological change in models of growth and distribution. The implications have been important and sometimes revolutionary, as in the case of international trade theory where the foundations of the theory have been challenged.

This chapter is a potpourri of research reporting applications of technological change. These areas form the *raison d'être* for the studies attempting to define and measure technological change: almost the whole of economic theory is being modified to a greater or lesser extent.

Economic Growth and Development

One of the principal reasons for the work in estimating technological change is the possibility that increased understanding will lead to ways of raising the rates of growth and productivity increase in the economy. In explaining the past, understanding might be gained of the extent to which measured inputs, capital and labor, have raised national income and the way in which technological change was brought about.[1]

---

[1]For a survey of the growth literature, see Hahn and Matthews (1964). The survey is especially valuable with respect to British literature.

So much for the general philosophy. In practice there seem to be two alternatives. One can measure the residual and then seek to allocate it among various changes in the economy as Denison (1962) has done. Or one may attempt to estimate directly all those factors that increase national income, such as education. This latter strategy has been discussed in Chapter 2 in the comments on Griliches. More general comments are contained in Carter and Williams (1957, 1958, 1959) and Nelson (1962).

In this section, the former position is examined. Denison begins in much the same way as Kendrick (1961): He measures inputs and outputs over the period 1909–1957 and uses an arithmetic index to calculate a figure for technological change. There are some differences in the measure of capital and labor, but on the whole the figures are quite close, as shown by Table 10.1 where Abramovitz (1962) summarizes the differences between the two.

But Denison doesn't stop here as did Kendrick; he proceeds to try to explain the residual and divide all of this unallocated technological change among its sources. The process is summarized in Table 10.2.

Denison carefully notes that there are no figures or studies for many of the areas he must investigate. Some examples will illustrate the point: Over the period, the average number of hours in the work week decreases substantially. Thus output per man should have suffered. On the other hand, the fewer hours a man works, the more alert and efficient he is while he works.

Clearly after some number (surely 18 hours a day is safe) there are absolutely diminishing returns to additional hours. Now, the more efficiency and alertness that are expected of the worker, the lower will be the number of hours that produce absolutely diminishing returns. For example, if a worker's mistake jams a machine which takes a week's time to repair, small decreases in efficiency will be costly. Denison assumes that the work week in 1929 (48.6 hours) was the point where further increases would produce absolutely diminishing returns. He also assumes that the 1957 work week (39.8 hours) produced a change in efficiency which offset 40 per cent of the decrease in hours. The estimates correcting for decreases in the work week are then interpolated.

These assumptions are not independent of working conditions and the level of technology. Current technology tires workers less yet demands more alertness. Investigating this question in any detail is certain to lead to problems. Yet Denison has managed to pull a measure out of this tangle and offered at least a plausible correction.

In similar fashion the estimates of the effect of education, and so on, are arbitrary but plausible. The result is a great bundle of numbers no one of which is more than a hunch, but the sum of which represent an exercise in exploring many areas of importance that have received only passing attention previously. Together, these hunches provide a basis for explaining United States growth.

As Abramovitz points out, Denison makes no correction for quality

Table 10.1   Allocation of Growth Rate of Real
National Income among the Sources of Growth

	Percentage Points in Growth Rate		
	1909–20	1929–57	1909–57
1. Real National Income	2.82	2.93	2.89
2. Increase in Total Inputs	1.63	0.92	1.22
3. Labor Input (unweighted man-hours)	0.88	0.47	0.65
4. Employment	1.11	1.00	1.06
5. Hours	−0.23	−0.53	−0.41
6. Capital	0.75	0.45	0.57
7. Increase in Output per Unit of Input (the residual)	1.19	2.01	1.67
8. Ratio: 7 : 1	0.42	0.69	0.58
9. Increase in Total Input (Kendrick)	1.96	1.10	1.46
10. Output per Unit of Input (1 minus 9) (the residual)	0.86	1.83	1.43
11. Ratio: 10 : 1	0.31	0.62	0.50

SOURCES:
From Abramovitz (1962)
Lines 1–7: Denison, Table 19.
Line 9: Based on Kendrick 14, Table A XIX.
Line 10: Line 1 minus line 9.

change in capital. This procedure leads to a picture quite different from that of Solow's new view. Denison assumes the role of the old-view economist and is subject to all Phelps' and Solow's criticisms. However, he is not a conventional old view economist since he uses gross rather than net capital stock.

In the light of his explanation of the past, Denison goes on to predict which policy variables will have the most effect on raising future growth rates. Although much of the past change was accounted for by education increases, this alternative does not offer the greatest hope for the near future. In the first place, education takes some time to have its effect, since only the entering labor force is subject to greater education. Secondly, there is a relatively high level of education now, hence it becomes relatively difficult to bring about any given percentage change.

Denison advises pursuit of growth along many lines and advises attention to many of the variables which will raise output.

Nelson (1964) picks up this work with an eye to synthesizing previous work. He focuses on the question: Just what does the study of technological change have to contribute to forecasts of the growth of real GNP and GNP per capita over the next dozen years?

Nelson's first conclusion is that estimates from the more general CES function hardly differ from Cobb-Douglas function estimates over the period

Table 10.2   Allocation of Growth Rate of Real
National Income among the Sources of Growth

	Percentage Points in Growth Rate	
	1909–29	1929–57
Real National Income	2.82	2.93
Increase in Total Inputs	2.26	2.00
Labor input (adjusted for quality)	1.53	1.57
Employment	1.11	1.00
Hours	−0.23	−0.53
Effect of shorter hours on quality	0.23	0.33
Education	0.35	0.67
Increased experience and better use of women	0.06	0.11
Changes in age-sex composition of labor force	0.01	−0.01
Capital input	0.73	0.43
Nonfarm residential structures	0.13	0.05
Other structures and equipment	0.41	0.28
Inventories	0.16	0.08
United States-owned assets abroad	0.02	0.02
Foreign assets in United States	0.01	0.00
Increase in Output per Unit of Input	0.56	0.93
Restrictions against optimum use of resources	n.a.	−0.07
Reduced waste in agriculture	n.a.	0.02
Industry shift from agriculture	n.a.	0.05
Advance in knowledge	n.a.	0.58
Change in lag in application of knowledge	n.a.	0.01
Economies of scale—independent growth of local markets	n.a.	0.07
Economies of scale—growth of national market	0.28	0.27

SOURCES:
From Abramovitz (1962).
n.a. = not available.
Denison, Table 32. Certain lines in Denison's table constituting subtotals not repro-
duced. One line referring to the contribution of "Land" is omitted. Denison puts the
contribution at zero on the ground that available land has been constant during the
period covered.

1929–60. Since the increased generality is costly, Nelson presents only the
Cobb-Douglas results. He also stops to take a closer look at the estimates
of the elasticity of output with respect to capital. Solow (1957) and others
used capital's share in income as the estimate of this series. Nelson is reluctant to follow this precedent and merely assumes W_K is in the range .25–.50.

Phelps' conclusion (that embodying technological change exclusively in
new capital makes no difference in the long run) does not hold for a period
as short as the one Nelson handles. Making the assumption that all tech-

nological change is embodied in new capital, Nelson comes out with Equation (1)

$$\Delta \frac{J}{J} = \Delta \frac{K}{K} + \lambda_K \Delta \bar{a} \qquad (1)$$

where J is a measure of effective capital, K is the usual measure of capital stock, λ_K is the rate per year at which machines improve, and $\bar{a}$ is the average age of machines. The formula indicates that the increase in effective capital is equal to the change in capital corrected for the rate at which machines improve plus a correction factor for changes in the age of capital.

If J is used in a Cobb-Douglas function in the place of K, the Johansen-Solow-Phelps assumption is realized. This new estimate differs from the standard one only by the term: $-(1 - b)\lambda_K \bar{a}$.

The two measures are compared in Table 10.3.

Table 10.3   The Components of Embodied Technological Change

	$\frac{\Delta A}{A}$	$(1 - b) = .25$ $(1 - b)\lambda K$	$-(1 - b)\lambda_K \bar{a}$
1929–60	2.1	2.1	0
1929–49	1.9	2.3	−0.4
1947–60	2.5	2.0	0.5
1947–54	2.9	2.3	0.6
1947–60	2.1	1.8	0.3
1929–60	1.7	1.7	0
1929–49	1.7	2.1	−0.4
1947–60	1.8	1.5	0.3
1947–54	2.1	1.7	0.4
1947–60	1.6	1.4	0.2

Over the period 1929 to 1960, the average age of capital changed very little; hence the embodied effect is negligible.

Another kind of embodiment that has been suggested is the changing quality of the labor force. A way of adjusting labor analogous to that of adjusting capital is presented in Equation (2).

$$\Delta \frac{Q}{Q} = \Delta \frac{L}{L} + \lambda_L \qquad (2)$$

Q is the adjusted labor figure and λ_L is the rate at which labor improves per year.

This index of quality changes of labor can also be added to the standard measure of technological change. When the equation is reestimated with $b = .75$, total technological change is about evenly divided between capital improvement and labor improvement as shown in Table 10.4.

Table 10.4 The Components of $\Delta A/A$

	$\Delta A/A$	$B\lambda_L$	$\Delta A/A - b\lambda_L$	$(1 - b)\lambda_K$
1929–47	1.9	1.0	0.9	1.1
1947–60	2.5	1.0	1.5	1.3
1947–54	2.9	1.0	1.9	1.5
1954–60	2.1	1.0	1.1	0.9

One thing that Denison neglected in his projections is the interactions between these two factors. The preceding formulas treat factors as independent. Neglecting interactions between factors can lead to trouble, since, for example, it seems likely that specially trained labor is required to run the new capital equipment. To handle this problem rigorously would require the estimation of production functions as discussed below.

In examining projections for the future, these interactions and the profitability of technological change lead Nelson to conclude: "We shall have full employment and rapid growth of potential GNP together or we shall have neither."

The existence of technological change brings into question many principles of the growth and development literature. For example, an early and rapid accumulation of capital is undesirable; it will become inefficient too quickly (Frankel 1956, Gordon 1956, Kindleberger 1961).

Some attempts have been made to finesse the problem by the argument that an "invisible hand" will regulate innovation and diffusion to the good of society. Habakkuk (1962) and Rothbart (1946) argue that labor saving technological change was stimulated by the scarcity of labor relative to land. Some further evidence for this proposition is presented in Chapter 11. On the other hand, Fellner (1961) and Kaldor (1961) argue there is no inherent tendency toward neutral technological change. Labor saving innovation will not necessarily appear to offset capital saving innovations.

Economic growth and development bring many adjustment problems. Technological change generally serves to exaggerate the difficulties and complicate the problem. Examples are given in Chapters 12 and 13. In particular, the United States agricultural sector has been experiencing rapid technological change for a century. The implications of this change for agriculture and the whole economy are spelled out by Heady (1962) and Tolley and Smidt (1964). A simple model might be used to illustrate the problem.

Expenditures on agricultural products at time t, F_t will be a function of population, P_t, and increases in income per capita Y_t/P_t as given in Equation (3).

$$F_t = \frac{F_o}{P_o} P_t + (Y_t - Y_o) M_f \qquad (3)$$

The first term in Formula (3) is a simple extrapolation of current expenditures per capita to take account of population increase: $(F_o/P_o)P_t$. The second term is the increase in income times the marginal propensity to buy agricultural products (M_f).

The growth rate will be dependent on time as can be seen by taking the derivative with respect to time as in Equation (4).

$$\dot{F} = \frac{F_o}{P_o}\dot{P} + \dot{Y}M_f \tag{4}$$

Assuming exponential growth of population and income, $\dot{P}$ can be shown to equal $(.015)P_o(1.015)^t$ while $\dot{Y}$ equals $(.03)(1.03)^t Y_o$. Then the percentage growth in food expenditures will be given by Equation (5).

$$\frac{\dot{F}}{F} = \frac{F_o(.015)(1.015)^t + M_f Y_o(.03)(1.03)^t}{F_o(1.015)^t + M_f Y_o(1.03)^t} \tag{5}$$

Assuming values for the parameters of $\dot{P}/P = .015$, $\dot{Y}/Y = .03$, $M_f = .05$, $F_o = \$90B$, $Y_o = \$500B$, the percentage increase in food expenditures for $t = 1$ is 1.82. This increases only slightly for $t = 2$ to 1.83. From Equation (5) it can be shown that the limiting growth rate is 3 per cent. Perhaps the most unrealistic part of the model is the assumption that M_f is constant. Were M_f to decline, it would tend to offset the asymptotic approach to Y. Thus, a value for $\dot{F}/F$ of 1.82 per cent would seem a good approximation.

With no technological change, agricultural prices would be constant were inputs to increase at a rate of 1.82 per cent per year (assuming a linear homogeneous production function). If the inflow of inputs is less than this figure, prices will increase and agricultural incomes rise; if more than 1.82 per cent, prices will fall and the absolute return to agriculture diminish. One complication arises because of technological change: inputs become more effective. But here the same conclusions hold when modified to account for the product of technical change and inflow of inputs.

An often mentioned problem of agriculture is the fixed nature of assets; they can move in easily enough, but have a higher book value than can be realized in selling them. If the rate of technological change is greater than 1.82 per cent, the fixed nature of assets will cause temporary inefficiency since assets must be released.

As measured by the Solow model, technical change in agriculture has taken place at a rate of 1.82 per cent or greater since about 1920. Since 1940, technical change has taken place at rates exceeding 4 per cent. In order to have kept agricultural prices constant over the last twenty years, factors would have had to leave at a rate of 3 per cent per year. Now, although labor has been leaving at a fairly high rate, about 2 per cent per year or perhaps a little less, capital has been increasing at about 1 per cent per year. Thus, inputs have been decreasing at a rate of only about 1 per cent instead of the 3 per cent required to maintain steady prices.

Note that the model gives some indication of the real magnitude of the farm problem. The 2 per cent difference cited is not a fair measure since output has been restricted substantially in the past two decades. If the 2 per cent figure is taken, however, the discrepancy between inputs that would give 1940 prices and the current situation is at least 49 per cent of the inputs currently devoted to farming. To the extent that acreage has been restricted, the discrepancy is just that much greater. It is easily seen that the problem is growing at a rate that could make it intolerable. It might be added that the rate of technological change has been accelerating in the postwar period and so the problem is growing at an even greater rate.

Learning by Doing

In going from macroeconomic to microeconomic levels, more theoretical structure may be introduced. Technical change in a process might be investigated in detail, but before measurement is fruitful, some difficulties with cost curves must be investigated. The classic theory of the firm proclaims that the marginal cost curve is U-shaped, that the long-run cost curve is flatter and lower than short-run curves, and that a firm might produce at a loss in the short run and then go out of business in the long run. All these propositions are viewed with suspicion by the businessman, since, for example, his cost curves seem to be L-shaped (see Johnston [1960]). Alchian (1959) has attempted to reconcile the businessman to the theorist; Hirshleiffer (1962) expands and improves the argument.

Alchian differentiates two dimensions related to output: the rate of output and the volume of output. He asserts that the larger the expected volume, holding the rate constant, the lower will be average cost. On the other hand, the higher the rate, holding the volume constant, the higher will be average cost. Economic theory implicitly holds the volume to be infinite or very large while it describes the changes in marginal cost due to changes in the rate of production.

He goes on to add two (not independent) dimensions: the time at which production begins and the length of the period in which output is produced. These two variables are particularly relevant in considering cost changes related to learning by doing. The later in the life of a firm that it attempts to produce a product, the more knowledge it will have and the cheaper should be the cost. Similarly, the longer the time taken to produce a product (the higher the volume), the more generalized and specialized learning will occur and so the lower the cost curve will be.

A further differentiation is useful between the width and length of an order. Examples of *Width* are the number of pages in a book to be produced or the amount to be transported. *Length* refers to the number of books or the distance the shipment is to go. Here again, the greater the width, the lower the average cost, *ceteris paribus*; and the greater the length, the lower will be marginal cost, *ceteris paribus*.

There are two possible interpretations of long-run cost curves; the first (Alchian's) depends on the time taken to set up an order, the second (Hirshleiffer's) depends on expected volume. The longer the time taken to set up an order (the more specialized the machinery acquired and training given to employees), the lower will be average cost. Although this proposition is plausible, it does not contain nearly the power of the classical assertion. Hirshleiffer's modification has to do with certainty. He asserts that the longer the expected production run, the more specialized equipment will be utilized. In addition, the longer the production run, the more learning will occur and so the lower the cost curve will be.

The notion of incurring short-run losses is debunked by Alchian on the grounds that, with correct expectations, a short-run loss either outweighs discounted future gains or it does not; if future gains offset the loss, then there is no real loss; if not, shut down. One problem not discussed is that of asset valuation. A short-run loss might be incurred by not paying interest or covering depreciation. Alchian might, however, argue that, insofar as the market value of the asset is great enough so that there is a real loss, the firm ought to go out of business and sell its capital equipment. If the asset has a high book value but low market value, the loss is only an accounting fiction.

Hirshleiffer takes a different view of the short-run–long-run controversy. There are two problems here, that of maximizing profit under uncertainty and that of getting optimal equipment. Now, there may be a short-run loss but, with an uncertain future, the possibility of long-run gain. Yet, here again, Alchian might argue that the discounted expected value of future profits ought to guide action. But the second point is that, with a long promised run or huge volume, it might pay to introduce specialized equipment. Thus, the firm might incur a loss on a short run or small volume, but make a profit on a long run or high volume of the same product.

In his discussion of average cost diminishing as length increases, Alchian talks about more specialized machinery and training for labor. In addition, the longer the job, the more chance a man has to learn his job and do it efficiently. This phenomenon is labeled "learning by doing."

The purest examples of learning by doing occur when a new product must be produced. In particular, various defense industries in the Second World War offer examples of industries with little or no prior experience and long, specialized jobs. Much data was collected on these industries since the government was anxious to maintain control.

Alchian (1963) attempts to measure the importance of learning by doing in the airframe industry. One standard assumption in the industry is the number of man-hours required to produce a pound of finished airframe diminishes in proportion to the number of airframes produced previously in that facility. The particular model that Alchian estimates is one that is linear in logs Equation (6)

$$\log m = a - b \log N + e \qquad (6)$$

where m is the required man-hours per pound and N is the number of airframes previously produced by that facility.

A number of questions are suggested by the form of the function and will be answered in turn:

1. How long does the decline continue? There is no evidence that it ever ceases in the range of N available.
2. Is Equation (6) the correct form of the function? The only answer seems to be the observation that the correlation coefficient exceeds .9 in 16 cases and .8 in the other six cases.
3. Are the intercepts and slopes identical for all model-facility combinations, or some proper subsets? An analysis of variance shows that neither the intercept nor slope is common to a subgroup based on type of airframe. Thus, insofar as a log linear curve is correct, the characteristics are peculiar to the model-facility combination.
4. How good are the predictions for individual facilities from industry estimates? The measure here is that of the accumulated hours necessary to produce 1000 airframes; the absolute differences between predicted and actual average 25 per cent of the actual.
5. How good are the predictions when estimated from airframe types, such as bombers or fighters? The error seems to be the same as for industry figures.
6. Is the reliability any different when extrapolated from the early history of a particular model-facility combination? The error here seems to fall to about 22 per cent.

One of the questions that Alchian doesn't consider is the effect of learning in the industry in general. A facility starting after other facilities have broken ground ought to begin at a higher level of efficiency and improve more slowly. Similarly, a facility starting to produce a new model after it had had extensive experience with similar models ought to be more efficient in the beginning and more quick to learn. Finally there is the effect of industry know how where the more airframes that are produced, the greater ought to be the knowledge of how to produce airframes and so the more efficient ought production to be.

A review of the literature on learning by doing can be found in Asher (1956). Much of it has been concerned with military operations for reasons cited before. A recent paper by Rapping (1965) follows this direction by considering improvements in the efficiency of shipbuilding in United States shipyards, 1941–44, by means of cross-section and time series data.

Wartime shipbuilding offers a particularly good example of technological change since (a) the shipyards were built especially for the war, (b) the management and workers were almost universally without previous experience, (c) they all produced Liberty vessels, (d) they were of quite different sizes, and (e) they all collected much data on inputs and output.

Rapping begins by estimating the parameters of the familiar Cobb-Douglas, linear in logs production function from cross-section data. Results are shown in Equation (7).

$$Y = 1.10L + .57K \qquad R^2 = .92 \qquad (7)$$
$$t = (22.1) \quad (4.0)$$

Rapping next attempts a conventional estimate of technological change by introducing a time trend, Equation (8).

$$Y = 1.12L + .63K + .23t \qquad R^2 = .96 \qquad (8)$$
$$t = (30.0) \quad (5.0) \quad (6.1)$$

The results improve and so he attempts to refine the estimate by using the time trend to measure the number of years each yard was producing ships, Equation (9).

$$Y = 1.14L + .29K + .28t_i \qquad R^2 = .96 \qquad (9)$$
$$t = (31.4) \quad (2.6) \quad (6.6)$$

Again the improvement is noted.

If learning by doing, rather than the more general notion of technological change, is correct, a better measure of the efficiency increase will be the accumulated output for each yard. Three measures of accumulated output are tried, the best of which is noted in Equation (10).

$$Y = .918L + .23K + .29C \qquad R^2 = .98 \qquad (10)$$
$$t = (30.5) \quad (2.9) \quad (11.4)$$

One final variable that might be relevant follows from the fact that some yards switched to Victory ships toward the end of the period. Thus a new variable, which should have a negative sign, is introduced to account for the diminution of effort put into the production of Liberty ships, Equation (11).

$$Y = .94L + .26K + .26C - .04X \qquad R^2 = .98 \qquad (11)$$
$$t = (29.6) \quad (3.4) \quad (10.9) \quad (2.2)$$

In order to test whether the relevant efficiency measure was learning by doing rather than the more nebulous technological change, Rapping introduced, Equation (12),

$$Y = .90L + .67K + .34C - .15t \qquad R^2 = .98 \qquad (12)$$
$$t = (24.3) \quad (.6) \quad (7.7) \quad (-2.7)$$

a regression with both variables present. A crude test of strength is provided by the question of which variable survives in the presence of the other. Since accumulated experience fares so well, there is evidence that it is the better explanatory variable.

However, Equation (12) is unsatisfactory for two reasons. The coefficient of time takes on a negative sign and is statistically significant. If this equation is correct, there has been significant negative technological change. The coefficient of capital is even more suspicious. It is grossly inconsistent in the analysis since the coefficient varies from .23 to .67. Finally, when time is added to Equation (12), the capital coefficient triples in size and loses significance.

Although the Alchian paper was written in 1949, before 1962 no one had placed this concept in a complete macroeconomic model. Arrow (1962) constructs a model of growth and technological change. The latter is embodied in increasingly productive capital goods since the labor used to produce them becomes more efficient over time. The model is similar to work by Solow (1960) where new machines were more productive through technological change.

Arrow defines two functions of G, the index of the total gross investment to date (of technological change): $\lambda(G)$ is the amount of labor used to produce with a machine of index number G; $\gamma(G)$ is the output of this capital good. For notation, X is the total output, whereas L is the total employed labor force. This formulation differs from Solow's insofar as Arrow has not made full use of all his powers to define. He could normalize either λ or γ by defining a capital good as a unit that gave one unit of output or requires one man to operate. (Solow chose the former.)

Output is defined in Equation (13).

$$X = \int_{G'}^{G} \gamma(G)\, dG \tag{13}$$

The demand for labor is defined in a similar fashion in Equation (14), where

$$L = \int_{G'}^{G} \lambda(G)\, dG \tag{14}$$

G' is the marginal capital that is just profitable to use. Generality can be obtained by defining $\Gamma(G)$ and $\Lambda(G)$ which are the indefinite integrals of Equation (13) and Equation (14), respectively. These new integrals result from knowing the labor force, solving for G', and then solving for output as a function of the known parameters. The result is the production function, Equation (15).

$$X = \Gamma(G) - \Gamma\{\Lambda^{-1}[\Lambda(G) - L]\} \tag{15}$$

The function does not display constant returns to scale.

Arrow specializes the form of γ by assuming that the capital output ratio is constant, Equation (16).

$$\gamma(G) = a \tag{16}$$

He further specifies the nature of λ to be the form typically found in the early literature on learning by doing as in Equation (17).

$$\lambda(G) = bG^{-n} \tag{17}$$

The wage rate can be derived as in Equation (18).

$$w = a\left(G - \frac{x}{a}\right)^{n/b} \tag{18}$$

The model does have a growth rate which satisfies all expectations and is internally consistent.

Finally, Arrow considers the difference between private and social product in this model. As noted previously, the production function displays increasing returns to scale. Yet this quality does not upset the model since there is a fallacy of composition of the sort that Frankel (1962) considers. Each individual gets his private marginal product, but the accumulated investment raises productivity and so raises the social marginal product above that of the private one. Thus, there is a difference between social and private product. Arrow shows that the consistent growth rates are the same under both pure competition and central planning in this model. The rate of investment under competition is, however, lower than the optimal rate.

The Accelerator and Technological Change

One of the more successful applications of the work on technological change is contained in a paper by Walters (1963). He starts with the usual Cobb-Douglas production function for a firm and differentiates it with respect to time. After solving for the change in capital, he derives Equation (19).

$$\dot{k} = \frac{1}{\alpha + \beta}(\dot{x} - \dot{a}) = \gamma(\dot{x} - \dot{a}) \tag{19}$$

where k, x, and a are the logarithms of capital, output, and technological change, respectively.

The accelerator is usually estimated as the coefficient of output change when it is regressed on capital change, Equation (20),

$$\dot{k} = b_0 + b_1\dot{z} + (v_1 + v_2) \tag{20}$$

where z is the foreseen value of x, and the error term $(v_1 + v_2)$ may be broken into $v_1 = -b_1\dot{a}^e$ (where a^e is the foreseen value of technological change) and the true error term v_2. The least squares estimate of b_1 is unbiased only if the independent variable is uncorrelated with the error term. However, the error term in this model contains $\dot{a}$ the measure of technological change. Because the measured correlation between technological change and output is very high, there is a bias in the conventional estimates of the accelerator. In fact, the bias is a downward one and helps to explain why the estimates of the accelerator have universally been smaller than those value predicted by theory.

The extent of the bias can be calculated from Equation (21)

$$E(\hat{b}_1) = b_1 + \rho_{zv_1}\frac{\sigma_{v_1}}{\sigma_{v_2}} \tag{21}$$

where $\hat{b}_1$ is the estimated accelerator.

Walters goes on to review the literature on technological change and estimates of the accelerator to discover the value of the bias. In all the data he explores, the correlation between output and technological change is positive, above .6, and generally above .9. The extent of the downward bias is therefore 30–60 per cent.

After correcting the accelerator for bias, the estimated values are much closer to theoretical expectations than the original.

Productivity Over the Business Cycle

The technological change measures of Chapter 2 were concerned with change over the long run and cyclical variations were regarded as unfortunate. An audacious theorist might connect these long-run and short-run concepts by the following line of reasoning. The economy contains long delays in adjustment and much slack. Thus whenever output is increasing, a constant number of workers is called upon to sustain the rise and productivity increases markedly. On the other hand, in a decline workers are kept much longer than they should be and so productivity declines. Furthermore, the decline may be sharpened if the firm ordered new capital equipment during the rise which is just being delivered.

This kind of reasoning, rather than answering the questions about short-run productivity behavior, tends to whet the appetite for work in the area. Hultgren (1960) examined the foregoing relation at the level of three-digit industries and found the data tended to substantiate this argument. There is a correlation over the whole cycle and the highest gains in productivity were registered in the first phases of recovery. Kuh (1960) got similar results with a simple one-equation model which included output, a time trend, and some cycle phase variations as explanations of productivity. Wilson (1960) got similar results in investigating both time series and cross-section data and Fromm (1960) got similar results with a more complicated approach.

Wilson and Eckstein (1964) have attempted to derive this relation from a neoclassical analysis of the theory of the firm. In attempting to estimate the man-hours required to produce a certain output, they develop Equation (22),

$$M_t = aC_t + \beta(Q_t^p - C_t) + \gamma(Q_t - Q_t^p) \qquad (22)$$

where M_t is the man-hours actually used to produce an output, C_t is the capacity at time t, Q_t^p is the output that was planned during the previous period to be produced at time t, and Q_t is the actual output at time t. The three terms on the right side of the equation are explained as follows: The first term might be interpreted as making man-hours a linear function of capacity, *ceteris paribus*, with a zero intercept. For a constant technology, this assumption is almost equivalent to the assumption of constant returns to scale. The second term is related to plant size. There is a certain labor requirement associated with a given-sized plant. When the firm is operating at less than the optimal size of the plant, it incurs high labor costs. Assuming that the firm produces a planned output, high labor costs will be related to the difference between planned output and capacity. The final term represents an attempt to take account of the possibility that the firm will produce an output different from the planned output. If the firm tools up for a particular output, it becomes inefficient to modify the plan later on.

The inclusion of technological change in this model is particularly easy since it is seen in shifts of the coefficients. Thus, the equation actually estimated is Equation (23),

$$\frac{M_t}{C_t} = \alpha_0 + \alpha_{1t} + (\beta_0 + \beta_{1t})\frac{Q_t^p}{C_t} + (\gamma_0 + \gamma_{1t})\frac{Q_t^p - Q_t}{C_t} \qquad (23)$$

where each of the coefficients depends on time and each has been divided by capacity. This equation is estimated using both quadratic time trends added to the coefficients and Equation (23) in logarithmic rather than linear form.

The equations were fitted to quarterly data for the manufacturing sector 1948–60. Three dummy variables were added to account for seasonal trends. Three different sets of equations were estimated for regular production workers, overtime hours, and nonproduction workers. The results follow. The coefficients are all significant and the worst feature of the model is the low Durbin-Watson statistic. The autocorrelation in the residuals casts doubt on the results.

α_0	351.83	γ_0	201.28	$R^2 = .9977$
α_1	-3.13	γ_1	-2.57	$DW = .58$
β_0	341.63	d_1	-5.94	
β_1	-4.42	d_2	-5.90	
		d_4	-2.04	

When the equation is used to forecast 1961 and 1962, the results are quite good, although there is some indication of an omitted variable. The equations were used to estimate the elasticity of employment with respect to output. From Equation (23) the elasticity is .57 in 1948 and .39 in 1960 for the short run, and .80 and .54 respectively for the long run. These elasticities have fallen over time as might be expected given the increase in capital per man.

International Trade

Along with deriving a new functional form that gave a constant elasticity of substitution, Arrow, *et al.* (1961) indicated there was evidence that one of the principal assumptions of the classical theory of international trade was invalid. Minhas (1964) extended the arguments, both theoretical and empirical, and came to much the same conclusion. The argument is that if industries within a country are ranked by the capital-labor ratio, shifts in the relative price of these factors might cause this ranking to change. If the elasticity of substitution of capital for labor is equal in all industries, there can be no change in the ranking. Should the elasticities be unequal, however, industries would respond differently to price changes and the ranking would shift.

Arrow, *et al.* concluded that there seemed to be a constant elasticity of substitution within the same industry across countries but different elasticities within different industries. Note that neither of the conventional functional forms used could have given them this conclusion; both the Cobb-Douglas and fixed coefficient forms assume a fixed elasticity of substitution (1 and 0 respectively) and so all industries must be the same.

Arrow, *et al.* concluded that there was a possibility of the axiom being invalid. They could not tell how serious their criticism was in practice. Minhas attempts to answer this question by means of a graph of log K/L against log w/r. If the elasticities of substitution are constant (across different K/L ratios, that is, across different countries), an industry would be seen as a straight line on this graph. If the elasticities were equal for different industries, the graph would show parallel lines whose intercept was defined by the country with the lowest capital-labor ratio in this industry.

If, however, the elasticities are not equal, there is the possibility that the lines will intersect and a crossover will occur. Thus, there will be a change in the capital-labor ranking and the classical axiom will be violated.

Minhas investigates the number of crossovers and concludes that they are frequent enough to vitiate the classical axiom. When Leontief (1964) uses Minhas' data to estimate the value, he finds that of the 210 possible crossovers that could occur, only 17 do occur. Further, the elasticities of substitution are so close that these contradictions do not imply important exceptions to the invariant ranking assumption. Thus, Leontief concludes that the Minhas conclusion is ill-founded and, indeed, concludes the classical axiom is substantiated.

Leontief goes on to present other criticisms of Minhas' work; he is simultaneously criticising Arrow, *et al.* The elasticity of substitution is estimated by *b* in Equation (24).

$$\ln \frac{V}{L} = \log a + b \ln W + \epsilon \qquad (24)$$

Since Minhas uses conventional regression techniques to fit this equation, Leontief points out that he is assuming that there are errors of measurement in V/L but none in W. This implicit assumption is hardly plausible. Yet, if there are errors in the measurement of W, the estimate of b is biased downward. This observation has substantial weight for Arrow, *et al.* since twenty of the twenty-four industries have an estimated b greater than .8 and eight of the industries have a b greater than .9. Correction for this bias would bring the estimates closer to unity, closer to the Cobb-Douglas form. Is the extra trouble in estimating the more general CES function justified?

Going back to two themes of long standing, Leontief first questions the assumption that a man-year of labor is the same in all countries. If this assumption is dropped and labor in different countries is assumed to differ, Minhas is no longer estimating the capital-labor elasticity of substitution by b, but is estimating a combination of the elasticity of substitution of labor for labor and capital for labor.

The second theme is a criticism of the use of elasticities of substitution. If the possibility of capital-labor substitution is possible only within a small range, the production function might be approximated by a fixed coefficient form and the elasticity of substitution would be a dubious concept. On the other hand, both the CES and Cobb-Douglas forms are based on the possibility of capital-labor substitution over all conceivable ranges of the function. Just as the fixed coefficient form is absurd when interpreted strictly, however, Leontief's argument must be qualified. Both functions serve only as approximations within the observed range. If the range of capital-labor ratios within a given industry is small, then either form might be used to fit the production function. The CES or Cobb-Douglas form would describe substitution possibilities within the small range (and one would have to be careful that it was not extrapolated outside the range) while the fixed coefficient form would describe the substitution possibilities outside the range.

Automation

The effect of technological change on United States agriculture is a cause of one of the great modern fears. As technology becomes more efficient and fewer men are required for a unit of output, as machines are better designed so that fewer men are necessary for operation and maintenance, the myth grows that technology is outdistancing the worker. It is argued that there will soon be a large pool of permanently unemployed workers who, because of lack of training or low intelligence, will have to live on relief the rest of their lives, who will be dependent on the charity of those who are working.

A glance at the principle of comparative advantage shows that although machines are getting better at some tasks, they can not be better at all tasks. Even if machines are more efficient at all tasks than men, it would be to the advantage of machines and men to specialize themselves to those tasks where they have greatest comparative advantage. Under general, plausible assumptions, all men will always have employment at positive wages.

The foregoing argument presents two problems: some wages, and possibly the share of labor in income, might fall. Employment at a positive wage is little consolation. After all, it is altogether conceivable that the wage might fall to $0.01 per hour for unskilled labor. This wage is positive and this example does fit in with the argument of comparative advantage. The other fear is that gradually men will be eliminated as the horse was eliminated. Although man does have comparative advantages, the total amount of income going to men may shrink until there are only a few around and machines "rule" the world.

The arguments are presented in detail in Simon (1960, 1965), Dunlop (1962), Cyert and Lave (1965) and in Chapter 12. The fear that wages may decline radically is not easily assuaged. Of course, it must be noted that automation and mechanization have been going on for thousands of years. At each new innovation, the same fear has appeared; in each instance, wages rose. Although it is conceivable that some workers, the most unskilled, may only be worth $0.01 per hour in the future, most of the workers will be earning much more than they are today. At worst, there may be a small group that suffers from automation, but the class of workers will gain.

This conclusion follows precisely from the fear that machines will take over. Simon argues that the share of labor in income will fall only under the most unusual conditions; W_L will rise or at worst stay constant over time. The only reason for adopting a technological change is that it gives more output for a comparable amount of input. The characteristic of technological change over three centuries has been that total income has risen rapidly. Thus, if labor's share stays constant, the total payments to workers will rise over time. Far from being a pessimistic subject, automation is one promising a rich future.

Production Functions

The interest in technological change has given rise to a derived demand for better estimates of production functions. If we are to measure technological change correctly, some general idea of the production function is necessary. If we are to explain the factors giving rise to technological change, a detailed knowledge of the production function is essential.[2]

In measuring aggregate technological change, aggregate production functions of one sort or another are necessary. Chapter 2 contains some brief

[2]For a survey of the production function literature see Walters (1963).

comments on the work in this area. Two of the more interesting contributions are those of Solow (1962) and Samuelson (1962). The former, described in Chapter 4, is an attempt to measure the cost of misspecification of a complicated heterogeneous capital, fixed-coefficient production function. The latter paper, to be described here, is an attempt to derive a neoclassical model of the heterogeneous capital, fixed-coefficients type that gives rise to an aggregate production function similar to one of the sort implied by an aggregate Cobb-Douglas function.

Samuelson's results are so unusual as to seem mystic; they seem to prove that things always turn out well under the masterful hands of Paul Samuelson. Heterogeneous capital models are complicated to handle except under some special assumptions. But Samuelson manages to produce a model that makes everything work.

He begins with the assumption that there is a single consumption good, Y. Under conditions of constant returns to scale and factors being paid their marginal product, the possible positions an economy may get to are defined by a curve in the wage-interest plane as shown in Figure 10.1. That is, there are tradeoffs for society between high wages and a high interest rate, given a technology; the tradeoff is determined by the stocks of labor and capital. Samuelson assumes that the capital-labor ratio is the same for both the production of capital goods and the consumption good. He assumes that only the nth capital good is used in the production of an nth capital good. One additional assumption and the stage is set: depreciation is assumed to be independent of the age of the capital good.

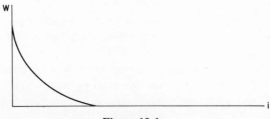

Figure 10-1.

For any given capital good, its profile in the wage-interest plane will be a straight line with intercepts determined by the interest rate when the wage is zero and wage when the interest rate is zero. The line is straight since total value added can be allocated either to wages or interest. Each "machine" (capital good) will have a straight line in the wage-interest plane as shown in Figure 10.2. Efficient production will keep the economy on the envelope of the lines.

The curve in the wage-interest plane for a linear homogeneous production function of two factors, where capital is a physical jelly as in the Clark-

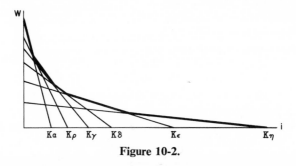

Figure 10-2.

Ramsey models, is shown in Figure 10.3. With a large number of different capital goods, the efficient envelope of Figure 10.2 will approximate the curve of Figure 10.3.

The simplicity of this argument is disarming. It depends rather strongly on assumptions which cannot be expected to obtain in general. Nevertheless, the effort in attempting to connect the functions that are estimated with those that have theoretical justification is noteworthy.

On a less macroeconomic level, the estimation of production functions has hardly progressed since Douglas fitted his aggregate linear in logs functions almost forty years ago. To be sure, there are more sophisticated econometric techniques and new functional forms, such as the CES function, but the basic objections remain. These functions are estimated from value data, are based on only the tradeoffs that the economic unit being investigated has actually experienced, and are subject to all sorts of errors of observation and misspecification.

Two notable exceptions to this trend are contained in the work of Heady (1961) in fitting production functions to physical units in agriculture, and a study by Kurz and Manne (1963) looking at capital-labor tradeoffs in machine shops (see also Chenery [1949]).

Markowitz and Rowe collected a large amount of data on the tasks that are normally encountered in machining, on the machines that can perform these tasks, the number of men required to operate each machine, and the

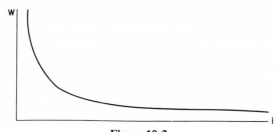

Figure 10-3.

output each day. Applying estimates of the capital costs of the machines, Kurz and Manne are able to get a rough idea of the capital-labor tradeoffs implicit in the Markowitz-Rowe data.

The tasks are described in terms of the operations that have to be performed, not the specific end part. Thus, a wide range of tasks are performed on a wide number of machines. One problem concerns inefficient machines, machines that cost more, use more labor, and produce less than other machines. In fact the data tend to show that increases in capital per man have relatively little effect on output per man. Kurz and Manne made the decision that they were attempting to estimate the optimal locus of capital-output tradeoffs; they eliminated inefficient machines, that is, machines which have a lower output per man for a given capital per man ratio of an efficient machine. In thus eliminating observations, they cut the number of observations from 1143 to 290.

With data from efficient machines, they attempted to detail the capital-labor tradeoffs by estimating a linear in logs regression. The first model specifies output as a function of capital, labor, and the various geometric characteristics of each job. The sum of coefficients of capital and output are assumed to add to unity and the geometric shapes are included as dummy variables.

The results are plausible with a capital coefficient of .3 and a high coefficient of determination. Some possible difficulties are concerned with the small number of observations in some categories and the assumption that the capital coefficient is constant over all tasks. Upon reestimation, the capital coefficient rises until it is about .5 for all geometric shapes except one. Since this one coefficient never reaches a reasonable level, they conclude that the data do not provide evidence allowing them to estimate the coefficient.

Fads being what they are, Kurz and Manne can hardly forbear to estimate a CES function for these data. After a rather ingenious estimation procedure, however, they find that the elasticity of substitution is so close to unity that nothing is gained over the Cobb-Douglas form.

As a final test of consistency, they examine the *U.S. Census of Manufactures* to see whether the relative shares are in fact approximately equal. There is difficulty insofar as no category lists the relative shares of a machine shop. As best they can estimate, however, the share of production workers is .548, which is extremely close to the .5 estimate they obtained.

The success of Kurz and Manne in estimating a physical production function was anticipated by estimates of agricultural production functions. Here investigators such as Heady have made full use of available data and techniques to derive production functions, isoquants, and cost functions both to describe the available tradeoffs and prescribe least cost functions for farmers.

Perhaps the major problem in estimating production functions is that the data fall into a narrow range and may be highly autocorrelated and colinear; the data are observed, not experimental data. Heady and his coworkers use experiments set up specifically to find the production function over a given range, to ward off the problems of autocorrelation and colinearity. There seems to be no reason why experimental techniques cannot be extended to firm production functions.

Of course, it might be argued that the agricultural examples are easily generalized. After all, there is not such a great difference between breeds of animals and type of feed from one year to the next. Thus, a weight-gained production function once done, has implications for many years to come. On the other hand, human workers are not invariant to most changes in the environment. It makes a difference how changes are introduced and how workers perceive management. Yet, these same objections seem to apply to agriculture since environment does make a difference to animals.

Kurz and Manne, however, demonstrate how these physical production functions may be estimated for machine shops. Perhaps if the work is done anew in a decade, one of the first real estimates of increase in technology in manufacturing will become available. Certainly in agriculture, there are functions which permit the measurement of the advance of technological knowledge. One example is given in the inclusion of antibiotics in diets of farm animals. The cost of feed and labor per pound gained decreases markedly and thus there is a technological change.

Thus, it is possible to calculate the savings due to specific innovations. Of course, for more general changes, such as the increase in education of the farm manager, we must go back to measures of efficiency in practice. But these examples provide a way of supplementing the estimates of technological change in practice with means of estimating the change in technological knowledge and ways of calculating the possible impact of specific innovations.

Data from public utilities using steam to generate electricity have been used in a number of production function studies. The industry has many desirable qualities: its output is relatively homogeneous; production decisions tend to be rational; and the data can be estimated through a wide variety of approaches.

In recognition of these merits, steam generation of electricity has been one of the most intensely investigated industries. In the postwar period, Lomax (1952), Nordin (1947), Johnston (1960), Komiya (1962), Barzel (1963), Nerlove (1963), Dhrymes and Kurz (1964), and McFadden (1964) have done studies. The approach and techniques have ranged over practically the whole of econometrics. Johnston attempted to estimate statistical cost functions; Barzel tried to measure the increase in efficiency, whereas Komiya, Nerlove, and Dhrymes and Kurz attempted to get some direct measure of the production function.

Nerlove is interested in estimating returns to scale. Assuming a Cobb-

Douglas production function, he estimates the implied cost function assuming that firms minimize cost under an output constraint. His results show that there are increasing returns to scale, although the degree of these returns is a decreasing function of the output level.

Komiya investigates steam power generation from 1938 to 1956 in order to allocate the increasing efficiency among three factors: (1) economies of scale, (2) factor substitution (non-neutral technological change), and (3) shifts in the production function (neutral technological change).

Two means of classification seem most appropriate for steam generating plants; the date when they were built and the kind of fuel they utilize. These plants represent a major investment decision: they are extremely expensive and long-lived. The tradeoffs between efficiency and flexibility appear to be small; a plant is designed for a given mode of operation, including the labor force and source of fuel. Once they are built, their operating requirements are more or less fixed until they are retired: a plant is retired rather than modified.

In particular, there appear to be four distinct generations of steam plants due to major changes in the design possibilities available. Since the plants represent an extremely large investment, it seems reasonable to assume that new plants use the latest technology.

Operating characteristics vary sharply between coal and other sources of fuel. The latter tend to be more capital-intensive, less labor-intensive, and more fuel-intensive. Thus, all plants built in the period under consideration are classified into one of eight categories (four age and two fuel variables).

Komiya first attempts to estimate a linear in logs production function to his data. The results, however, tend to be inconsistent both with themselves and with economic theory. He is led to a model which doesn't allow substantial substitution between factors. The new model is embodied in a set of three equations concerned with the amount of fuel required, the amount of capital required, and the labor requirement. These functions are linear in logs and specify the fuel energy as a function of the size of the generating unit. The capital requirement for a plant is a function of the size of each unit and the number of units. Finally, the labor requirement is also a function of the size of the units and the number of units. The double measure of capacity, average size of each unit and the number of units, arises from the inability to specify whether scale effects will be related to unit size or plant size.

The three equations in eight groups are investigated by means of a modified covariance analysis. In each case Komiya begins by estimating the equation, treating each of the eight groups as if all parameters differed between groups. Then he reestimates the model, assuming that one after the other of the parameters remains the same across one or the other means of classification. If the explained variance has not diminished substantially, the more general model is accepted.

He concludes that, for the fuel input function, the improvements in efficiency are due primarily to increasing returns to scale. He also finds that noncoal plants require 2 to 3 per cent more energy then coal plants.

For the capital input function, the first conclusion is that returns to scale are a function of both the average size of the generating units and the number of units. The decline in capital costs is due primarily to the scale effect. Finally, the data show that noncoal plants cost up to 25 per cent more than coal operations.

The shifts in labor requirements are much more variable than for the other two inputs. His method is able to isolate the largest reduction in labor as between the first and second periods in the coal plants. The over-all reduction in labor is greater for coal operations. In general, the reduction in labor is by far the most substantial of the three factors. Finally Komiya finds that noncoal operations require 25 per cent to 35 per cent less labor for a plant of equal size.

Dhrymes and Kurz have done a later investigation of these data. They use a generalized CES function so as not to be restricted to assumptions of linearity and homogeneity. Their objective is threefold: (1) to measure the elasticity of substitution of capital for labor, (2) to measure technological change, (3) to measure returns to scale. Their approach and initial classification of the data are similar to that of Komiya.

The equation estimated for labor is linear in logs and shows labor as a function of the price of labor relative to that of capital and the amount of capital. As with Komiya, the results of the estimation are unsatisfactory, since the coefficient of the price ratio sometimes has the wrong sign and generally is insignificant. It seems to be difficult to get a direct estimate of the elasticity of substitution in these data.

Komiya modified his model to a fixed coefficients one to get around the difficulty, Dhrymes and Kurz use a fixed coefficients function in logs. The effect of the transformation as well as its justification don't seem completely clear.

Their fuel input equation is again linear in logs and shows fuel (measured in energy units) as a function of the price of fuel relative to that of capital and of the amount of capital. This form seems particularly well suited to the data and generates estimates that seem to accord with the theory.

Their modified logarithmic fixed coefficients production function gives estimates that are considerably more reasonable than the form that allowed estimation of the elasticity of substitution. They find increasing returns to scale on the order of 1.7 which seem constant through time. They also find some significant relations in differences between regions. This difference is, however, explained by Komiya's work which shows significant differences between coal and oil plants, which tend to specialize over regions. Thus, this regional effect is probably no more than a surrogate for coal versus oil plants.

The elasticity of substitutions of capital for fuel is estimated from the fuel equation. The estimates are distributed around .1 and range from .02 to .20. They tend to fall with increases in the size of the plant. For the larger-sized plants, the elasticity increases over time.

Finally, Dhrymes and Kurz investigate neutral technological change over the period (1937–59). The measure is an implied one coming from changes in the constant terms of the production functions over time. In most cases the measures are significant as shown in Table 10.5. The coefficients of size II require some explanation since they imply a fall in neutral technological change over the period. Such a fall might be explained by a great deal of non-neutral technological change that more than offset this fall in neutral change.

Table 10.5   Implied Measure of Neutral
Technological Change (steam generation of electricity)

Size of Operating Plant	Technology			
	1937–45	1946–50	1951–54	1955–59
I	1	1.18	1.29	—
II	1	0.84	0.63	0.765
III	—	1	2.07	3.32
IV	—	—	1	1.24

Dhrymes and Kurz have a rather novel definition of capital; they measure it in megawatt hours. Calculating the time a generator of a given size was operating, they multiply this time by rated capacity to derive a measure of capital's services. As a consequence of this definition, the price of capital also looks a bit unorthodox. After subtracting the cost of fuel and labor from total cost, what remains is capital cost and possibly unmeasured profit. This residual measure of capital cost is divided by the measure of capital to get the unit cost of capital.

Early in the paper, the authors spell out their conception of an empirical production function:

> ... once a plant is established, little substitution is permitted among the various inputs. Yet it may not be unrealistic to suppose that, in the planning stage at least, the entrepreneur is confronted with the possibility of choosing from a variety of input combinations. ... Hence, the production function we envisage is to be understood as a frontier of technological possibilities in the ex ante sense.
>
> Dhrymes and Kurz (1964, p. 292)

Whether their measure of capital is appropriate for the estimation of this *ex ante* production function depends on whether the entrepreneur could have anticipated the number of hours his new plant would be operated. This possibility is likely to be the case only when the plant is operated essentially all the time. The authors give no data to indicate this is so, although the possibility seems plausible.

This *ex ante* anticipation of hours operated must be combined with *ex ante* knowledge of costs in order to justify the price of capital. If the entrepreneur knew all requisite costs, including the cost of building the plant, and the number of hours the plant would be operated, the estimated unit cost of capital would be an accurate reflection of the true cost. For the particular case of steam electricity generation, this assumption seems plausible. The measure appears to be the superior one they claim it to be. However, it must be realized how restrictive are the assumptions and how unlikely it is that this technique will generalize.

The Dhrymes-Kurz measure of capital illustrates a basic difficulty in the estimation of production functions: is the relevant measure one of capital services or of the available capital stock? Hicks (1932, 2nd edition, pp. 342–50) has done a good job of untangling at least part of this question. Any measure of capital services must come down to a dollar measure: wear and tear on capital, replacement cost, or any other measure. The Dhrymes-Kurz measure, megawatt hours, must implicitly assume various constancies in the cost of capital. It is not an overstatement to note that dollar measures of capital have no place in a real (physical) production function. A real production function must relate physical factors to a physical output. Dollar measures of either inputs or outputs serve only to confuse the issue.

One example of a real production function was just described: Kurz and Manne estimated a production function whose individual points are existing machines, their labor requirement in men and their physical outputs. Such a production function is precisely what is discribed in economic's texts.

However, nothing is changed if the inputs or outputs are measured by one index instead of another: a linear translation of indices does not change the physical facts. Thus, in certain cases, the physical measures can be expressed in dollar units. If a man capable of operating machine X is paid $30 per day, the formulation is not basically changed by measuring labor in dollars.

But the transformation that occassionally allows physical inputs to be measured in monetary units should not be confused with attempts to estimate production functions from monetary data. For example, knowing that a firm spends $X on labor, $Y on capital, and gets $Z in output, is of not the slightest help in estimating a physical production function without some other facts. Only in the unique case where these dollar measures are precise indices of physical quantities can these data be used to estimate a real production function.

However, available capital and available labor make no more sense than crude dollar measures in estimation. If thirty men are employed, but only half are actually used in production, the former figure will generate nonsense when used for estimation. The correct data for estimation should be man-days actually used in production (or better still, man-hours or man-minutes).

Thus, the argument seems to have gone around 360° and capital services are being argued as the correct measure. However, service figures will only give rise to real production functions if physical capital, available capital, is constant. In the particular case of Dhrymes and Kurz, capital services are used as a measure within the constrained class of generators of a limited capacity range built within a short time span. This limitation seems a reasonable approximation to holding physical capital constant.

A General Comment on Macroeconomic Production Functions

When Dhrymes and Kurz estimate a production function, their data and results are well understood. There is, of course, inherent difficulty in measuring labor; nonetheless, one has some confidence that the labor series is a reasonable approximation. Again, many objections can be raised to the output and capital series: output is not really homogeneous, it has different values at different times and places, and so on. Although such comments might form the basis of a more comprehensive study, they are not of the character to discredit the current study. The estimated function is clearly an approximation, but probably a good one.

On the other hand, the estimation of a macroeconomic production function starts from quite a different basis. To begin with, not many economists would agree that there is a single valued function relating capital and labor in the total economy to output; if there is such a function, it is certainly complex and extraordinarily sensitive to factors such as relative prices. Thus, the notion of a macroeconomic production function is an approximation to begin with; so, to be sure, is a microeconomic one of the smooth, continuous variety. But these are two quite different levels of approximation.

Note that accepting the notion of an aggregate production frontier does little to help the macroeconomic production function. Certainly one could describe this aggregate function, probably even by a simple function because of averaging effects of the law of large numbers; but the aggregate would have the property of agreeing with almost any hypothesis but rarely being consistent with alternative tests. It would be a smooth aggregate with constantly changing, or a completely amorphous, economic structure.

But even this level of approximation seems exact compared to the character of available data. Aggregate measures of national product, productive wealth, and an employed labor force can be subjected to endless streams of criticism. Other series such as the return to capital, the share of capital in output, and price indices offer even greater problems. A succinct comment on these problems is offered by Arthur Grant (1963). Although most economists agree that the share of labor in output rose from .43 to .63 between about 1890 and about 1955, a careful re-examination of the Department of Commerce series led him to the conclusion of no change. If reasonable research can support the claim that this basic series could be mismeasured across such a large change, what confidence can be placed in the aggregate functions?

At this point one must abandon the whole venture or reaffirm Solow's (1957) comment that some poeple like this sort of thing and others don't; that these measures provide an oblique approximation. However, the moral to the story seems to go deeper than constant reaffirmation that one is blind in a land of blind men; there are some uses of the data that are less sensitive than others. In particular, the more straightforward and obvious a model, the more likely it will be that conclusions can be understood and the data giving rise to them carefully examined. When one gets to multistage estimation procedures which are top heavy with assumptions, results may be dubious. The data indicate only the grossest changes with any assurance; why use an estimation procedure that requires many significant digits? Isn't it likely that if estimation requires the inversion of a large matrix, or complex adjustment of data by estimates from previous calculations, that the result will have the character of random numbers? Virtuoso work in developing models may include complex general functions and even more complex estimation techniques; but when applied to macroeconomic data, the result seems to have less to offer than some very simple models.

Neutrality of Technological Change

One of the critical assumptions of the Solow formulation is that of netural technological change; that is, the rate of substitution of capital for labor depends only on the magnitudes of these factors and not on time.[3] Solow (1957) employed one test to check his hypothesis and found that no deviation from neutrality was evident, although he admitted the test was extremely weak. Robert Resek (1963) set out to find a better measure of deviations from neutrality. If change were found to be non-neutral, some of the increases in output per man might be due to the interaction of capital or labor and technological change. For example, suppose the share of labor increases from .6 to .7 while capital per man does not increase at all, although there

[3]The definition of neutrality has been argued over by Hicks (1932), Robinson (1938), Harrod (1957), Salter (1960), Uzawa (1961), Kennedy (1961, 1962), and Asimakopulos (1963). The definition becomes complicated when more than a single good is involved as analyzed by Kennedy (1961, 1962), Meade (1961), Asimakopulos (1963), and Weldon (1963).

is gross capital formation. If the labor force is increasing, this non-neutral shift in the production function would cause an increase in production. Assuming technological changes were neutral, all the increase would be attributed to the residual since capital per man did not increase at all. On the other hand, capital (that might have caused the shift in the production function) has interacted with technological change to produce all the increase in output per man. There would have been no increase in output per man without the gross capital formation; capital had a substantial share in the increase.

Resek attempts to devise a test of neutrality that is free of the assumptions of constant returns to scale and pure competition among firms. He assumes that firms maximize profit subject to constraints. Unfortunately, his derivation is both complicated and implausible. Even given his particular assumptions, why should firms know enough to maximize profit? Why is this a better assumption than pure competition? The answer that both derivations assume profit maximization is not a defense since competition tends to eliminate inefficient firms whereas Resek strongly depends on rationality and complete knowledge.

The derivation does give an expression for the marginal rate of substitution. Unfortunately, this expression depends on a number of data series not easily available, such as the life of capital, the discount rate for tax deduction, the interest paid on long-term debt, and the proportion of equity in long-term debt. Resek sets arbitrary, though plausible values for these variables and then proceeds to test for neutrality.

An epoch is defined as a linear relation between the capital-labor ratio and the marginal rate of substitution of capital for labor. When annual data are graphed from 1919 to 1959, three "epochs" seem to emerge. The data from 1919 to 1929 cluster around a line nicely; the data from 1930 to 1939 don't seem to fit a line well; and the data from the 1950's don't exhibit any relation.

He concludes that, between 1919 and 1959, the increase in output per man is accounted for by capital, technological change, and an interaction term. The importance of these three terms are 10.3 per cent, 60.5 per cent, and 29.2 per cent, respectively. It is not at all clear what these results mean since they depend on a derivation based on strong assumptions and further, on arbitrary values of parameters.

One might estimate the extent and effects of non-neutrality directly by estimating a production function and observing the extent to which it shifted non-neutrally over time. In particular, a Cobb-Douglas function would give evidence of non-neutrality if the coefficients shifted. Brown and Popkin (1962) attempt to estimate an aggregate Cobb-Douglas function and use it to measure the extent of neutral and non-neutral technological change.

As with all of the aggregate measures of technological change, the model is plausible for a firm, but suspect at more aggregate levels. The Brown-

Popkin "representative" firm has a production function which is linear in logs, whose arguments are capital and labor, and has a time trend representing neutral technological change.

Aggregate productions were discussed above; another problem arises from the notion of the "rational" behavior of a sector. What is plausible for individual firms may not be plausible for a sector. The possibility of a fallacy of composition renders the rationality argument suspect. For example, Brown and Popkin argue (page 404) ". . . but no rational entrepreneur would choose a technology that yielded less rather than more output with the same inputs." Observing such a phenomenon at the aggregate level would not necessarily cast doubt on the rationality of individual entrepreneurs; there may have been either a fallacy of composition or some shift in structure or composition of production to cause "irrational" behavior in aggregate data. Unfortunately, these difficulties are inherent in all of the aggregate technological change indices. Only an aggregate production function built up from the firm level would get around the difficulties.

Their notion of technological advance is that of technological epochs during which only neutral technological change takes place. These epochs are distinguished by a uniform technology where there is a non-neutral shift of the function from one to another. Of course, this abrupt shift is merely an approximation. During the end of an epoch the new technology is gradually going into use just as, during the first part of the next epoch, the old technology is gradually going out of use. Thus, these abrupt shifts mean that their function is misspecified at the ends and beginnings of all periods.

These epochs are estimated by choosing an initial period of say twelve years. The coefficients for the initial twelve-year period are compared with those for the period extended one year. If the coefficients have changed significantly, the first epoch is over. If not, another year is included and again the coefficients are tested for a difference.

Brown and Popkin use Kendrick's data for the nonfarm, domestic economy from 1890 to 1958. They find that there were three distinct technological epochs: 1890–1918, 1919–37, and 1938–58. The following table summarizes their results.

Table 10.6 Technological Change Epochs
in United States Nonfarm, Private Economy, 1890–1958

Epoch	Capital Coef-ficient	Labor Coef-ficient	Returns to Scale	ΔY Due to Non-neutral Technological Change (per cent)	ΔY Due to Δ Inputs (per cent)	ΔY Due to Tech-nological Change (per cent)
1890–1918	.49	.98	1.47			
1919–37	.60	.44	1.04	−10	16.6	47.3
1938–58	.53	.51	1.04	4	68	67.8

Some criticisms of the method include the assumptions that (1) no non-neutral variation is allowed during an epoch; (2) the production function is linear in logs; (3) there are problems associated with (a) the aggregate nature of the investigation, (b) a bias toward overestimating the returns to scale of the production; (4) the data contain errors of measurement; (5) the estimates are known to be biased and inconsistent.

Innovations and Their Diffusion

Technological change has been treated throughout the majority of the literature as an ill-defined process that seems to occur independently of economic or scientific events. In only a few instances have there been attempts to connect it to some measurable event, such as education of the labor force or learning by doing. The literature on diffusion offers a way of examining the processes and ways by which ideas and inventions were brought to economic prominence. The general investigation has been of a noneconomic character and generally been within the body of sociological theory. Some economists, however, have attacked the problem and attempted to isolate economic variables.

The relevance of diffusion questions is illustrated by the conclusions of Chapter 7. Contrary to what might have been expected, it was found that the rate of technological change did not vary significantly between different agricultural regions. It would seem as if the important agricultural innovations have been specific to particular crops, and therefore to particular geographical regions. Some obvious examples are the combine for wheat, hybrid corn and the corn picker, and more productive breeds of cattle. How could it happen that different regions experienced substantially the same rate and time pattern of technological change?

At least two factors operate to insure that the rate of innovation and diffusion are homogeneous throughout the agricultural sector. First, there are important externalities in innovation. Once a basic invention or discovery occurs, the applications to different uses should follow more or less simultaneously. The demonstrated effectiveness of mechanization in wheat tended to promote mechanization in corn: the combine was the father of the corn picker.

Second, there are important externalities in diffusion. The diffusion of a radical innovation is slow. Mechanical reapers were built in the first half of the nineteenth century, but few were adopted until late in the second half. However, once the effectiveness of these reapers was proven, other harvesting devices were adopted with far less trouble. Indeed, the externalities extended far outside wheat farming because the success of mechanical reapers seemed to make adoption of mechanical harvesters easier for other crops.

The importance of these two externalities is seen in the result of Chapter

7: technological change throughout agriculture has proceeded at approximately the same rate and with the same time profile. The importance of questions of diffusion is also illustrated by industrial innovations.

Woodruff (1962) examines one of the most important innovations of the nineteenth and twentieth centuries, the use of rubber in commercial goods. Perhaps the central point of his work is the widespread and simultaneous nature of invention. Charles Goodyear in the United States is generally given credit for inventing vulcanization whereby natural rubber is chemically stabilized against changes in temperature. Yet, men in England, Germany, and Holland were successful at almost the same time. The reason for the widespread nature of the experimentation is probably to be found in the commercial value of the invention. The inventors tended to be businessmen who were concerned with exploiting natural rubber for commercial purposes. Their experiments led them, via trial and error, to a process of vulcanization.

Goodyear's particular virtue was that he knew when he had succeeded and was successful in turning the invention into commercial value. It might not be entirely correct to say that necessity was the mother of invention, but it was certainly the mother of commercial exploitation.

Goodyear's invention was diffused throughout Europe with great rapidity because of his need for capital. He sought this capital in Europe and then later on, Americans built European plants. There were a number of reasons for these plants. First of all, there was a boom in rubber that collapsed, leaving skilled workers and excess capacity in America. Secondly, Europe levied a high duty on imported rubber. The logical conclusion was that the American workmen emigrated to Europe. Indeed, all the secrets of the rubber industry were in the methods of production; thus, nothing short of the emigration of workmen would have been satisfactory, Finally, the joining of American skills and European capital speeded the diffusion.

The discovery of synthetic rubber, in contrast to the vulcanization of natural rubber, was made by scientists. The first discoveries were of more scientific than commercial interest and the work was much more technical. Indeed, the process of discovery involved many small steps taken by scientists of different countries who relied on the work of previous investigators.

In exploiting the discovery, however, commercial and social interests again came to the fore. Since Britain controlled the sources of natural rubber, it had little interest in the synthetic product and did not produce any until quite late. On the other hand, Germany and the United States wanted supplies that did not depend on the whims of Britain and her colonies.

Woodruff's final point is the leading role played by Europe and the United States in diffusing the industry to other parts of the world. Companies set up branches in other parts of the world and sold their technology to local companies. Woodruff attributes this diffusion to the availability of capital for foreign investment.

The greatest lessons to be learned from the case of rubber concern the role of social, political, and economic forces in the diffusion. Britain had no role in synthetic rubber until after the Second World War because of its investment in colonies producing natural rubber. The United States has diffused the rubber industry around the world because of the availability of capital for foreign investment. The commercial interest in synthetic rubber came from the desire of Germany and the United States to develop a source of rubber that would free them from dependency on British colonies. Finally, the discovery of vulcanization, which started the industry, came from businessmen looking for ways to make use of the properties of rubber under conditions other than normal temperatures.

The investigation of diffusion assumes a more quantitative form under the hand of Edwin Mansfield (1962). He investigates factors having to do with the entry and relative growth rates of firms. The areas of investigation are (1) factors affecting entry and exit, (2) the effect of innovation on size, (3) factors influencing the relative growth rates of firms.

The first model is a relatively simple one investigating the effect of two factors: rates of return and the capital cost of the minimum efficient firm on entry into an industry. Entry is defined as the proportion of firms that entered and survived divided by the total number of firms at the beginning of the period. Profitability is measured by the average rate of return in the industry. Thus, the model predicts that entry is greater as the average rate of return increases and is inversely proportional to the cost of entry. Mansfield fits Equation (25)

$$\ln E_{it} = .49 + 1.15 \ln \pi_{it} - 27 \ln C_{it} \quad \bar{R}^2 = .49$$
$$t = \qquad (2.7) \qquad (1.9)$$

(25)

where E_{it} is entry at time t_1, π is profitability, and C is the cost of entry. He finds that the signs of the variables are as expected and the coefficients are significant.

The second model is concerned with explaining the proportion of firms that left an industry during a given period. The proportion of firms of size S is considered to be a function of the ratio of S to $\hat{S}_{it}$ the minimum efficient size of a firm in a given industry, of the average rate of return in that industry π, and of a coefficient measuring the distribution of firm sizes V_{it}. The relation Equation (26) is fitted and again the coefficients have the proper signs, although the results are not as significant as could be desired.

$$\ln R_{it} = -1.68 - .41 \ln \left(\frac{\bar{S}_{it}}{\hat{S}_{it}}\right) + .10 \ln (1 - V_{it}^2) - .60 \ln \pi_{it} \quad \bar{R}^2 = .49$$
$$t = \qquad (2.9) \qquad (0.4) \qquad (1.8)$$

(26)

The next relation attempted is that of the effect of successful innovation on firm size. Mansfield finds that successful innovation is unrelated to the previous growth of a firm. Thus, any later growth cannot be attributed to a previously strong tendency to grow. Secondly he finds that a successful innovation tends to raise a firm's growth rate by 4–13 percentage points, depending on the time and industry.

Finally, Mansfield investigates the degree of mobility within an industry. $P(S)$ is the probability that a firm of size S will be smaller than a firm that was 60–70 per cent of its size at the beginning of the period. The change in size is hypothesized to be a function of the distribution of firm sizes at the beginning V_{it}, of the age of the industry A_{it} (since a new industry ought to display more variation) and of the number of firms in the industry at the beginning of the period N_{it} (since the greater the number of firms, the more chance there is that a firm will switch position). The results are given below in Equation (27) and provide an amazingly good fit. With the exception of the variable on the distribution of firm sizes, the signs of the coefficients are all in the expected direction and all are significant.

$$\ln P_{it} = -.55 - .57 \ln (1 + V_{it}^2) - .15 \ln A_{it} + .29 \ln N_{it} \quad \bar{R}^2 = .81$$
$$t = \quad\quad (2.9) \quad\quad\quad (2.1) \quad\quad (3.6)$$
(27)

Mansfield (1963) continues his study of diffusion of new inventions by examining factors affecting the speed with which firms accept such inventions. He begins by enumerating four factors that help to determine the time taken to adopt an innovation: (1) waiting time is inversely related to firm size; (2) elaborating the first factor, waiting time decreases at an increasing rate with increases in firm size; (3) waiting time will be inversely related to the profitability of the innovation to the firm; (4) this relation decreases at an increasing rate.

Remember that the four propositions are alleged to hold for the firm of average size and average profitability. Thus, the very first firm to innovate may be a small one, yet Mansfield predicts that by the time the average small firm has adopted the innovation, the average large firm will long since have gone over.

The relation between the two factors, size and profitability, is assumed to be multiplicative, giving rise to Equation (28),

$$\ln d_{ij} = a_{it} + a_{12} \ln P_{ij} + a_3 \ln S_j + e_{ij}$$
(28)

where d_{ij} is the delay in introduction of an innovation, P_{ij} is the profit of the innovation to the firm, and S_j is the size of the firm. Figures for the potential profitability of an innovation are not easily come by, however, and Mansfield was reduced to using surrogates in some cases and to have no estimates at all in others. Thus, firms are divided into two groups, those with data on profitability and those without. The elasticity of response with respect to firm size is $-.40$ for the former group and $-.32$ for the latter. The elasticity with respect to profitability ranges from $-.03$ to -1.53, depending on the innovation and industry. The coefficients are significant at conventional levels.

Mansfield attempts to expand his model by introducing more variables that affect waiting time. The fifth proposition states that waiting time is inversely proportional to the firm's rate of growth. The sixth proposition gives waiting time an inverse relation with the firm's profitability. Finally, he conjectures that waiting time is directly related to the age of the firm president, inversely related to liquidity of assets, and directly related to past profits. The results are inconclusive since the coefficients often have the wrong sign and are almost universally insignificant.

Next, Mansfield examines the probability that a firm which was quick to adopt one innovation will be quick to adopt a second. He conjectures that a firm attains technical leadership in an industry and innovates when this happens. Such leadership decays over time, however; hence the longer the time between innovations, the less likely it should be that a firm that was first to innovate will continue to be first. In particular, he hypothesizes that the correlation between the time it takes a firm to introduce one innovation with the time it takes to introduce a second ρ_{qv} is a constant term V plus a term t_{qv} that decays as the time between innovations rises, Equation (29).

$$\rho_{qr} = V + wt_{qv} + e_{qr} \tag{29}$$

The estimated range of the constant term is .28 to .66, depending on the industry, whereas the coefficient of decay w is $-.012$ and is statistically significant.

Once an innovation has been adopted, what determines the time it will take to have it completely replace the old way of doing things? Mansfield essays this question for the diesel locomotive. This innovation was introduced in the United States in 1924 but gained slow acceptance. By 1930, only eleven roads owned diesels and they were used only where there were fire hazards or smoke problems. The diesel was not fully developed until 1934 when General Motors came out with a small, fast, highly powered locomotive. In 1935 half of the major roads had begun to use diesels, although the biggest single factor governing their adoption and spread seemed to be the amount of coal hauled by the road. Roads seemed to be reluctant to alienate their coal customers. Only at the end of 1941 had railroads decided that many of their tasks would be handled by diesels. It was not until 1945, however, that most of the roads decided to dieselize completely.

Mansfield (1963) investigates the factors affecting the time it took thirty randomly selected railroads to go from 10 per cent diesels to 90 per cent diesels. The model implies that the proportion of diesels is a logistic function of time. He estimates Equation (30) where $\rho_i(t)$ is the proportion of road i's

$$\ln\left[\frac{\rho_i(t)}{1 - \rho_i(t)}\right] = a_i^1 + V_i t \tag{30}$$

locomotives that are diesels at time t. V_i is used in Equation (31).

$$V_i = C_1 + C_2\pi_i + C_3L_i + C_4S_i + C_5C_i + E_i \tag{31}$$

π_i is the rate of return a road could obtain by filling a place with a diesel; L_i is the difference in years between the time the ith road introduced diesels and 1924; S is a measure of the size of a firm; and C is a measure of its liquidity.

Equation (30) fits the data well (R averages .90); hence Mansfield concludes that the proportion of diesels is a logistic function of time. The estimate of V_i is used to estimate Equation (31):

$$\hat{V}_i = -.163 + .900\pi_i + .048L_i + .0028S_i + .115C_i \quad R^2 = .69$$
$$t = \qquad\quad (1.8)\quad\;\; (6.0)\qquad (1.2)\qquad (2.9)$$

Mansfield now investigates four additional factors, the age composition of steam locomotives when the road had attained 10 per cent diesels, the number of diesels that a road needed to attain 90 per cent changeover, the road's average length of haul, and the average railway operating income as a per cent of total adjusted capital in the two years prior to and including the year when the ith road began to dieselize. All the factors have the correct sign when they are introduced into Equation (31), one at a time, although none of them is statistically significant.

Finally, a new model is tried with dependent variable corrected for utilization data on freight service. The change does not substantially change the previous results.

Gibrat's Law

Innovation and diffusion have had marked effect on the growth of firms. Some empirical regularities have been observed with respect to firm size. Investigation of concentration and firm size in United States manufacturing shows that plotting firm size against number of firms of that size gives approximately a straight line on double log paper. The distribution looks like the Pareto, Yule, or log normal distribution, a result quite different from what one would expect from explanations based on static cost curves (see Simon and Bonini [1958]). The investigation takes a turn toward stochastic processes when it is realized that simple assumptions about firm growth will give rise to distributions like those observed. The simplest form of Gibrat's law postulates that the probability of a proportionate change in firm size over a period is independent of the initial size of a firm. Thus, additional sales of $500 million for a $5 billion firm are just as likely as a growth of $5000 for a $50,000 firm in the same industry.

This simplest form of the law can be formulated in three ways depending on what account is taken of firms that fail or which firms the law is supposed to govern. Mansfield (1962) makes these tests on United States manufacturing data. The first test simply applies a χ^2 goodness of fit test to all firms over the period. Mansfield finds that growth is significantly nonproportional in seven out of the ten industries investigated. Thus, this simplest form of the law fails.

A second test excludes all firms that failed over the period on the grounds that the law covers only growth. This modification helps only slightly (growth is nonproportional in four out of ten industries).

The third modification excludes firms that were below the minimum efficient size at the start of the period. It is argued that these firms are handicapped or inefficient and so have little chance of growing. Yet, again growth is nonproportional in six out of ten cases.

In looking at the data Mansfield develops a hypothesis that should explain growth in these data. He defines a unit firm as one that has the minimum size necessary to be efficient in the industry. Thus a large firm is made up of many units. If each of these units had the same probability of growth, small firms (that consisted of a single unit) would display variable rates of growth, whereas large firms (consisting of many units) would tend to be less variable, since some of their units would be moving up while others stayed constant or moved down. This averaging process is hypothesized to account for the differences in volatility in small firms.

Ijiri and Simon (1964) attack the problem from a different angle by attempting to modify Gibrat's law. They define a process where the growth rate of a particular firm is proportional to a weighted average of past growth rates of this firm. Thus, we can predict that a firm which grew quickly last period will grow this period, although it may not grow nearly as quickly as last period. They show that this new process gives rise to a distribution of firms which approximates the Yule distribution and is approximately linear on double log paper.

Bibliography

Section A: economic growth and development. Abramovitz 1956, 1962; Amano 1964; Ames and Rosenberg 1963; Aukrust 1964; Balogh 1958, 1964; Banerji 1956; Becker 1964; Bell 1964; Blaug 1960; Christensen and Yee 1964; Denison 1961, 1962; JPE Supplement on Education 1962; Galenson and Leibenstein 1955; Gourvitch 1940; Haavelmo 1954; Hahn and Matthews 1964; Heady 1962; Kendrick 1964; Knowles 1960; Meade 1961; Mills 1952; Nelson 1964; Neville 1964; Rosenberg 1964; Rostow 1960; Schmookler 1965; Schultz 1960, 1962; Swan 1956; Terleckji 1958, 1959; Tinbergen and Correa 1962; Tolley and Smidt 1964; Tweeten and Tyner 1964.

Section B: learning by doing. Alchian 1959, 1963; Arrow 1962; Asher 1956; Hirsh 1956; Hirshleiffer 1962; Levy 1964; Rapping 1965; Robinson 1963; Schultz 1956; Sturmey 1964; Verdoorn 1949.

Section C: the accelerator. Bowen 1954; Walters 1963.

Section D: productivity over the business cycle. Balogh 1959; Fromm 1960; Hultgren 1960; Kuh 1960, 1965a, 1965b; Nield 1963; Soligo 1963; Streeten 1962; Wilson 1960, 1964; Worswick 1958.

Section E: international trade. Ames and Rosenberg 1963; Arrow, *et al.* 1961; Bardhan 1963; Bhagwati 1964; Finley and Grubert 1959; Leontief 1964; Michaely 1964; Minhas 1963; Posner 1961.

Section F: automation. Brown and de Cani 1963b; Brozen 1958; Cyert and Lave 1965; Dunlop 1962; Eels, Hazelwood, Knowles, and Winston 1959; Simon 1960, 1965.

Section G: production functions. Amey 1959; Anderson 1961; Bernard 1964; Bhalla 1964; Black 1962b; Brown and Conrad 1962; Bruno 1964; Charnes and Cooper 1952, 1954, 1962; Chenery 1949, 1953; Dhrymes and Kurz 1964; Diwan 1964; Ferguson 1963, 1965a, 1965b; Frankel 1962; Frisch 1965; Green 1964; Griliches 1957, 1963, 1964; Heady and Dillon 1961; Hildebrank and Liu 1965; Intrilligator 1965; Johnston 1960; Kamien 1966; Komiya 1962; Kurz 1963; Kurz and Manne 1963; Lomax 1950, 1952; McFadden 1963, 1964; Morrissett 1953; Nerlove 1963; Newman and Reade 1961; Nordin 1947; Pyatt 1964; Simon and Levy 1963; Solow 1960; Walters 1963a, 1963b.

Section H: neutrality of technological change. Amano 1964; Asimakopulos and Weldon 1963; Fellner 1961, 1962; Hicks 1932; Horowitz 1962; Resek 1963; Uzawa 1961.

Section I: innovations and their diffusion. Blaug 1963; Carter and Williams 1957, 1958, 1959; Commandor 1965; Ewell 1955; Griliches 1957, 1958; Grossfield 1962; Habakkuk 1962; Hamberg 1959, 1964; Hart and Prais 1956; Hymer and Pashigan 1962, 1964; Ijiri and Simon 1964; Jewkes, Sawers and Stillerman 1958; Kennedy 1962; Lave 1963; Little 1963; Lydall 1959; Mansfield, 1961, 1962, 1963a, 1963b, 1963c, 1964, 1965a, 1965b, 1965c; Mansfield and Brandenberg 1965; Markham 1965; Nelson 1959, 1962; Phillips 1956; Robinson 1938; Rogers 1962; Rosenberg 1963; Ruttan 1959; Scherer 1965; Schmookler 1959; Shen 1961; Simon and Bonini 1958; Strassman 1959; Sutherland 1959; Terleckji and Halper 1963; Usher 1964; Villard 1958; Woodruff 1962; Worley 1961.

CHAPTER ELEVEN

Appalachian Agriculture : Its Problems 1870–1975*

Introduction and Setting of the Problem

Two words characterize the American economy over the last century: growth and prosperity. Increases in Gross National Product (GNP), capital, and real income have been unprecedented in the world. The figures (as measured by the Department of Commerce) are so large that one is continually amazed at reviewing them. Between 1870 and 1960, GNP increased 2755 per cent; GNP experienced a twenty-eight-fold increase. Output rose from $17.65 billion in 1870 to $503 billion in 1960 (both in 1960 dollars). The nation's wealth also expanded during this period: the capital stock rose 1830 per cent.

At the same time income and output per worker rose precipitously over this period. Output per man increased 453 per cent; capital per man increased 274 per cent.

The picture for the nation's agricultural sector is every bit as impressive. Although total output increased only 553 per cent over this period, the rise in productivity (output per man) is much higher, 949 per cent, than the total economy. Similarly, the increase in capital per man is slightly higher than the total economy: 411 per cent. Table 11.1 sets out these relationships.

*The research embodied in this chapter was supported by the President's Appalachian Study Commission. The opinions expressed are those of the author.

Table 11.1   Growth between 1870 and 1960

	Series	Growth (percentage)
U.S.	GNP: Y	2755
U.S.	Capital: K	1830
U.S.	Labor Force: L	416
U.S.	Productivity: Y/L	453
U.S.	Capital per worker: K/L	274
U.S.	Capital output ratio: K/Y	−42
Agriculture	Y	553
Agriculture	Y/L	949
Agriculture	K/L	411
Agriculture	K/Y	−51
Appalachian Agriculture	Y	353
Appalachian Agriculture	Y/L	674
Appalachian Agriculture	K/L	344
Appalachian Agriculture	K/Y	−49

1960 Value of

Agriculture K/L (in 1960 prices)	$27,000
Appalachian Agriculture K/L	$14,000
Appalachian Agriculture L (for 1959)	626,000

SOURCE: The agricultural figures 1870–1950 come from Tostlebe (1957). The manufacturing figures come from *Historical Statistics* (1957) and *Statistical Abstracts* (1964).

These figures indicate that American agriculture has been spectacularly successful in improving productivity and contributing to higher per capita incomes. If prices had stayed constant, the agricultural sector would be among the richest and highest-paying sectors. The increase in production exceeded the increase in demand, however (the demand for food increases less rapidly than income). Distributing it more widely has been nearly impossible due to tariffs, quotas, and other barriers to the movement of food in international trade. It is precisely the spectacular increase in productivity that has given rise to the set of issues labeled "the farm problem."

Yet the farm problem is not nearly so easily defined as one might suppose. Over the period 1870 to 1960, changes in income per capita were approximately proportional to productivity changes: income per capita increased 850 per cent for agriculture as against 600 per cent for manufacturing. Since the wage in agriculture rose more than the wage in manufacturing, the farm problem is certainly not one of stagnation. In 1960, however, the average agricultural wage was only seven-tenths of the manufacturing wage. This comparison offers the first clue of the extent of a problem in agriculture. This sort of comparison might also be used to get a first glance at the problem in Appalachia: manufacturing wages in Appalachia were only about

83 per cent of the average for the rest of United States manufacturing; agricultural wages in Appalachia were under 60 per cent of the national manufacturing wage in 1960.

But the problem of Appalachian agriculture is not low income or low productivity; these are only symptoms. The distribution of income, prices of commodities, and productivity are the result of adjustments over time. Why has Appalachian agriculture not come up to the standard of the economy? The basic answer lies in the dynamic adjustments of the economy.

Without recognition of the deeper problem, policies are likely to aggravate the current problem. The focus must be on examining the way in which Appalachian agriculture has adjusted over time in response to economic forces. One must describe the present state of the sector in terms of its history and then one can make predictions about the future by extrapolating past behavior. These investigations of the past, present, and future should give some clue to whether changes in the sector must be induced to aid the adjustment mechanisms, and what such changes ought to be.

Technological Change in United States Agriculture

The problem of Appalachian agriculture is first of all a problem of United States agriculture. The extent of the problem cannot be appreciated unless Appalachia is put into its setting.

The increases in output, capital, and labor for agriculture and ten sub-regions are presented in Table 11.2. A glance shows the increases in output

Table 11.2 A Comparison of the United States and Ten BAE Regions

	Y/L for 1870 in 1960 Prices		Y/L for 1960 in 1960 Prices		Percentage Change from 1870–1960									
					Y		K		L		Y/L		K/L	
U.S.	755		8110		425		206		−40		949		411	
App.	512	8	3960	10	227	9	86	9	−58	8	647	9	344	7
N.E.	1235	2	9760	5	122	10	−06	10	−75	10	689	8	148	9
S.E.	398	10	6330	9	482	6	169	7	−63	9	1488	2	627	4
L.S.	905	4	11,250	2	657	5	385	5	−39	5	1139	5	582	5
C.B.	977	3	10,010	4	362	8	108	8	−51	6	927	7	326	8
D.S.	575	7	6,660	8	397	7	245	6	−57	7	1064	6	703	2
G.P.	714	5	9450	6	4190	2	2430	2	227	3	1222	4	672	3
T-O	580	6	7980	7	2480	4	950	4	87	4	1279	3	463	6
M	481	9	11,100	3	10010	1	5440	1	332	2	2205	1	1181	1
P	1895	1	12,500	1	3100	3	505	3	400	1	557	10	21	10
	rank		rank		rank		rank		rank		rank		rank	

Source: see Table 7.1.

to have been much more rapid than could be accounted for by increases in labor or capital. This additional increase stems from a change in efficiency and the introduction of new products and methods: technological change.[1] A series of measured technological change for United States agriculture from 1870–1960 is presented in Table 3.3. The figure of 7.58 for 1960 might be interpreted as a 2-1/4 per cent annual growth in efficiency over this ninety-year period.

Another way of interpreting the measure of technological change involves comparing agriculture with the private, nonfarm sector of the economy. Such a comparison over the period 1910–1950 appears in Figure 3.1. The rate of technological change in agriculture has been spectacular viewed either relative to other parts of the economy (it is almost twice as rapid) or an absolute rate (2-1/2 per cent per year).[2]

The State of Appalachian Agriculture

The total agricultural sector has had incomes that rose only slightly faster than incomes in manufacturing, even though the rate of technological change was much more rapid. The 1960 differential between agriculture and manufacturing wages was still very large.

The farm problem is all the more acute in that the efficiency increase has not been distributed uniformly across the ten regions. Productivity increase in Appalachia lagged behind the national average by at least 50 per cent over the ninety-year period as shown in Table 11.2. Problems with land or labor have kept this region from keeping pace with the rest of agriculture.

The region's farmers improved their efficiency faster than workers in the economy as a whole (674 per cent as against 453 per cent) and yet their income slipped relative to all workers. Their more efficient competitors

[1]The relation of technological change, productivity, and the average wage can be seen from the Solow Index. The average wage is simply productivity times labor's share in output, W_L. Technological change is productivity corrected for capital increase. The relation between these variables is used repeatedly throughout this analysis as the focus changes from one variable to another.

[2]In making the comparison between agriculture and manufacturing many problems reemerge. For example, the manufacturing figures are based on a reduction in the work week. In order to make the agricultural figures comparable, a 25 per cent reduction in the work week was assumed. The agricultural figures are in man-years and are something of an overestimate since men are counted who may have full-time or part-time jobs off the farm. The amount of this working off the farm seems to have increased over the period (1910–1960). Even without this adjustment, however, technological change in agriculture is much greater than in the private nonfarm sector.

Additional problems come in through the questions of whether figures are really comparable over time; in particular does the labor series in agriculture have a bias? Are there underlying differences in structure that make some regions different from others in adjusting the figures? At present, there doesn't appear to be anything to be done about these problems other than hoping that they do not significantly affect these conclusions.

increased production faster than demand increased thereby causing prices to fall. Appalachia's relatively smaller productivity increase was an insufficient bulwark against these falling prices and so incomes have hardly risen.

This situation requires explanation and a close look at Table 11.1 will reveal some indications of the performance of Appalachia over this period. In 1870 the absolute level of productivity of the region's agriculture was considerably lower than the national average (the ratio was .66) This relatively low level of productivity implies that resources were earning relatively low incomes in Appalachia. Economic theory would predict that, if resources were free to move in and out of the region, the region should experience a more rapid increase in productivity until it came up to the national standard. Thus, the economy should work to bring a substandard region up to the average except for fixed resources, such as land of different quality. Even the fixed resources should experience price changes that bring their rate of return into line with the national average.

A rough check of this hypothesis can be derived from Table 11.3. A simple rank ordering shows Appalachia to be at the bottom of the heap in all categories. If anything, the position of the region, relative to others, seems to have deteriorated over time.

Table 11.3   Adjustments of the Ten BAE Regions over Time

	Correlations of Data in Actual Figures			
	Y/L 1870	Y/L 1960	Per cent increase Y/L	A(1960)
Y/L 1870	1			
Y/L 1960	.66[s]	1		
Per cent increase in Y/L	−.62[s]	.10	1	
A(1960)	−.39	−.21	.49[s]	1

s: significant at $\alpha = .05$, one-tailed test.

Table 11.4   Correlations Using Ranks Instead of Actual Data

	Y/L 1870	Y/L 1960	Per cent increase Y/L	A(1960)
Y/L 1870	1			
Y/L 1960	0.65	1		
Per cent increase in Y/L	−0.66	−0.13	1	
A(1960)	−0.43	−0.67	0.62	1

Although the hypothesis of adjustment toward equality doesn't seem to hold for Appalachia, it seems to do better for comparable regions. The Delta states and Southeast are neighboring regions that started out in positions comparable to Appalachia but improved a great deal over time. They each displayed productivity increases over the national average. The Mountain states offer a region with terrain comparable to that of Appalachia. This region is first in productivity increase over the period. Thus, there is no tendency apparent in the data for Appalachia to adjust toward the national standard; if anything, its relative position seems to have deteriorated over time.

The Distribution of Technological Change

Indices of technological change for the ten BAE regions over the period 1870–1960 are presented in Table 7.3. A glance at the 1960 figures shows the wide variation in rates: the cumulative index goes from 5.89 to 12.35. Some caution must be used in interpreting these figures since they measure increases in efficiency. Insofar as they have anything to do with absolute efficiency, there might be an inverse relation. As argued earlier, regions that started with high levels of efficiency should tend to experience relatively low growth, whereas the regions starting with low efficiency should show a relatively high growth.

The data of Table 11.2 can be used to test a hypothesis that the market is working to adjust the returns and values of factors toward greater equality. Since the data cover a ninety-year period, there should be substantial evidence of adjustment. If the adjustment were complete, productivity (Y/L) would be the same in all regions and would give rise to a correlation of zero. Insofar as the market is bringing regions toward equality, the rich should still be rich, but not quite so rich. The poor should still be poor, but not quite so poor. The rich are getting relatively poorer whereas the poor are getting relatively richer. Of course, it is possible that the market might have overadjusted, but this is extremely unlikely.

Given that the rich are expected to become relatively poorer, the following relations should hold: productivity in 1870 should be positively correlated with productivity in 1960: the rich are still rich and the poor still poor. However, 1870 productivity ought to have a high *negative* correlation with the increase in productivity over the period: the rich are getting relatively poorer. Finally, the greatest technological change should have occurred in the regions that were initially so poor: 1870 productivity ought to have a high negative correlation with technological change.

The relations concerning productivity in 1960 should parallel those for 1870: 1960 productivity should be positively related to the increase in productivity, and negatively related to technological change. The reasons for these relations are parallel to those given for 1870 productivity.

Two of the relations for the increase in productivity have already been set out: it should be negatively related to productivity in both 1870 and in 1960 with the stronger relation being that with 1870. Of course the increase in productivity should have a strong positive relation to technological change: the greater the increase in productivity, the higher will be technological change, *ceteris paribus*. The relations of technological change with the other variables have all been described: it is negatively related to productivity in 1870 and 1960, and positively related to the increase in productivity.

These four variables, observed from 1870 to 1960 on the ten BAE regions, were entered in a correlation analysis with results shown in Table 11.3. The results accord with the predictions listed above and most of the results are significant at the .05 level. The only failure to predict comes in the relation between 1960 productivity and the increase in productivity. It appears that there is a slight positive relation: the higher was productivity in 1960, the higher was the increase in productivity. Even though a plausible argument could be made for this relation, the correlations were reworked using ranks instead of the detailed data. The results, shown in Table 11.4, now accord completely with the elaborated predictions. It is significant that Appalachia is the only definite exception to the prevailing pattern of adjustment.

The Real Cost of Appalachian Agriculture: A First Approximation

Perhaps the best way to dramatize the cost of this failure to adjust is an extrapolation to 1975. The trends for this fifteen-year extrapolation come from the period 1930–60, the period of most rapid productivity increase. Thus, the conditions are as optimistic as they could reasonably be. Of course, such an extrapolation is suspect for many reasons. It assumes that no government plans will be put into operation and that the economy will merely continue in the same direction and at the same speed it has for the past thirty years. Nonetheless, this extrapolation is probably the best point estimate of what the future of Appalachian agriculture would be without additional intervention.

Extrapolating the indices of Table 11.2 from 1960 to 1975 gives a cumulative technological change index of 14.03 for the total United States agricultural sector and of 9.74 for the Appalachian sector. Output per man will have increased to $15,700 (in constant 1960 dolalrs) for total United States agriculture and to $5630 for Appalachia. This picture is clearly one of subsistence agriculture with small farmers earning far less than a national standard. Indeed, if account were taken of the probable fall in farm prices (see Chapter 10, first section) it is more than conceivable that output per man in current prices would be lower than the 1960 figure. This extrapolation presents the real possibility of what could happen to Appalachia without

Table 11.5 Growth in Appalachia

Year	Y Output (Millions of 1910–14 Dollars)	K Capital (Millions 1910–14 of Dollars)	L Labor × 1000	Y/L Total U.S. (A)	Y/L Appalachia (Tostlebe) (B)	Y/L Appalachia Census (C)	K/L Total U.S. (D)	K/L Appalachia (Tostlebe) (E)	K/L Appalachia (Census) (F)
1870	271	335	891	329	216	304	2880	1570	376
1880	236	343	1071	414	276	220	3240	1750	320
1890	317	347	1243	445	272	225	3380	1670	279
1900	352	338	1377	528	322	256	3710	1680	245
1910	641	338	1612	535	346	398	3100	1780	209
1920	916	364	1262	650	367	726	4350	1950	288
1930	410	361	1219	829	496	337	4690	1990	295
1940	1007	373	861	1030	620	1169	5310	2260	433
1950	296	385	682	1700	986	434	7750	3370	564
1960	409	376	325			1258			1159

Column (A) Output per worker for total United States agriculture (1910–14 prices, from Tostlebe [1957]).
Column (B) Y/L (1910–14 prices), from Tostlebe, for Appalachian region).
Column (C) Y/L (1910–14 prices for 340 Appalachian counties).
Column (D) Capital per worker for United States agriculture (1910–14 prices, from Tostlebe).
Column (E) K/L (1910–14 prices, from Tostlebe for Appalachian region).
Column (F) K/L (1910–14 prices for 340 Appalachian counties).

intervention; it presents perhaps the best argument for why there is a special need to help the adjustment process in Appalachia to bring productivity up to national standards.

Differences within Appalachia

Tables 11.6–11.8 disaggregate the Appalachia figures to the state level in an attempt to pinpoint the problem. These tables illustrate the first problem arising in these data: there is a great deal of variation between years within the same region. Since the Solow measure of technological change is sensitive to errors of measurement in the data, these series were adjusted by fitting a curve that had a steady rate of growth. (This procedure is discussed in Chapter 4.) The regressions had uniformly high coefficients of determination. In all cases, the 1960 observation fell below the regression line, indicating

Table 11.6   State Figures for Productivity
(in 1910–14 prices)

Year	Ala.	Ga.	Ky.	Md.	N.C.	Ohio	Pa.	Tenn.	Va.	W. Va.
1870	104	106	215	371	100	369	539	388	247	470
1880	82	76	166	356	74	346	437	213	185	223
1890	127	118	241	352	150	365	345	276	251	281
1900	122	119	227	388	150	412	414	262	284	297
1910	240	228	346	587	209	821	711	388	389	451
1920	405	483	733	913	548	880	975	744	933	1145
1930	148	148	288	650	193	541	675	305	353	471
1940	2240	1423	802	791	1181	705	814	1076	637	691
1950	267	458	281	888	156	557	779	398	416	468
1960	1145	2155	894	1265	1021	1291	1434	1135	997	1491

Table 11.7   State Figure of Capital per Worker
(in 1910–14 prices)

Year	Ala.	Ga.	Ky.	Md.	N.C.	Ohio	Pa.	Tenn.	Va.	W. Va.
1870	223	364	521	316	364	201	350	433	546	655
1880	135	286	469	173	277	288	256	427	484	551
1890	207	319	431	273	280	218	148	381	426	429
1900	127	238	255	443	234	208	223	285	370	380
1910	114	178	285	326	144	186	192	261	282	335
1920	122	268	309	208	303	294	266	366	290	487
1930	148	313	316	305	204	386	324	318	335	496
1940	204	494	394	642	444	471	429	441	412	839
1950	277	874	554	809	401	606	639	509	567	953
1960	565	1949	1314	924	1057	1198	848	1016	1165	2793

Table 11.8 Technological Change Index, 1960

Ala.	Ga.	Ky.	Md.	N.C.	Ohio	Pa.	Tenn.	Va.	W. Va.	Appa-lachia
9.11	11.46	3.22	3.87	6.63	2.70	2.90	3.18	3.52	3.05	4.26

$A(1960)$, where $A(1870) = 1$.

the productivity increase over the period was underestimated and thus so was technological change. The index of technological change was calculated from the regression coefficients of the growth over time with results summarized in Table 11.8.

Disregarding the variation over time, it is apparent that there is as much variation between states as anywhere in the whole economy. In Table 11.8 Alabama and Georgia stand out with technological change indices good by even the national standard. North Carolina forms an intermediate point and then the other states have very low indices. In particular, the Appalachian counties in Pennsylvania and Ohio show themselves as backward as any counties in the study. This comparison might be explained in part by an observation in the Appendix to this chapter that Appalachian counties contain farms that were smaller and more labor-intensive than the farms of non-Appalachian counties in the same states.

As shown in Table 11.6, however, Pennsylvania and Ohio had productivity (Y/L) figures that were among the highest in Appalachia. These states started from relatively high levels of productivity and never improved much. Table 11.6 also gives an gives an indication why Alabama, Georgia, and North Carolina had such high rates of technological change: they had extremely low productivity in 1870 and improved to about the average for Appalachia by 1960. Finally, it should be noted that the productivity figure for Appalachia (Table 11.2) in 1960 is less than half the national average in that year.

A Measure of Adjustment

This section is concerned with the problem of how Appalachia has evolved over time and is likely to continue evolving. How rapid is technological change? What causes it and how can it be speeded? The statement that Appalachian agriculture is substandard in 1960 offers little comment on whether additional intervention in the market is necessary. In addition one must know the relative growth rate of the rest of the economy: will the relative position of Appalachian agriculture improve, stand still, or get worse? If the region had a high growth rate and had merely started from a low base, it could be argued that the best policy would be to leave the market as it is.

Statements about absolute rates of growth of the region are not sufficient to form the basis of policy decisions. The economy is growing and there are continuing price adjustments. The assurance that Appalachia is improving is not sufficient to assuage doubts. One must know how the growth of Appalachia compares to that of the rest of the nation.

These growth rates have been examined in previous sections and the overwhelming conclusion has been that the relative situation is bad and getting worse. As a first approximation to the cost of pulling the region's agriculture out of its present state, increases in capital would raise productivity. An upper bound to capital's effectiveness is provided by the assumption that raising capital per worker to the national standard would raise output per worker to the national standard. Approximately $10 billion in new capital would be required on the basis of the figures in Table 11.2. This amount is one sort of lower bound for the cost of solving the farm problem in Appalachia. It is a lower bound since, in addition to the above assumption, it rests on the doubtful assumption that the increase in production resulting from the new capital is desired at current prices.

Alternatively, total production might not be sensitive to the number of workers. The assumption is one of disguised unemployment in agriculture. It might be argued that there has been disguised unemployment in United States agriculture since the First World War; increases in productivity have been directly related to the number of workers leaving agriculture. If the problem is one of underemployment, Appalachian agriculture might be brought up to the national standard by providing jobs for approximately 50 per cent of the 1960 agricultural labor force, about 300,000 new jobs. This calculation also carries a doubtful assumption: production is assumed to remain constant in spite of losing half the labor force.

Although saddled with doubtful assumptions, these calculations provide a lower bound for the cost of necessary action. They provide two very optimistic estimates of the cost of bringing Appalachian agriculture up to the national standard.

Factors Affecting Technological Change

The measures of productivity increase and technological change are more representative of our ignorance than of our knowledge. They give no clue to the reasons why the indices of one region are different from those of another; they tell nothing about what brought about the increases and how the process might be helped.

Denison (1962) and Griliches (1963) have attempted to decrease this ignorance by quite different means. Griliches fitted aggregate production functions which included terms for various improvements. Any increased productivity not explained by this variable is technological change. Denison has attempted to explain changes in production, using more informal means. He divides the productivity increase into segments due to more capital, more labor, changes in the work week, and so on. The analysis is highly informal and highly interesting.

The method here is much like that of Denison.[3] Technological change, that is, output corrected for increases in labor and capital, is "explained" by variables hypothesized to shift the production function. The basic tool is regression analysis with two dependent variables: technological change, 1870–1960 and 1950–60. These two variables should separate the difference between long-run and short-run influences.

Seven sets of variables should be the prime determinants of technological change: (1) type of farm (what crops are raised); (2) the quality of soil in the farm; (3) state differences; (4) nonfarm economic variables; (5) changes in the educational level of farmers and hired workers; (6) changes in the skill levels of operators not related to education; (7) the rate of inventions and discoveries in agriculture.

It proved impossible to get data on all these series. In some cases, such as (4) nonfarm economic variables, some surrogates were tried and discarded. For variables (5) through (7) no data series were found that seemed capable of explaining the dependent variables.

Perhaps the least justified of the independent variables is (3), state differences. There is nothing indigenous to a state that explains technological change. These state variables might, however, serve as surrogates for some of the variables that are not in the analysis. For example, they might pick up differences in the levels of education of the farmers of different states. Since these variables are not likely to be good surrogates, they should prove less hardy than the other two sets.

The 1959 Agricultural Census lists twelve categories for type of farm. These categories were observed in each of the 342 Appalachian counties. In order to make the counties comparable, the variables were transformed so that the data used in the analysis were the percentage of farms of the specified type in the county in 1959. These percentages do not sum to one since there are a number of unclassified farms which become part of the constant term.[4]

The Department of Agriculture has prepared extensive studies of the quality of soil; there are eight classifications of soil capability, running from

[3]Terleckyj (1959) seems to have also used this method.

[4]Since farm types are as of 1959, this set of variables seems to be the correct one for explaining technological changes over the short period, 1950–1960. The justification for inclusion in the 1870–1960 regression is not so strong, although it might be argued on the grounds that the long run trends toward efficiency were always in this direction over the ninety-year period.

Table 11.9 Regression with $A(1960)$

Variable	Reg. Coef.	t	R.C.	t	R.C.	t	R.C.	t	R.C.	t
1. Constant Term	5.8	(10.8)	1.2	(.6)	4.2	(3.0)	4.5	(2.5)	4.7	(2.4)
Type of Farm:										
2. Cash grain	−11.7	(1.1)					−2.2	(.2)	−9.8	(1.1)
3. Tobacco	−3.9	(2.4)					−3.2	(2.0)	−4.1	(2.9)
4. Cotton	10.2	(5.1)					10.6	(4.8)	−11.1	(4.3)
5. Other field crop	−36.4	(1.6)					−36.2	(1.6)	−53.7	(3.0)
6. Vegetable	58.7	(3.1)					46.2	(2.5)	16.5	(1.1)
7. Fruit and nut	9.1	(.7)					11.4	(1.0)	12.4	(1.3)
8. Poultry	16.8	(9.8)					14.1	(8.0)	1.8	(1.0)
9. Dairy	−5.6	(5.2)					−6.1	(4.8)	−2.0	(1.5)
10. Livestock	−10.9	(3.7)					−9.8	(3.4)	−4.7	(1.9)
11. Miscellaneous	−5.0	(.8)					−10.0	(1.5)	−.6	(.1)
Type of Soil:										
12. Class 1			−34.3	(2.7)			−23.0	(2.5)	−23.7	(2.8)
13. 2			−1.3	(.4)			.0	(.0)	2.6	(1.2)
14. 3			5.8	(2.1)			2.0	(.9)	1.1	(.6)
15. 4			10.5	(3.3)			3.3	(1.3)	−2.2	(1.0)
16. 5			54.9	(3.2)			36.4	(2.5)	2.0	(.2)
17. 6			8.2	(3.0)			6.2	(2.9)	4.6	(2.7)
18. 7			1.8	(.9)			−.2	(.1)	−.3	(.2)
State Dummy Variable:										
19. Ala.					5.6	(3.9)			7.9	(5.2)
20. Ga.					8.2	(5.7)			8.0	(5.5)
21. Ky.					−1.1	(.7)			.0	(.0)
22. N. C.					2.7	(1.9)			2.6	(1.9)
23. Ohio					−1.4	(.9)			−1.2	(.8)
24. Pa.					−1.0	(.7)			−1.2	(.9)
25. Tenn.					−.8	(.6)			−.7	(.6)
26. Va.					−.7	(.4)			−.3	(.2)
27. W. Va.					−1.5	(1.1)			−1.2	(.9)
R^2	.49		.15		.66		.55		.73	
$\bar{R}^2$	.48		.13		.65		.52		.71	

Table 11.10 Regression with 1950–60 Technological Change

Variable	R.C.	t	R.C.	t	R.C.	t	R.C.	t	R.C.	t
Constant Term	.26	(15.0)	.12	(2.1)	.16	(3.0)	.24	(4.1)	.26	(3.3)
Type of Farm:										
2	.11	(.3)					.24	(.7)	.04	(.1)
3	−.21	(4.1)					−.19	(3.6)	−.24	(4.1)
4	.11	(1.7)					.18	(2.4)	−.17	(1.6)
5	−.53	(.7)					−.78	(1.0)	−1.23	(1.7)
6	.57	(.9)					.34	(.5)	−.24	(.4)
7	.01	(.0)					.12	(.3)	.13	(.3)
8	.21	(3.8)					.21	(3.5)	−.02	(.2)
9	−.24	(6.9)					.21	(4.9)	−.17	(3.1)
10	−.50	(5.3)					−.46	(4.7)	−.33	(3.2)
11	−.34	(1.6)					−.26	(1.2)	−.10	(.5)
Type of Soil:										
12			−1.20	(3.1)			−.81	(2.4)	−.66	(1.9)
13			−.08	(.8)			−.04	(.4)	−.01	(.1)
14			.11	(1.4)			.02	(.3)	.02	(.3)
15			.12	(1.3)			−.03	(.3)	−.09	(1.0)
16			1.12	(2.2)			.60	(1.4)	.03	(.1)
17			.10	(1.2)			.07	(1.0)	.05	(.8)
18			.67	(1.1)			.01	(.2)	.03	(.5)
State Variable:										
19					.12	(2.0)			.10	(1.6)
20					.16	(2.7)			.11	(1.9)
21					−.00	(.0)			−.01	(.2)
22					.06	(1.1)			.03	(.5)
23					−.05	(.8)			−.05	(.8)
24					−.03	(.5)			−.02	(.4)
25					−.03	(.5)			−.03	(.6)
26					−.02	(.3)			−.03	(.6)
27					−.03	(.5)			−.06	(1.1)
R^2	.35		.07		.34		.37		.45	
$\bar{R}^2$	.33		.05		.32		.34		.40	

165

unrestricted to rocky, shallow soil suited only to recreation. Allowance is made for the availability of water, etc. The variables used in the analysis are of the percentage of agricultural land of each of the first seven categories in a particular county. The effect of the eighth category is part of the constant term.

The results of the regressions are shown in Tables 11.9 and 11.10. Five equations are shown for each dependent variable. The first three are limited to one of the individual sets of independent variables. The fourth equation shows the type of farm and soil capability variables together. The fifth equation shows all variables together. With 342 observations and cross-section data, there are enough degrees of freedom to estimate all these equations. All regressions are significant as shown by the value of R^2. The individual coefficients can be judged by noting that a t value of 1 shows significance at $\alpha = .32$, whereas a t value of 1.96 shows significance at $\alpha = .05$.

There is a marked similarity between regressions with technological change over the whole period and over the decade of the 1950's. The consistency of the two regressions can be seen in Table 11.11. Here the coefficients of both regressions are presented together. The coefficients for technological change, 1950–60, have been multiplied by a factor of 28 to account for the difference in mean between the two dependent variables. In general, the coefficients are of the same order of magnitude and sign. Only six differences in sign occur, none of which is significant statistically. The comparison is even better without the state dummy variables. There are differences in the signs of only three coefficients. All comments will be on the regression involving the whole period.

The regression involving only state dummy variables explains more than half the variation in technological change. Only two variables, however, are significant at conventional levels: the above-average technological change in Alabama and Georgia. As noted earlier, these two states have levels of technological change good even by national standards and far above the average level for Appalachia. There is hardly any difference between the other state coefficients, except for North Carolina, which is high, and West Virginia, which is quite low.

It might seem that the higher the percentage of land in the top soil categories, the higher should be technological change. Insofar as new discoveries and inventions are responsible for technological change, however, the greatest effect might be in the lowest grades of soil still being used for farming. The table seems to bear out this reasoning since the coefficients get larger as the grade decreases from 1 to 5, but then fall off again in strict order. Apparently, little technological change took place on first-grade land; land worse than level 5 was not good enough for farming, even in 1960.

These coefficients change a good deal in the regression involving all

Table 11.11   A Comparison of Dependent Variables

Variable	A(1870–1960)	A(1950–60)
Constant Term	4.7†	7.2‡
Type of Farm:		
2	−9.8*	1.1
3	−4.1†	−6.7‡
4	−11.1‡	−4.7*
5	−53.7‡	−30.4*
6	16.5*	−6.7
7	12.4*	3.6
8	1.8*	−.6
9	−2.0*	−4.7‡
10	−4.7*	−9.2‡
11	−.6	−2.8
Type of Soil:		
12	−23.7‡	−18.4*
13	2.6*	−.3
14	1.1	.6
15	−2.2*	−2.5*
16	2.0	.8
17	4.6†	1.4
18	−.3	.8
State Variable:		
19	7.9‡	2.8*
20	8.0‡	3.0*
21	.0	−.3
22	2.6*	.8
23	−1.2	−1.4
24	−1.2	−.6
25	−.7	−.8
26	−.3	−.8
27	−1.2	−1.7*
R^2	.73	.45
$\bar{R}^2$	.71	.45

*Indicates significance at $\alpha = .32$.
†Indicates significance   .05.
‡Indicates significance beyond $\alpha = .02$.

twenty-seven variables. Thus, it might be conjectured that this low quality land is associated with some particular type of farming. In regression 4, which involves type of farm and soil, however, the coefficients hardly change at all. Thus, it seems likely that certain types of soil are concentrated in some states.

The regression involving type of farm must be interpreted with some care. The coefficients are estimates of the technological change experienced by each type of farm over the period. Interpreted in this way, however, the coefficients must be treated carefully. It is not likely that cash grain farms experienced negative technological change of 5.9 ($-11.7 + 5.8$) over the period 1870–1960. Nor is it likely that vegetable farms experienced technological change of 66.9 ($58.7 + 5.8$). The relative order of the coefficients does make sense.

The coefficients for technological change over the 1950–60 period seem more justified. It is plausible that cash grain experienced a technological change of 1.27 ($1 + .11 + .26$) over the decade of the 1950's; it is also plausible that vegetable farms experienced technological change of 1.83 ($1 + .57 + .26$) over the decade. But again, the coefficients must be interpreted with some care. Although these coefficients are probably minimum variance, unbiased estimates of the amount of technological change experienced by each type of farm, this form of estimation strains the interpretation of coefficients.

The relative, rather than absolute, values of the coefficients are safer figures to focus on. It is plausible that positive coefficients, or small negative ones experienced technological change above or near the value of the constant term, 5.8. The seemingly wild value of some coefficients might be due to very small samples. Vegetable farms, for example, tend to be only .4 per cent of the region's farms.

In going from the three regressions involving a single set of variables to the one involving two sets (type of farm and soil capability), virtually no change in the coefficients takes place. This fact indicates there is little relation between type of farm and soil capability. This fourth regression provides perhaps the best estimate of the effects of type of farm and soil capability on technological change.

The coefficients change a bit more in going to the regression involving all twenty-seven variables. Three important changes take place. Tobacco farming goes from one of the farm types enjoying a high rate of technological change, to one involving a very low rate. This change is due to some correlation between tobacco farming and the state dummy variables and indicates that tobacco is concentrated in certain states. The set of variables measuring soil type generally fares badly in the larger regression. Soil types 2 and 4 change sign and the strict ordering is generally destroyed. Again, this change is due to correlations with state variables.

Although the state variables themselves don't shift much, only two coefficients are statistically significant. The level of adjusted R^2 rises with the introduction of state variables, indicating they are surrogates for variables not in the analysis. The principal influence of these variables is in explaining the extraordinary performance of Alabama and Georgia. Since the other two sets of variables don't do much of a job here, some important variables have been left out. On the whole, however, the state variables tend to confuse the analysis. They are sufficiently collinear with the other variables to change their coefficients and confuse their affect.

It is interesting to note that livestock farming comes out near the bottom in all regressions. The results indicate that livestock farming has experienced technological change far below the average. Some of the programs for helping Appalachia have emphasized the role of livestock farming. They advocate encouraging this type to the exclusion of other types. The low rates of technological change can make no direct comment on this policy measure, but they do indicate that this activity has not improved rapidly in the past. Unless efficiency in Appalachian livestock farming increases markedly, this policy measure is likely to be unproductive in solving the region's problems.

Summary and Conclusion

Over the period 1870–1960, the United States enjoyed a spectacular increase in GNP (2755 per cent), capital (1830 per cent), and productivity (453 per cent). The agricultural sector paced this growth with an increase in productivity of 949 per cent and in capital per worker of 411 per cent. All these increases are in constant prices. But prices did not stay constant. Although income increases were roughly proportional to productivity increases, agricultural incomes were only 70 per cent of manufacturing incomes in 1960.

Appalachian agriculture lagged behind the national average with a productivity increase of 674 per cent. Incomes were under 60 per cent of the national average for manufacturing in 1960. This relative decline in Appalachian agriculture is corroborated by figures for measured technological change and productivity increase. The region is unique in not having adjusted to prices in the economy.

Furthermore, there are wide differences within the region's agriculture. Alabama and Georgia showed rates of technological change good by any standards, whereas most of the region showed very little increase.

A first estimate of the cost of the region's failure to adjust might be gained from the extrapolation to 1975. Productivity in 1975 rises absolutely, but decreases to one-third of the national average. The relative technological change index will also have slipped further behind.

To have brought the region up to standard in 1960 would have cost at least $10 billion in new investment if farms were to be supplied with enough capital to bring them up to the national average. Alternatively, if the problem was one of disguised unemployment, 50 per cent of the farmers would have had to be released to bring productivity up to the national average. Thus, 300,000 new jobs would have had to be created.

Regression analysis is used to explore the factors affecting technological change in the 342 Appalachian counties. The regressions are highly significant and indicate the relations between three classes of variables. For the soil capability classifications, technological change was most rapid on the poorest types of soil used in farming. The type of farm variables pinpoints kinds of crop specialization that showed the highest rates of technological change. State dummy variables indicate differences between the counties in the ten Appalachian states. Finally, the regressions show an enormous consistency between the factors affecting technological change over the long period (1870–1960) and over the short period (1950–60).

Appendix : Derivation of the Data

Two sources of data were used in this study. The first consists of the Department of Agriculture figures for the ten regions that make up United States agriculture. These figures, running from 1870 to 1950, are presented in Tostlebe (1957). The second set of figures is taken from the agricultural and population censuses, 1870–1960. The latter figures are collected at the level of the 342 counties in the Appalachian region.

The analysis was carried along at three levels using the latter figures: at the level of the individual counties, at the level of the counties aggregated into their states, and at the level of the entire Appalachian region. The last figure was used as a gross consistency check on the Census figures, since the USDA figure for Appalachia was also available. These figures were not strictly comparable, since the BAE Appalachian region consisted of the states of Delaware, Kentucky, Maryland, North Carolina, Tennessee, Virginia, and West Virginia. The Census figures involved a more exact definition of Appalachia and consisted of 342 counties in these same states (with Delaware omitted) as well as in the states of Georgia, Alabama, Pennsylvania, and Ohio.

The process of aggregation from the level of counties to that of an entire region was found justified in Chapter 7. The disaggregated data should provide a better view of the areas having the greatest problems. The process of aggregation may be accomplished in any of three ways. The first involves computing the county estimates and then averaging these to get the state and regional figures. The second involves using these unweighted averages for output per man and capital per man and using regional figures for the share of capital in income. The final way involves aggregating the output, capital, and labor series to the regional level and then computing the aggregate figures. All three computations were made and found to be extremely close.

Thus, only the figures from one method are reported. The last method should give higher-quality figures since this aggregation should tend to wash out spurious variations in the data.

The sources of these data are described in detail in Chapter 7. The only major difference is that no adjustments were made here for the undercounting of labor in the late nineteenth century. These underestimates may tend to bias the technological change series downward, but the error in the labor series is not large.

Until 1940 the Census listed laborers only at the state level. Thus, some way had to be found of allocating these over the counties in each state. In Chapter 7 it was assumed that the number of men per farm was approximately constant across all counties in the state. Another suggested way of allocating laborers was by assuming that the number of laborers per acre was constant across all counties in the state. These two methods were compared with the Census figures for farm labor in each county in 1940, 1950, and 1960. The criteria for judging them was the sum of the squared errors. The results are given in Table 11-12. The previous method provides the better fit in general and was used here.

It is interesting to pursue this issue a bit further. Considering the Agricultural Census figures for laborers per county as the correct one, the two estimates were regressed on it. These regressions provide a more general way of estimating the county labor figures; they permit the inclusion of an intercept and slope different from unity. In general these coefficients were such that Method A, allocating laborers per farm, had a higher coefficient than Method B, allocating laborers per improved acre. In general it was also true that the coefficient of A was slightly greater than unity, whereas that for B was much less than unity. These regressions were not used to fill in past labor estimates since they were unstable over the three years they could be estimated.

One final test involved comparing the state sums of the two estimates, for all Appalachian counties within each state, with the state sum of the Census estimates. Note that, since not all counties were in Appalachia, these state sums were different. A distinctive pattern emerged from this comparison. The total estimates of Method A were almost always greater than the sum of the Census estimate; those of Method B were almost invariably smaller. The first difference implies that there are fewer laborers per farm in Appalachian counties than in the average counties in the state. The second difference implies that there are more laborers per improved acre in Appalachian counties than for the average county in the state. These statements taken together describe counties that contain many small farms which have fewer improved acres than the average farms of the state. In this day of returns to scale and efficiency machinery, these statements characterize inefficient, subsistence farms.

Table 11.12 Comparison of Two Ways of Finding County Labor

	1940		1950		1960	
	$\sum (A - C)^2$ $\times 10^6$	$\sum (B - C)^2$ $\times 10^6$	$\sum (A - C)^2$ $\times 10^6$	$\sum (B - C)^2$ $\times 10^6$	$\sum (A - C)^2$ $\times 10^6$	$\sum (B - C)^2$ $\times 10^6$
Ala.	28	74	16	37	3	10
Ga.	19	29	15	5	5	5
Ky.	24	190	19	21	8	5
Md.	3	0.5	2	0.6	0.9	4
N.C.	53	50	21	10	12	12
Ohio	8	52	3	11	3	2
Pa.	17	43	14	16	9	6
Tenn.	22	98	9	16	3	10
Va.	12	48	9	7	6	4
W. Va.	14	51	9	6	3	1

Method A: Labor per farm for state times number of farms in county.
Method B: Labor per improved acre for state times number of improved acres in county.
Method C: County labor estimates from Agricultural Census.
The figure is $(A - C)^2$ summed across all Appalachian counties in state.

The output and capital series were derived by taking the Census figures for the amount of a commodity sold and multiplying it by the 1910–14 price. This procedure was followed from 1870–1940. In 1950 and 1960 output figures were deflated by total product as given in the Census. The capital series was computed in this same fashion. The price of improved land was assumed to be three times that of unimproved land in 1910–14. Wherever dollar magnitudes were given for value of fences and buildings, and so on, they were deflated to 1910–14. The Census did not, however, list machinery figures for the last part of the series.

The measures used to estimate capital seem drastically to have underestimated it, if Tostlebe's figures are taken as correct. Of course the figures are not quite comparable, but capital figures for Appalachia are about five times as high for Tostlebe as the estimate from Census data. On the other hand, the increase in capital per man over the period is quite comparable for the two estimates.

Now, the Solow measure is independent of scale and so it appears that this underestimate in the capital series has no affect on the measure of technological change; however, as $W_K = K/(20\,Y)$; thus the W_K series was underestimated over the period. The extent of the bias is about .10 at most. Calculations were made to determine the bias in the technological change index caused by this underestimate of W_K. It was found that $A(1960)$ would have been about 10 per cent lower if W_K had been uniformly larger by .10. Thus, all figures should be corrected by this amount if the Census-derived estimates of capital are believed to be less accurate than the estimates of Tostlebe.

CHAPTER TWELVE

The Falling Rise of Indistan, A Fable*

> ... and a labourer in Hindostan may continue to work with perfect vigour, though receiving, as his natural wages, only such a supply of covering as would be insufficient to preserve a labourer in Russia from perishing.
> R. Torrens, *An Essay on the External Corn Trade*, 1815.

Prologue

The following is a tale; a fable with heroes, villains, and a moral. Of course, the hero will triumph; though his means may not be honorable, they are common. Perhaps, since the fable is not so witty, it should be reclassified as a medieval morality play whose hero, Everyman, is struggling toward fulfillment. Everyman: Indistan, a pleasant little nation, unchanged for centuries, is ruled by an enlightened dictator, that rare man economists dream about. This dictator realizes one must run to stand still in this shrinking world; he has decided to go full tilt into a development program.

And so he received the loan of a group of prominent economists from distinguished American institutions to plan his development. These planners learned that Indistan had a predominant agricultural sector employing 80

*Any clarity in this chapter results from the efforts of Martin Bronfenbrenner, Mike Lovell, Roman Weil, Arnold Lieberman, and John Gurley.

174

per cent of the labor force with an output per worker of $200.[1] The manu-
facturing sector was small, but comparable with 20 per cent of the labor
force and an output per worker of $200.

After a short survey, the planners agreed that Indistan was a textbook
case: its previous stability provided assurance that little would happen
without their efforts; productivity was low in the economy. Although
agriculture and manufacturing had comparable levels of productivity, the
only real hope for improvement lay in emphasizing the manufacturing sector
and introducing advanced technology so as to bring it up to the standards
of the developed nations.

They decided that primary attention must be given to the agricultural
sector. Agriculture had to be strengthened to support this industrialization and
had to be made efficient to provide workers for a growing manufacturing
sector. No real progress was likely without radical changes.

Two problems of immediate importance concerned the land in agriculture
and capital in manufacturing. These resources were owned by the peasants
who worked them; they were notoriously uncooperative in adopting new
means of production. The Planners devised the ingenious scheme of buying
these resources and thus assuring government control.

So convincing were their arguments and predictions, an international
agency agreed to lend $3200 in foreign exchange, interest free, based on
land value and capital value. When this foreign exchange was given to the
peasants, it was immediately hoarded and so no inflationary boom con-
fronted the government. Again, since the money never found its way out of
Indistan, the agency felt it was merely transferring the location of some of
its free reserves.

There were those who argued that implementing the full development
program would not be so easy; they said major investments in health and
education would be necessary and even then some non-neutrality might ruin
the whole plan. But the prevailing feeling was toward going ahead, and so
a memorandum was prepared.

The Plan

"The basic problem of Indistan's agriculture," read their report to the
dictator, "is that the people don't possess the technological knowledge for
technological change." They went on to present the audacious plan of
educating every farm worker to permit him to adopt and utilize the advanced
technology of the rest of the world and thus increase his efficiency. Thus,
education should set off the yearly shift in the production function, which

---

[1]Production is governed by a Cobb-Douglas function, see Table 12.1. $200 is the average
product of labor; the marginal product is $100.

had made American agriculture so prosperous, and release workers to speed industrialization.

Such a task could be accomplished for $250 per worker and could be done within a few months. All was made ready and the entire 400,000 workers were educated in period 1.

Production was not interrupted by the education process, and everyone agreed that much useful knowledge was passed on. While they were present, the visiting educators suggested that great increases in output per man could be achieved by introducing a special new capital from abroad: M. At the end of the first period this suggestion was implemented, and output began to grow at a rate of 5 per cent per period after correction for price changes. An even more spectacular achievement was that output per man grew at a rate of 16.5 per cent per period and settled there. Finally, 10 per cent of the labor force was released each period to the manufacturing sector. Best of all, the education and new capital resulted in technological change (according to the Solow [1957] measure) at a rate of 10 per cent in the first period, 8 per cent in the second, 7 per cent in the third, and so on. Surely the progress was better than could have been anticipated.

The planners made sure that all men released from agriculture found jobs in manufacturing with no delay. There was a slight $100 relocation cost, but the government could bear that cheerfully. During the fourth period, the planners decided they would turn their attention to manufacturing, since agricutlure was now so prosperous. Here production had increased 45 per cent in the first four periods and all seemed to be going well.

A previous study had hinted that the expenditures on education had not been quite as profitable as they might have been. And so the planners decided to forego this particular way of starting in manufacturing. However, no one could suggest that the introduction of a new type of capital had not benefited agriculture greatly; and so they tried the same scheme with manufacturing. Introducing another new imported capital C in the fifth period, they were encouraged to find that output rose by 3.5 per cent. But increases had to be larger than this, and effort redoubled. And lo, the sixth period produced a 10.9 per cent increase in output and the seventh period topped even this with a 13.3 per cent increase. Furthermore, the production function started shifting during the fifth period just as it had done in agriculture. Technological change took place at rates of 10 per cent in the fifth period, 9 per cent in the sixth period and 8.4 per cent in the seventh period.

Before the planners turned their attention to manufacturing in the fourth period, output per man had been dropping somewhat. They considered this natural since there was such a large influx of new workers and the difficulties of absorbing them were tremendous. However, they were determined to overcome this difficulty and set to work. By the seventh period, output per man began to turn up and they counted their efforts a success.

By the end of the seventh period, the planners felt they had accomplished their task with spectacular success. They drew up a memorandum describing their successes and cautioning that the only way to ensure that this growth would continue was to be eternally vigilant. They formally asked leave to return home to their universities for a well-earned rest.

Some Difficulties

Before the planners had a chance to leave, they were informed that there was heavy speculation against Indistan's currency. Investors had refused to lend additional money for the capital goods M and C and were demanding a comprehensive plan under which the old loans would be paid off. The dictator was completely confused as to whether to build statues to the planners or to expel them for bankrupting his country. To determine the facts, he summoned the planners and speculators for a conference. They jointly presented him with Tables 12.1, 12.2, and 12.3 giving the figures for the agricultural sector, the manufacturing sector, and the whole economy in each period. All figures are in constant prices of period zero.

The Planners Defend

The representative of Indistan's planners noted that measuring the success of a development program was generally difficult, yet here there could be no doubt. In agriculture, output per man rose 158 per cent over the seven periods, technological change was rapid, and the sector had produced more than enough food for the economy while releasing almost 50 per cent of its workers to manufacturing. In manufacturing, output had risen by 88 per cent with rapid technological change over the last few periods, and the sector was obviously prospering. For the economy, output had risen 45 per cent with a constant labor force. In short, the economy had lived up to every expectation and the planners couldn't think what the trouble was all about.

A Speculator on Capital Evaluation

The representative of the speculators proceeded to give the reasons for their position against Indistan's currency. He viewed the foregoing figures as somewhat less than convincing since they were not consistent across

Table 12.1 The Agricultural Sector (in period 0 dollars)

Period	Y (value output) $C̄*	L (no. laborers) C̄	T (initial value land) $C̄	M (units new capital) C̄	A (tech. change index)	$\frac{\Delta A}{A}$ rate of T.C.	Income to L $C̄	Income to T $C̄	Income to M $C̄	L + T $C̄	Y/L Output Per Man $
1	800	4	3200	1	7.07	...	400	400	...	800	200
2	840	3.6	3200	3598	7.78	.1	420	378	42	798	233
3	882	3.24	3200	4422	8.40	.08	441	357	84	798	272
4	926	2.92	3200	5122	8.99	.07	463	337	127	800	317
5	972	2.63	3200	5380	9.53	.06	486	318	168	804	370
6	1021	2.37	3200	6411	10.00	.05	510.5	302	208.5	812.5	432
7	1072	2.14	3200	6544	10.40	.04	536	285	251	821	502

Table 12.1 The Agricultural Sector (Cont.)

Period	$\Delta T'$ Capital Loss Land ($C)	Capital Loss Labor ($C)	Capital Loss Total ($C)	Interest on Cost of Education ($C)	$\bar{Y}$ (net income) ($C)	$\bar{Y}'$ (net internal income) ($C)
1	...	...	...	...	800	800
2	-176	-140	-316	36	482	446
3	-168	-126	-294	32	504	472
4	-164	-112	-276	29	524	495
5	-144	-103	-247	26	557	531
6	-128	-91	-219	23	593	570.5
7	-133	-81	-214	21	607	586

*$C = 100,000$

PRODUCTION FUNCTIONS

(1) $Y = A(1) L^{.5} T^{.5} M^{.0}$

(2) $Y = A(2) L^{.5} T^{.45} M^{.05}$

(3) $Y = A(3) L^{.5} T^{.405} M^{.095}$

(4) $Y = A(5) L^{.5} T^{.365} M^{.135}$

(5) $Y = A(5) L^{.5} T^{.328} M^{.172}$

(6) $Y = A(6) L^{.5} T^{.295} M^{.205}$

(7) $Y = A(7) L^{.5} T^{.266} M^{.234}$

Table 12.2 The Manufacturing Sector (in period 0 dollars)

Period	Y (value output)	L (no. laborers)	K (value capital)	C (units new capital)	A (tech. change index)	ΔA/A (rate of T.C.)	Income to				Y/L (output per man)	ΔK (change in value of K)	Ȳ (net income)	Ȳ' (net internal income)	Ȳ'/L
							K	L	K + L	C					
	$C̄*	C̄	$C̄	C̄			$C̄	$C̄	$C̄	$C̄	$	$C̄	$C̄	$C̄	$
1	200	1	400	...	10	0	100	100	200	...	200		200	200	200
2	236	1.4	400	...	10	0	118	118	236	...	168.5	+72	308	308	220
3	265	1.76	400	...	10	0	132.5	132.5	265	...	150.5	+58	323	323	184
4	289	2.08	400	...	10	0	144.5	144.5	289	...	138.6	+48	337	337	161
5	299	2.37	400	50	11	.1	134.6	149.5	284.1	14.9	126.1	−39.6	259.4	244.5	103
6	332	2.63	400	100	12	.09	132.8	166	298.8	33.2	126.1	− 7.2	324.8	291.6	111
7	376	2.86	400	150	13	.084	131.5	188	319.5	56.5	131.2	− 5.2	370.8	314.3	110

*C̄ = 100,000

PRODUCTION FUNCTIONS

$$Y = A(1-4) \; L^{.5} \, K^{.5} \; C^{.0}$$
$$Y = A(5) \; L^{.5} \, K^{.45} \; C^{.05}$$
$$Y = A(6) \; L^{.5} \, K^{.4} \; C^{.1}$$
$$Y = A(7) \; L^{.5} \, K^{.35} \; C^{.15}$$

Table 12.3 Total Economy (in period 0 dollars)

Period	Y (value output) $\$\bar{C}$*	L (no. laborers) $\bar{C}$	T (initial land) $\$\bar{C}$	T (value capital) $\$\bar{C}$	M (units of agric. capital) $\bar{C}$	C (units of new mfg. capital) $\bar{C}$	Y/L (output per man) $	ΔK (change on capital) $\$\bar{C}$	interest on debt $\$\bar{C}$	$\bar{Y}$ (net income) $\$\bar{C}$	$\bar{Y}'$ (net internal income) $\$\bar{C}$	Y'/L (net internal income per man) $\$\bar{C}$
1	1000	5	3200	400	1	...	200	...	40	1000	1000	200
2	1076	5	3200	400	3598	...	215	−244	78	790	754	151
3	1147	5	3200	400	4422	...	229	−236	116	827	795	159
4	1215	5	3200	400	5122	...	243	−229	156	861	832	166
5	1271	5	3200	400	5380	50	254	−253.6	208.9	816.4	775.5	155.1
6	1353	5	3200	400	6411	100	271	−230.2	266.7	917.8	861.1	172
7	1448	5	3200	400	6544	150	290	−226.2	329.5	1020.8	900.3	180

*$\bar{C} = 100{,}000$

181

sectors. Although the rise in manufacturing output was 88 per cent, the rise in agricultural output was only 34 per cent. Similarly, although the rise in agricultural output *per man* was 158 per cent, there was a *fall* in output *per man* in manufacturing of 33 per cent.

Furthermore, the figures did not show the earnings of the new imported capital. Since these earnings were paid abroad, they were not part of income. Nor had the interest charges on education been included. After making corrections for imported capital and education, the speculators found that output in agriculture actually fell over the period. The problem seemed to worsen the more they examined the figures.

One of the greatest problems in measuring economic development is the valuation of capital. Indistan has been experiencing both neutral and non-neutral technological change, and central planning that had interfered with the market. However, one rule of thumb is that agricultural land has always been worth about eight times its income. Table 12.1 shows the return to land had fallen over the period, both as a percentage and as an absolute. Thus land was worth less as shown in Table 12.1. Accordingly, the loan which permitted the government to buy this land was changed each period; since the land was worth less, Indistan was subject to a large capital drain.

"That's nonsense," charged the planners. "We started with a given amount of land that has neither been improved nor worn out, nor changed in any way. It is sophistry to charge us with a supposed capital loss on a productive asset which, if anything, has become more productive and which has changed in no physical way."

"Our way of evaluating investments is based on present value of future revenues," said the speculators primly. "Since the revenue paid to land has declined, the value of land must have declined (interest rate rising or constant) and so there must have been a capital loss. We have noted some regularity across countries: where technological change is so rapid that assets must leave a sector, and there is a certain non-neutrality in the technological change, the value of fixed assets may fall as the mobile assets leave.

"Another capital loss occurs every time a farmer leaves agriculture. You were so successful in inducing technological change that the money spent on educating the farmers is a capital loss in large part."

"If capital valuation is a problem, education valuation is even more so," sighed the planners. "When we realized the cost of this education we attempted to do without it in manufacturing. We accepted Schultz's argument (1960) that education contributes to technological change. But we could not approximate its effect as had Denison (1962) and Griliches (1963). However, the migrating workers caused manufacturing capital to be used more intensively thereby increasing its marginal product and value."

"But over all," noted the speculators, "there was a substantial capital loss over the period as shown in Table 12.3. The table also shows that income fell substantially. Even beyond that, the tables are in constant prices whereas the prices of both food and manufactured goods fell as the result of a shift in Indistan's terms of trade. Thus, we took our position against Indistan's currency and feel sure we will profit substantially."

During the last few remarks, one of the conferees had started muttering and agitating among the group. To placate their disgruntled conferee, they decided to consider the problem of the relation of wealth to income.

"Two things disturb me about the last remarks. How can there be capital loss when the physical capital (land) is unchanged? Secondly, isn't it unfair to charge the first seven periods so heavily for the development plan? Consider the capital loss in education; surely it is not equitable to charge off the investment in seven periods. Education gave agriculture its start and the cost should be amortized over a long enough period to be off set by profits."

"Yet, if the education was specific to the farmers who were educated, then there must be a capital loss when one leaves the farm. On the first point, you are quite correct that there is a difference between the physical nature of capital and its earning power. While we generally think of capital as physical, it is only the congealed (discounted) profit that is relevant."

"All right, it is not profit that is relevant, only the welfare of society. Now, society is no worse off than before since it is satisfying tastes better than ever before. We may have built capital which was too durable, such as blacksmith's shops, or capital which did not satisfy people's tastes, such as Edsel factories, but Indistan has a greater welfare today than ever before and so there has been no capital loss."

"With a less sure intuition, I must find more pedestrian ways of assuring myself that the economy is satisfying tastes better and giving everyone a higher real income. In calculating real income, I am beset by all the index numbers that have plagued economics. Current prices don't give consistent measures, yet the conclusion depends on what base is used for constant prices."

"But you are forgetting that tastes in Indistan have not changed. Any price changes, at least in the capital stock, are due to technology changes. And changes in the capital stock are easier to evaluate than you indicate. If we take capital to be the productive capacity of the economy (neglecting inventories and intermediate products), we can examine some of the relations between national product and wealth. As long as national product is rising, the real productive capacity of the economy must be increasing. Any loss in the capital goods is just so much internal bookkeeping. Since the national income in Indistan has risen, there can have been no capital loss."

"This is precisely the problem I stated a moment ago: how can you be sure that national income has risen? The tables show income in constant prices of period zero. What if we had used period 7 prices as the base?[2]

"The real problem with your argument is that capital has become a residual category, something that is implied by the level of real income. There is a confusion between productive capacity and capital. You may have gotten around the aggregate problem of the relation of wealth to income, but you have thrown out everything else. How can we measure this elusive 'productive capacity'? Would we merely define it as three times the measured output? What would you do with capital goods which were potentially productive, but for one reason or another were not being currently used?

"What you seem to have done is to marry technological change to the stock of capital. You have finally accomplished the goal of defining all increases in output per man as increases in the economy's 'total productive capital.' I'm afraid that my tastes run toward measuring capital directly and calling any residual: technological change."

"Tastes change in the measurement of capital, and I certainly would not try to convince you that my kind of capital tastes are better than yours. However, you must note that your capital has diminished precisely at the time when output has been rising. You must admit that you have only a partial measure of the economy's capital stock."

Free Enterprise or Planning?

At this point the planners were seen exiting quietly through a side door. Amid the ensuing furor, the representative of the Chamber of Commerce managed to gain the microphone and began to castigate the planners. He contended that the central error with this plan was that it was too central. If the planners had merely indicated a direction and given free enterprise

---

[2]One argument that has grown out of comparing the national income of two economies at the same time is that an economy will become efficient in producing the kinds of goods it concentrates on. Thus, United States' consumption goods are cheap compared to military goods. Using this argument intertemporally, it would seem that, as long as there is full employment, using constant prices with the current year as base will underestimate the growth of the economy; conversely, using the initial period as the base year will tend to overstate the amount of growth. This argument relies on many assumptions including full employment, tastes changing slowly enough to allow full adjustment, and no scarcities that cause increasing cost in the area of concentration. Perhaps the one of greatest concern to the question of capital loss is that of changing tastes. Unless capital is built flexible or short-lived, rapidly changing tastes will diminish the relevant productive capacity of society. Tastes and technology have changed in this society. The changing of tastes is reflected in the drop of export prices. Period zero prices obscure this change. Finally, the changing technology has tended to shift some of the income to capital into the hands of foreign investors through the imported capital goods.

its way, the economy would have developed properly and there would have been no reason for this conference.

The Polish representative jumped to his feet and charged that this was capitalist propaganda. The only way this situation could have been avoided was through a strong central plan. After all, he said, consider the small capitalist farmer. He sees that he can increase productivity if he can be educated, so he contracts for a course in agriculture. His neighbors are soon forced to see the profit in this approach. And so they all become educated as well. And, having been educated, a farmer sees that there is profit for him to introduce M, a new capital good. And having done so, he is recognized as extra profitable and is imitated. The agricultural sector is in the same straits as previously. In similar fashion a manufacturing firm sees that it is profitable to adopt a new capital good C, and forces everyone else to do likewise. The whole problem with free enterprise, the distinguished Polish representative contended, is that what is best for one firm is not best for all firms. Thus, capitalism contains the seeds of its own destruction. The only way to have avoided all this was to have efficient central planning.

And Indistan's dictator meanwhile muttered to himself that some witchcraft was at work. After all, everything his country had had previously it still had. It still had all its land and capital. It still had all its workers. It still had all the knowledge of agriculture that the workers had gained. And it even had much additional output. What could be wrong?

A Happy Ending

But the distinguished Polish representative turned out to be wrong. Indistan followed a long tradition in obtaining all of the capital required for development: a military force marched into the conference, arresting the dictator and declaring that he had been a capitalist stooge who had exploited the nation. They declared that he had had no power to make any contracts and so they were nationalizing all foreign property. Thus, Indistan was by this one stroke turned from bankruptcy to prosperity, and lived happily ever after.

What Really Happened in Indistan?

It might be helpful to describe the underlying structure of Indistan's economy to provide an account of how a rather formal economist or computer might view the situation, sort of *deus ex machina*. The production functions for agriculture and manufacturing are three factor Cobb-Douglas functions. Along with being functions frequently used to describe an economy or sector, they offer all the usual nice properties of constant returns to scale, homogeneity, etc. With inputs measured in constant prices, the absence of quality changes means these are real production functions which relate combinations of physical inputs to a physical output. These thoroughbreds should not be confused with geometrically weighted indices (Domar 1961), distribution functions (Ferguson 1963), or surrogate production functions (Samuelson 1962). That the units of labor and capital are value units makes no difference here except to the value of A, the constant term.

Initially, Indistan had a stable economy where laborers in agriculture and manufacturing were equally worse off. The planners made the judgment that the only real hope for improvement lay in manufacturing. In order to release workers and provide the food for them, they first turned their attention to agriculture. To increase efficiency, they educated farm workers and introduced a new imported capital. Without ever knowing precisely what the mechanism was, they induced technological progess. While they were shifting labor out of agriculture, they were pleased to find that total output rose while output per man skyrocketed. However, the parameters of the function also began shifting in favor of the new capital. This non-neutral shift in technology represents perhaps the most important problem for Indistan.

Another important problem is the valuation of assets. Since the return to land declined, the value of land declined (interest rate rising or constant). On the other hand, the value of manufacturing capital appreciated by the same criterion. Thus, the value of two physical assets changed, even though their physical description never varied. Further capital loss occurred when labor was shifted to manufacturing: Both the cost of moving and the cost of education were lost. All these changes represent interactions between parts of the economy that upset previous values.

These problems make the gross income values misleading. Net output, $\bar{Y}$, is gross output net of capital loss and service on the education debt. Subtracting the income paid to foreigners from $\bar{Y}$ gives rise to net internal income, $\bar{Y}'$. These corrections change income from a rising series to a sharply falling one.

Having initially focused on agriculture, the planners did not turn their attention to manufacturing until period 5. The influx of workers had raised income but lowered income per worker. In their attempt to copy agriculture without the "mistake" of educating all workers, the planners relied on another new imported capital. This new capital did serve to bring about technological change although it resulted in both neutral and non-neutral shifts. As in agriculture, non-neutral shifts in technology transferred a great deal of income to foreign investors.

The picture for the whole economy is a combination of changes in agriculture and in manufacturing. Aggregate capital fell in value during the development period since the manufacturing appreciation was not sufficient to offset the agricultural loss. Gross income, Y, rose sharply over the period.

Net income, $\bar{Y}$, rose, but much less rapidly than Y. Finally, net internal income, $\bar{Y}'$, and $\bar{Y}'/L$ fell sharply over the entire period, although they rose slightly near the end.

The development program, if measured by Table 12.3, has been a failure. Part of the difficulty (not shown in the table) is the fall in the terms of trade. While the planners could have done little about the terms of trade, they had more control over shifts of labor and prices of land and capital. More attention to these internal guides might have changed the situation. However, there is the fundamental difficulty of the interactions between sectors; either sector might have been considered a success had it been paired with a different partner. The combination of the two sectors, though, is what brands the program a failure.

But Table 12.3 does not tell the whole story. The future may be bright for Indistan's economy if there are favorable shifts in the terms of trade, or if the manufacturing sector manages to make use of its new labor. Depending on one's view of the future, Indistan may either grow into considerable prosperity or lapse into even lower incomes.

Indistan's planners seemed to discover that development is not a matter of slogans or rules of thumb. They got their workers out of agriculture and into manufacturing; they induced technological change and introduced education. Yet, they were failures. They sometimes handled the variables within their power badly, and they fared worse with variables outside their control.

Development is indeed a complicated problem and not amenable to easy solutions.

Epilogue

The circumstances cited in Indistan provide more than an interesting but isolated example of some problems that can occur under technological change. This sort of conclusion might have been derived over shorter periods or with less dramatic losses using any number of different, plausible happenings.

In particular, a case that corresponds more closely with observable reality is shown in Table 12.4. The new production function is Cobb-Douglas with a share of .75 for labor and .25 for capital. As labor leaves agriculture, the share of labor falls, although productivity and wages rise. Here the fall in $\bar{Y}'$ is not subject to questions about capital losses from land.

This fable provides some illustrations of the dynamic or short-run problems that might come to an economy with technological change. Are these problems inherent in technological change? Are they merely short-run problems, or do they have long-run implications? These problems are taken up in the next chapter.

Table 12.4 The Agricultural Sector: A Second Case

Period	A (tech. change index)	Income to				Y/L	$\bar{Y}'$
		L	T	M	$L+T$		
1	37.7	600	200	0	800	200	800
2	41.4	588	210	42	798	233	622
3	44.7	574	220	88	794	272	636
4	47.9	555	231	140	786	317	645
5	50.7	535	243	194	778	370	649
6	53.4	510	255	256	765	432	651
7	55.5	483	268	321	751	502	649

The following are unchanged from Table 12.1: $Y, L, T, \Delta A/A$, Capital loss labor, Interest on Cost of Education

Production Functions:

(1) $Y = A(1) L^{.75} T^{.25} M^{.00}$ (5) $Y = A(5) L^{.55} T^{.25} M^{.20}$

(2) $Y = A(2) L^{.70} T^{.25} M^{.05}$ (6) $Y = A(6) L^{.50} T^{.25} M^{.25}$

(3) $Y = A(3) L^{.65} T^{.25} M^{.10}$ (7) $Y = A(7) L^{.45} T^{.25} M^{.30}$

(4) $Y = A(4) L^{.60} T^{.25} M^{.15}$

CHAPTER THIRTEEN

Structural Unemployment and Technological Change: A Theoretical Analysis

Introduction

Objections are legion to aggregate production functions. One of the principal ones is argued on the ground that many diverse capital goods cannot be aggregated into a single K. Indeed, a recent controversy between Professor Solow (1962, 1963) and Mrs. Robinson (1962) has centered on the qualitative and quantitative aspects of the error in treating heterogeneous capital goods as if they were homogeneous.

If this objection were to be interpreted symetrically, it would also have to be applied to heterogeneous labor which the aggregate function treats homogeneously. Although it does seem a bit more logical to assume that men are more homogeneous with regard to their productive characteristics than are machines, machines wear out and are adapted from generation to generation. The progress in man does not manifest quite the same speed.

A machine that is rendered inefficient can be scrapped, a man who can no longer earn his living must be supported. And, should a class of machines, such as anvils, become obsolete, the present ones need merely be scrapped and no new ones built. If a set of men should become obsolete because they

Note: Herbert Simon and Martin Bronfenbrenner criticized this chapter in an early draft.

haven't enough intelligence or skill, they and their ilk in future generations present a continuing problem.

Questions of this sort and the fears they imply have given rise to the current unrest about the question of automation and its implications for workers in the future. Although much of this fear proves to be groundless,[1] there is a problem which is not easily dismissed. The question of heterogeneous labor in a heterogeneous capital model is taken up in this chapter along with an attempt to answer questions concerning structural unemployment, wage rates, and the place of labor.

The Model: Capital

Productive capacity resides in sets of machines and in the men trained to operate them. Each machine is a piece of steel that is incapable of being modified once it is built. (See, for example, Solow [1960] and Phelps [1963].) Once built, it continues to require the same raw materials and labor; it continues to turn out the same finished product. Initially, each type of machine might be thought of as requiring an operator of a minimum skill level. If an operator has less than the required skill, he and the machine will produce nothing. Using what appears to be a natural ordering, capital can be partitioned into α classes ordered $\{1, 2, 3, \ldots \alpha\}$ such that the skill needed to operate m_i is greater than the skill needed to operate m_{i-1}. It is convenient to define units of capital: one unit of machine m_i requires the services of one laborer. M_i will be the number of units of machines in $\{m_i\}$.

At this point, assumptions about maintenance and depreciation are required. Different assumptions have different implications; the ones to be made here are simple, plausible, standard, and cover a wide range of actual cases. All machines are maintained at full capacity; thus there is no difference between the output of a brand-new machine in a given class and one that is old. The life of a machine is expressed by either of two assumptions: (a) machines last forever and are retired only when obsolete; (b) machines last for k years and then fall apart with no scrap value. Case (a) might be rationalized as a machine wearing out gradually, with one part after another being replaced. At some time, no part of the orginal machine remains, although it is still regarded as the same machine and still produces at the same capacity. Case (b) is the familiar "one hoss shay" assumption ubiquitous in models of growth and technological change. These two cases tend to merge as the life of a machine increases. Further, they also have similar implications if the capital supply is considered to be infinitely elastic at a given rate of interest $\bar{r}$. The only difference (other than one in $\bar{r}$) occurs when a

---

[1]For a good debunking see Simon (1960).

machine is being utilized but is earning a rate of return less than the equilibrium.

A fixed rate of interest is convenient in this model and not terribly unrealistic, considering United States historical evidence. Furthermore, it tends to concentrate attention on comparative static aspects of the model, the important aspects for this chapter. Finally, a fixed rate of return is realistic in a model where the rate of adjustment is rapid compared with the changes in disturbing influences.

Labor

The assumption concerning the various grades of machines induced a natural partition and ordering of capital. This same partition is relevant in dividing labor into α classes ordered $\{1, 2, 3, \ldots \alpha\}$ such that l_i can operate m_i. A man can operate all machines requiring less skill than his own.

In defining the production function which connects these heterogeneous machines and classes of labor, two cases seem to cover the available range of possibilities. In the first, the production function is of the fixed coefficient variety where one man operates one unit of machine to get one unit of output. This function is described in Equation (1),

$$f(m_i, l_j) = 1 \quad \text{if} \quad j \geq i$$
$$= 0 \quad \text{otherwise} \tag{1}$$

with x units of m_i, y units of labor of skill i or greater will produce either x or y units of output, whichever is smaller.

A second possibility, involving a production function that permits substitution both of men and skill levels, is shown in Equation (2).

$$Y_i = z_i \left(\frac{n_i}{n_i + \lambda_i} \right)^{\alpha_i} \left(\frac{S_i}{S_i + \sigma_i} \right)^{\beta_i} \tag{2}$$

Here, the higher the skill and the greater the number of men, the greater will be the output, although first there are increasing returns to scale and then decreasing returns. The output of the ith machine is equal to some constant term, z, a measure of efficiency, times the ratio of n, the number of men employed on this machine, divided by the sum of n and λ, the number of men this machine was designed to employ, all to the α power. Similarly S is the skill level of the men employed, whereas σ is the skill level the machine was designed for. The function is approximately linear in logs and the α and β serve to weight the relative importance of manpower and skill.

A digression is in order here to explain the units with which output is measured and the difference they might make. In the model there is an index number which permits comparisons of output bundles; or equivalently, there is a single output which is used alternatively for capital and consumption. Raw materials are assumed to be available in unlimited quantitities at the current prices. Thus, their cost can be subtracted from the value of output to give each machine a value-added measure of output. This complicated string of assumptions is equivalent to there being no raw materials.

In this model, education is a capital-intensive process analogous to aging wine; that is, all men can be educated to any desired skill level. The economy emerging from these assumptions is a Ricardian one. As recently modeled by Samuelson (1959) and Sraffa (1960), this economy leaves nothing to demand forces and all prices are determined strictly by technology. Perhaps the greatest advantage of these assumptions is that any generalization to many final goods holds no difficulties.

The Wage Rate

There is competition in the model and so all workers of a given skill level are paid the same wage: w_i is the wage of l_i. For the fixed coefficient production, some l_i will be hired on an existing machine if and only if $Y_i \geq w_i$ (output exceeds the cost of wages). Now, labor will be hired until Equation

$$Y_i = w_i \qquad (3)$$

or

$$\delta_i = M_i$$

whichever is smaller (where δ_i is the number of machines of class i being operated). Certainly in all cases $w_1 \leq w_2 \leq w_3 \leq \ldots \leq w_\alpha$ since a man of skill i would seek employment on a machine requiring less skill if the wage on the higher-skill machine were not at least equal to that of the lower one.

Beyond these two statements, nothing can be said for the wage rate under a fixed coefficient production function. There is a wide area of ambiguity since the marginal product of each factor is not determinant between zero and one. Any wage between zero and the output of this unit machine is consistent with the prescription that the wage equal the marginal revenue product.

For the factor tradeoff production function, the partial derivative with respect to employment gives Equation (4).

$$\frac{\partial Y}{\partial n} = w = z\alpha\left(\frac{n}{n+\lambda}\right)^{\alpha-1}\left(\frac{1}{\lambda+n} - \frac{n}{(\lambda+n)^2}\right)\left(\frac{S}{S+\sigma}\right)^{\beta}$$

$$= z\alpha\left(\frac{n}{n+\lambda}\right)^{\alpha}\left(\frac{S}{S+\sigma}\right)^{\beta}\left(\frac{\lambda+n}{n}\right)\left[\frac{\lambda+n-n}{(\lambda+n)^2}\right] \qquad (4)$$

$$= Y\frac{\alpha\lambda}{n(\lambda+n)}$$

The return to skill is derived in the same fashion in Equation (5).

$$\frac{\partial Y}{\partial s} = s = Y \frac{\beta \sigma}{S(S + \sigma)} \tag{5}$$

The expression $\alpha\lambda/[n(\lambda + n)]$ can be interpreted as the percentage of output going to each of n workers. Further, it can be broken down into the ratio of planned labor requirements to the sum of planned and actual employment multiplied by α, a proportionality constant.

This is a model that aggregates easily. National product, for example, is merely the sum of outputs of all machines that are being utilized. The demand schedule for labor is also easily described. Within the context of the fixed coefficient function, a worker of skill α can work with any machine in the economy; a l_α can work with any m_i for all i. The number of workers of skill α that will be demanded will depend on w_α. Writing out the demand schedule (under the assumption that $w_i = w_{i-1}$ if l_i are working on any m_{i-1} and that the most highly skilled worker will be hired first):

$$D(w_\alpha) = 0 \quad \text{for} \quad w_\alpha > Y_\alpha$$
$$= M_\alpha \quad \text{if} \quad Y_{\alpha-1} < w_\alpha \leq y_\alpha$$
$$= M_\alpha + M_{\alpha-1} \quad \text{if} \quad Y_{\alpha-2} \leq w_\alpha \leq Y_{\alpha-1}$$

However, $w_\alpha = w_{\alpha-1}$ because of competition. Or, in general:

$$= \sum_{i=n+1}^{\alpha} M_i \quad \text{if} \quad Y_{\alpha-n} < w_\alpha \leq Y_{\alpha-n+1}$$

where $w_\alpha = w_{\alpha-1} = \ldots = w_{\alpha-n+1}$. The preceding relation can be graphed as a conventional demand curve, as shown in Figure 13.1, neglecting workers of lower skill. Note that the height of each step is dependent on α, the number of classes of labor. One might treat α as a continuous variable instead of letting it take on only integer values. If α were continuous, the demand schedule would be a more conventional demand curve with no corners.

Generalizing to workers of skill i is relatively straightforward. The formula is exactly the same, except that an additional correction term is subtracted to account for labor of a higher skill which is not employed at a higher wage. The result is given in Equation (6),

$$D(w_i) = \sum_{j=n+1}^{i} M_j - C \quad \text{if} \quad Y_{i-n} < w_i \leq Y_{i-n+1} \tag{6}$$

where $w_i = w_{i-1} = \ldots = w_{i-n+1}$. Thus the demand curve for l_i is defined recursively starting from $i = \alpha$.

The correction term, C, focuses attention on an inherent problem: the demand curve for labor of skill i cannot be defined without knowing the supply curves for labor of every skill in the economy. The labor of highest skill has a well-defined demand curve only when its wage rate is greater than $Y_{\alpha-1}$. For wages below $Y_{\alpha-1}$, the assumption of competition requires that all laborers who could run a given machine get at least the wage paid

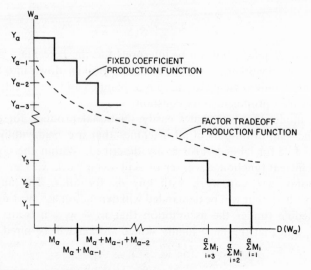

Figure 13-1.   The Demand for Labor Under Two Production Functions

on that machine. Thus, if there were a systematic excess of labor, all wages might be zero, even though only one man were unemployed and he of skill 1. The elegance of the formulation is battered by the necessity of knowing the supply curves of all skill levels in order to define a single demand curve, but deficiencies of this sort have little history of invalidating models. For now, it is simply assumed that the number of laborers of each skill is known, and that all men wish to work a fixed amount at any positive wage.

In the model skill has a definite meaning and it is entirely plausible that the L_i would be known. Without so strict a definition of skill or the possibility of recursion, the demand curve for labor is ambiguous.

If might be helpful to spend a moment exploring the conditions that would lead to a zero wage in the system. If any wage is zero, all lower wages must also be zero since a man can always take a job requiring a lower skill level. Consider a case where there are exactly as many workers as machines in each skill level except for level α. Here there is one excess man. This excess man will have to work on an $m_{\alpha-1}$, which means that all l_α must be paid the same wages as men in $l_{\alpha-1}$. But, this man has displaced a $l_{\alpha-1}$ who is forced to operate a $m_{\alpha-2}$. Thus, all $l_{\alpha-1}$ must be paid the same wage as men in $l_{\alpha-2}$. This bumping will continue until finally an l_1 is displaced and can find no machine to work on. Thus, w_1 will be zero and hence w_2 will also be zero, and so on until w_α must also be zero.

Now zero wages seem unlikely, particularly since m_1 is likely to be a simple hand tool, or no tool at all. The critical assumption that gives rise to zero wages is the fixed coefficient nature of the production function. If there is even a slight possibility of substitution, zero wages will be ruled out. (Capital is implicitly assumed to be available, if not abundant.)

Going on to consider the demand curve for labor under the factor tradeoff production function, the derivation is very much as before. Now, however, there are no sharp drops in the curve since it is possible to use fewer men of a higher skill, or more men of lower skill to derive the same output from each machine. As a result, the demand curve will be continuous and will also become more horizontal. The possibility of a zero wage is ruled out. The second curve is plotted in Figure 13.1.

Since it would take a brave theorist to argue there is no possibility of substitution, the preceding argument has essentially ruled out the possibility of a zero wage. There does remain the possibility that men of the lowest skill level will be earning a wage which is too low to sustain life, or more generally, lower than society wishes it to be. The system does not necessarily lead to small skill differentials and men of the highest skill stand to earn substantially more than men of the lowest skill. When the technological change function is defined, output per man in society will be rising, yet it is not necessary that the wage of the unskilled worker should rise. Thus, a completely unfettered free market may give rise to a wage structure which is not optimal according to society's utility function.

In principle, the answer is quite simple: charge a lump sum tax to those men of higher skill levels and pay a lump sum subsidy to those of lower skill levels. In implementing such a policy, one would be getting close to a Lerner (1944) notion of a social dividend paid to all men which they can supplement by working.

In spite of the analytic simplicity of its solution, this problem, with the attendant one of slow rates of adjustment, seems to be the focus of popular discussions of automation. It seems to be unassailable logic that if society can produce more, there will be more to distribute. It would not seem difficult to get workers to see that jobs must change and old skills be replaced by new ones, that each man will still have a job. But, what assurance does a worker have that his share of national income will continue to be at some reasonable level?[2]

---

[2]The model has some immediate implications for several policies currently pursued by society. It suggests that the notion of a minimum wage is a bad one for allocation. A minimum real wage would tend to make the lowest-skilled workers unemployable if it exceeds y_1. If it is below y_1, it has no effect. Given the expected rate of return, $\bar{r}$, a minimum real wage is a fifth wheel or additional constraint that can either do no good or play havoc with the system. If the incomes of workers are to be supported, this should be done through lump sum income transfers, and should have nothing to do with the wage allocation mechanism.

Competition is an important assumption in the model. It is an assumption that rules out the usual monopsony argument for minimum wages.

Retraining

Just how do displaced workers become skilled and what are the costs of increasing their training? One possible form of the function relating the cost of attaining a given skill level is given in Equation (7).

$$\xi_i = \xi_0 \sigma^\epsilon \tag{7}$$

ξ_0 and ϵ are constants greater than zero. This function has the property that education becomes increasingly expensive as the absolute level increases.

For the moment assume that this function and its parameters are known for a worker of skill i. This man is attempting to determine whether he should raise his skill level. He should do so if the present discounted value of the future wage increase will pay for his training. If m is the number of years of working life left, a worker should get further trained, Equation (8).

$$\xi_{i+1} - \xi_i \leq (w_{i+1} - w_i) \sum_{j=0}^{m} (1 + \bar{r})^{-j} \tag{8}$$

Note that for m large and $\bar{r}$ reasonably large, the inequality is approximated by Equation (9).

$$\Delta\xi \leq \frac{\Delta w}{\bar{r}} \tag{9}$$

There is the possibility of workers being heterogeneous with respect to their ability to receive additional training as well as their present training. In such a case, ξ and ϵ would change between workers, and it would always be an individual decision as to whether it is profitable to contract for additional training.

In the case of workers being homogeneous with respect to further training, pure competition would guarantee that skill increases were worth no more than the cost of attaining them. Thus, the skill level takes on the aspect of additional capital investment. On the other hand, heterogeneous workers can earn an economic rent on their ability to be trained. The heterogeneous assumption seems to characterize the world, since it is "obvious" that not all men can be trained to the highest skill levels. As long as there are men in each skill level who can be further trained, however, there are no economic rents for skill increases.

Investment

So far the capital stock has been fixed. In order to consider tradeoffs between capital and labor, Equation (10) is introduced,

$$C_i = C_0 \lambda_i^{-\gamma} \sigma_i^{-\eta} \tag{10}$$

where C_i is the cost of constructing m_i. The smaller is the required labor (λ); i.e., the higher is productivity, the larger will be the capital cost. Similarly, it costs less to construct a machine which inefficiently uses highly skilled labor (σ).

The function might be interpreted as if a machine shop were to be built. The fewer the number of men to be employed, given a constant level of output, the greater must be the capital investment (cost of machines). Similarly, the lower the skill level of the men to be employed, holding output constant, the greater must be the capital cost.

In order to derive the return to capital and investigate the question of returns to scale, it would be helpful to explore some of the properties of the factor tradeoff production function [Equation (2)]. The marginal product of a worker, his wage, was given earlier as $y[\alpha\lambda/n(\lambda + n)$.] Multiplying the wage by the number of workers gives the total return to labor: $y[\alpha\lambda/(\lambda + n)]$. Finally, dividing by output gives the share of labor in output $\alpha\lambda/(\lambda + n)$. In similar fashion, the share of skill in output is $\beta\sigma/(S + \sigma)$. Adding the two shares together, $\alpha\lambda/(\lambda + n) + \beta\sigma/(\sigma + S)$, it is apparent that the function can display decreasing, constant, or increasing returns to scale, depending on the values of its parameters.

Consider the degree of returns to scale in the region of employment and skill at their prescribed levels. Taking $N = \lambda$ and $S = \sigma$, the sum of shares simplify to: $(\alpha + \beta)/2$. Thus, the sum of α and β greater than one guarantees increasing returns to scale, whereas the sum less than one permits decreasing returns.

But all the factors haven't been increased proportionately: capital is implicit in this function. To investigate a proportional increase in the factors in the cost function, let θ be the proportion λ and σ may decrease. Take $\mathbf{k} = \mathbf{b} = .735$, as one example

$$2C = C_0(\theta\lambda)^{-\gamma}(\theta\gamma)^{-\eta} \quad \text{from the cost function}$$
$$= C_0\theta^{-\gamma-\eta}\lambda^{-\gamma-\eta}$$
$$= C\theta^{-\gamma-\eta}$$

or $\qquad 2 = \theta^{-\gamma-\eta}$

Take $\gamma = \eta = .735$, as one example

$$\theta = .6234$$

Now, let $N = \lambda$, $S = \sigma$

$$Y_0 = z_i\left(\frac{N}{\lambda + N}\right)^\alpha\left(\frac{S}{S + \sigma}\right)^\beta$$
$$= z_i\left(\frac{1}{2}\right)^{\alpha+\beta}$$

Now take $\alpha = \beta = 4/5$. (Thus, the relative shares are each 2/5.)

$$Y_0 = z_i \frac{1}{3.031}$$

$$Y_1 = z_i \left(\frac{2n}{.6234\lambda + 2n}\right)^\alpha \left(\frac{2S}{.6234\sigma + 2S}\right)^\beta$$

$$= z_i \left(\frac{2}{2.6234}\right)^{\alpha+\beta} \quad \text{letting } \alpha = \beta = \tfrac{4}{5}$$

$$= z_i \left(\frac{1}{1.525}\right)$$

Thus, $Y_1 = 2Y_0$ which implies constant returns.

This example shows that the function can display constant returns to scale at the planned levels of employment and skill. The function displays decreasing returns to scale at $N > \lambda$, $S > \sigma$ *ceteris paribus*, and increasing returns at $N < \lambda$, $S < \sigma$ *ceteris paribus*.

Let

$$k = \frac{N}{\lambda} = \frac{S}{\sigma}$$

then

$$Y_0 = \left(\frac{k}{1+k}\right)^\alpha \left(\frac{k}{1+k}\right)^\beta$$

$$= \left(\frac{k}{1+k}\right)^{\alpha+\beta}$$

$$= \left(\frac{k}{1+k}\right)^{8/5}$$

$$Y_1 = \left(\frac{2k}{.6234 + 2k}\right)^{8/5}$$

for $k = 1$

$$Y_0 = \left(\frac{1}{2}\right)^{8/5}$$

$$= \frac{1}{3.031}$$

$$Y_1 = \left(\frac{2}{2.6234}\right)^{8/5}$$

$$= \frac{1}{1.525}$$

Since $Y_1 = 2Y_0$, the function exhibits constant returns for $k = \tfrac{1}{2}$:

$$Y_0 = \left(\frac{1/2}{3/2}\right)^{8/5}$$

$$= \left(\frac{1}{3}\right)^{8/5}$$

$$= .146$$

$$Y_1 = \left(\frac{1}{1.6234}\right)^{8/5}$$

$$= .46$$

now $Y_1 = 3.2\, Y_0$ which implies increasing returns for $k = 2$

$$Y_0 = \left(\frac{2}{3}\right)^{8/5}$$

$$= .441$$

$$Y_1 = \left(\frac{4}{4.6234}\right)^{8/5}$$

$$= .795$$

$$= 1.8\, Y_0$$

which implies decreasing returns.

Application of the Model

So far the investigation has been conducted on the level of a thought experiment where the function was potentially estimable in case all relevant data were present. How feasible, however, is the collection of data? Is there an easy interpretation of the function?

Although machines are easily classified by their input-output and operating characteristics, labor presents a problem. How can one tell that a man is of skill 21 and not 20 or 22? One way involves using years of education as a surrogate variable. Yet, though there is likely to be an observable difference between a man with a college education and one with a fourth-grade education, finer differences may be meaningless. Certainly it would be a brave man who predicted that of two men operating identical machine tools, the one with eleven years of schooling was more skilled than the one with seven.

Another conventional way of measuring skill uses wages as a surrogate. The problem here is that there tends to be rough uniformity within a particular class of job, and the wage is tied to issues of seniority and experience and not productivity. The wage would offer a good surrogate under perfect competition, but in its absence, remains suspect.

Recent work in learning by doing offers one hope of getting a measure. Alchian (1963) and Rapping (1965) have concluded that productive efficiency increased as a function of the amount of time spent gaining experience. Among other things, this work provides a rationale for tying wages to seniority. Thus, one way to measure a worker's skill on a machine might involve a weighted average of the time he has spent working with this particular machine and the time he has spent in the industry on similar machines. For the particular application of a machine shop, this index of skill is probably a good one.

Skill measured by experience also offers a particularly easy way of estimating the cost of acquiring additional skill: it is the foregone value of production when a man is placed on a new machine. It is the difference between the output of an old hand and that of a neophyte discounted back to the present. Again, such data ought to be easily available.

Measuring the requirements of machines seems particularly easy. In general a machine comes equipped with a guide for the manpower and skill requirements. Since the machine also comes with a price tag, the cost function ought to be easy to estimate.

Finally, the estimation of the production function might come either from experimental data or from investigations of peak and slack periods when the labor and skill levels were varied—for one investigation see Kurz and Manne (1963). In the particular case of machines where the labor and skill requirements are quite rigid, the fixed coefficient production function is available.

Thus, the three functions, cost of education, cost of capital, and production, might be estimated in the context of a machine shop.

Technological Change

The usual view of technological change is a shift in the production function over time. In the present model there is the more general possibility of shifts in any of the three functions: cost of education, cost of machines, and production. Unfortunately, the model is too limited to incorporate the factors that might shift these functions, for example, learning by doing in the production function and cost functions, or technological advance.

There are six kinds of shifts that might be present in the model either separately or simultaneously (dots over variables indicate time derivatives):

(1) $\dot{z}$ > 0 which implies neutral, nonembodied change

(2) $\dot{C}_0$ < 0 implying neutral, embodied change in the cost of capital function

(3) $\dot{\xi}_0$ < 0 implying neutral, embodied technological change in the cost of education function

(4) $\dot{\gamma}$ or $\dot{\eta}$ < 0 implying non-neutral, embodied change in the cost of capital function

(5) $\dot{\epsilon}$ < 0 implying non-neutral, embodied change in the education function

or

(6) $\dot{\alpha}$ or $\dot{\beta}$ < 0 giving rise to unembodied, non-neutral change in the production function

So far as the embodied technological change is concerned, (2) and (4) are changes in capital whereas (3) and (5) are changes in education.

The situation gets further complicated on noting that the changes in education (3) and (5), and in production (1) and (6) may occur uniformly across all classes or nonuniformly within specific classes. The analysis will confine itself to some general comments. Consider the question of the welfare of workers under change.

Capital losses are possible given adjustments in the model. A machine may be rendered obsolete or a worker may find that the skill differential that holds him above the next lower level is now irrelevant. Yet, even under these changes, no single worker loses absolutely by change. A machine is rendered obsolete only when a machine of lower cost and skill requirements becomes relatively more productive than this machine. Workers may lose some of their comparative advantage, but their absolute wage never declines.

A more formal argument would consider the welfare of labor under change as exemplified in three variables: individual wages, the total return to labor, and the share of labor in output. The preceding paragraph hints that no individual wage can fall under the impact of automation; its assumptions are (a) a fixed interest rate, (b) fixed prices for raw materials. This argument is plausible and can be elaborated.

The assumption that raw materials are available at fixed prices allows a value-added measure of output that is independent of demand conditions in the factor markets. With this two-factor production function, the assumption of a constant interest rate induces a further simplification. The owners of capital are now indifferent to how machines are built or operated as long as they receive a fixed return. Suppose that a proposed technological change implied a reduction in wages. In order to put it in over the opposition of the workers, someone would have to argue for it. But the producers of raw materials could not be benefited since their prices could not rise. And the capitalists could not be benefited since their return could not rise. Thus, no one would be taking the case and the proposed change would die for lack of support.

The argument can be restated in more general terms. Given the following five conditions, every worker will be employed in the long run. There is no guarantee that a worker will earn a wage deemed sufficient, merely that he will have a job at a positive wage. These conditions need not hold in general, merely within the relevant range.

Condition one is the familiar one of competition. In this argument it can be a very weak form of competition since it merely serves to guarantee that the possible will be realized.

The second condition is more controversial: raw materials are assumed to be available at constant prices. This assumption is necessary to stay off the Ricardian shoal. Population pressures obviously can wreck any argument of this sort. One need merely listen to a pessimistic demographer to learn of the possibility of men literally covering the earth's surface. As long as population growth is kept under control, this assumption seems a good approximation. Science and technology are continually finding ways of conserving or substituting scarce resources. For example, it has recently become possible to run an automobile on ammonia at a cost comparable to that of gasoline.

Assumption three precludes consumers being satiated with goods; the prices of consumption goods are assumed to stay greater than zero. This assumption rules out stagnation arguments and the possibility that all consumption goods will become free goods and no human labor will be necessary for their production.

The fourth assumption is a dual one concerning the amount of available capital and the range of technology: all grades of labor have a positive marginal physical product. Technology must be broad and flexible enough to provide production processes which will make use of all grades of labor. This assumption is subject to historical verification.

The last assumption is a behavioral one and subject to question: relative wages are flexible and a man will accept a job at any positive wage. Since this wage might be low for some workers, one might think of it being supplemented by the social dividend mentioned earlier.

The general argument is that assumptions three and four imply a positive marginal physical product for a worker, a positive price, and therefore a positive marginal revenue product. Assumption one guarantees that the marginal revenue product will be offered to the worker and assumption five guarantees that it will be accepted. Assumption two really serves as a partial justification for the positive marginal physical product of each worker; it reduces assumption four to a statement about the range of technology.

These conditions do not serve as the minimum set necessary for the argument. However, they are fairly plausible and within the framework of contemporary economic models. The conclusion is a strong one and may help to clearify some of the arguments about "structural unemployment."

Adjustments to Technological Change

Consider the question of the power of this model to adjust to technological change. Perhaps the worst conditions for adjusting occur when no further education is possible and the production function is of the fixed coefficient variety. If a particular machine is rendered more productive, the workers operating it benefit. It is possible that more highly skilled workers may also benefit if the change is large. Unless income is redistributed, however, no worker of lower skill receives benefit (the effects would spread throughout the labor force under the factor-substitute production function). Of course, the owner of an obsolete machine suffers a capital loss.

A second case involves the polar assumption that all men can be further trained (the form of the production function is not important). The average wage in this case rises more rapidly than the previous one since workers can shift machines more easily; the general level of skill should also rise more rapidly. This case has an appealing property: since all men can be further trained, wage differentials reflect only the capitalized cost of training; all wages are equal save for the cost of training. Finally, this case allows output per man to rise as rapidly as technological change will allow.

In the intermediate case of some men being capable of further training, the properties are a compromise. As long as there are workers at each skill level who can be further trained, this case is identical to the previous one. As soon as all workers have received as much training as they can take, however, the case reverts to the one of no workers being capable of further training. As the system moves through these two stages, the relative welfare of the least skilled worker declines. When no more men can be trained, the payment for skill begins to rise above the cost of training. Unless there is some redistribution of income, the system is likely to move into a welfare disequilibrium.

Some Generalizations

At this point it would be profitable to pick up some loose ends and explore some further cases. The analysis has been conducted under the assumptions of an infinitely elastic supply of raw materials and a single final output. Generalizing these two assumptions is quite easy within the framework of a Ricardian economy. (See Samuelson [1959].) As long as there is a single scarce resource that is fixed in quantity, prices in the system will be determined strictly by technological considerations, quite independently of the market.

In order to achieve the condition of a single limited resource, workers must all be equal. Thus, the whole of the discussion so far fits into the Ricardian framework if all men can be trained to all jobs. Of course, these same conditions are achieved when some men can still be trained.

Going outside this framework, the prices of raw materials might be subject to variation. If a raw material were in short supply, its price would rise. The first effect would be a decrease in the value added of machines using this material. Wages connected with this machine, as well as the return on the machine, would fall. Eventually, workers would leave this machine if the wages paid to lower-skilled workers were higher; if so, the machines would pass out of existence because they were now inefficient. Certainly the wages of workers connected with these machines would have to fall. In case men could be further trained, the new equilibrium would have all wages slightly lower than previously, and some workers would have suffered capital loss.

The case of many final goods leads to insolvable difficulties outside the Ricardian framework. Whether raw materials are involved or not, the combination of many different labor skills and many final goods gives rise to all the index number problems that have plagued neoclassical economics. This chapter makes no attempt to handle such a problem. The fundamental structure of the preceding analysis, however, generally applies to this problem.

Some Implications of the Model

In the model, education was seen as a capital-intensive process. Thus, total capital expenditures are highly correlated with the amount of training, and the expenditure of capital on new equipment would be a poor explanatory variable of technological change. If the amount spent on training exceeds net capital formation, the model would produce the kind of empirical results that Solow (1957) and others have derived where capital increase accounts for only 10 per cent of the total increase in output per man.

Within the limited span of this mode, education and skill are not synonymous. The number of years of schooling has no direct relation to productivity. In the parts of the economy where this model is a reasonable approximation, the analyses of Griliches (1963) and Schultz (1962) that use education as a surrogate for skill might give misleading conclusions.

The model exhibits properties relevant to the discussion of structural unemployment: (a) if there is even a slight possibility of substituting labor for capital, there can be no unemployable workers in the long run; (b) the wage paid to some workers might, however, be lower than that prescribed by society; (c) in this case, lump sum income transfers offer a solution that does not change the optimal properties of the equilibrium.

The third conclusion can be elaborated by noting that, under the assumptions here, the real wage of no single worker can fall under the impact of technological change. Thus, at worst technological change can work to reduce the relative wage of a class of workers while holding their absolute wage fixed.

Finally, a new production function has been presented here. This new function, designed to incorporate variables dealing with skill level, rigidly designed machines, and training, might be applied to a microeconomic unit, such as a machine shop.

Summary and Conclusion

The model could be described as the manufacturing sector of an economy. The sector neither makes its own capital goods nor supplies its raw materials. Productive machines are partitioned into α classes ordered by the amount of skill required of the operator. The labor force is similarly divided into α classes corresponding to the classes of machines. The demand curve for labor has the property that the curve for any skill level depends on the supply and demand curves for labor of all other levels.

Assuming that capital is infinitely elastic at an expected return of $\bar{r}$, the long-run equilibrium of the economy can be specified. When the possibility of education is introduced, three cases are prominent: (1) when no man can be educated, the equilibrium stays as before; (2) when all men can be educated, all wages become equal except for the capitalized cost of education; (3) when some men can be educated, case (2) prevails until all possible men have been educated; then the system reverts to a case (1) solution.

When technological change becomes possible, again there are three cases of importance: (1) when no men can be educated, technological change is only interesting insofar as it operates on existing machines; large wage shifts can occur if technological change favors some machines. (2) When all men can be educated, wages continue to be equal except for the capitalized cost of education; capital losses may occur as one machine falls into disfavor, but these can have no long-run importance. (3) When some men can be educated, a combination of these first cases occurs. Much as before, the third case is identical to the second as long as some men can still be educated, but reverts to the first case as each skill level comes to contain only men incapable of further training.

Attempts to generalize the model are successful only (a) when all men can be educated and all raw materials are still available at fixed prices, or (b) if there is a single final good. The first case is that of a Ricardian economy and has the property that prices of final goods depend only on the technology; since they are independent of demand, output is measured without difficulty. The second case is just as tractable, although its solution depends on the values of the parameters of a particular system. The case of many final goods, outside of case (a), becomes entangled in all the neoclassical problems of index numbers, measures of real income, demand equations, etc.

Bibliography

Alchian 1963; Griliches 1963; Kurz and Manne 1963; Lerner 1944; Phelps 1963; Robinson 1962; Rapping 1965; Samuelson 1959, 1961; Schultz 1962; Sraffa 1960; Simon 1960, 1964; Solow 1962, 1963b, 1956.

Bibliography

Journal Abbreviations

A.E.R.	American Economic Review
B.E.S.	Bulletin of Economics and Statistics
B.O.I.S.	Bulletin of the Oxford Institute of Statistics
C.J.E.P.S.	Canadian Journal of Economics and Political Science
Em.	Econometrica
Ec.	Economica
E.J.	Economic Journal
E.R.	Economic Record
I.E.R.	International Economic Review
Jahr	Jahrbuch fuer National Okonomic und Statistik
J.F.E.	Journal of Farm Economics
J.I.E.	Journal of Industrial Engineering
J.B.	Journal of Business
J.P.E.	Journal of Political Economy
J.R.S.S.	Journal of the Royal Statistical Society
Kyklos	
K.K.	Keizai Kenukyu
M.E.	Metroeconomica
O.E.P.	Oxford Economic Papers
P.M.R.	Productivity Measurement Review
Q.J.E.	Quarterly Journal of Economics
R.E.S.	Review of Economics and Statistics
R.E. Stud.	Review of Economic Studies
S.Z.V.S.	Schweizerische Zeitschrift fuer Volkswitschaft und Statistik

Abramovitz, M., 1956, "Resource and Output Trends in the U.S. since 1870," AER.

Abramovitz, M., 1962, "Economic Growth in the U.S., A Review Article," AER.

Alchian, A., "Costs and Outputs," in Abramovitz, M., 1959, *The Allocation of Economic Resources.* Stanford: Stanford University Press, 1959.

Alchian, A., 1963, "Reliability of Progress Curves in Air Frame Production," Em.

Akihiro, Amano, 1964, "Biased Technical Progress and a Neo-Classical Theory of Economic Growth," QJE.

Ames, E. and Rosenberg, N., 1963, "Changing Technological Leadership and Industrial Growth," EJ.

Amey, L., 1959, "Measuring Productivity in Absence of Records," BOIS.

Anderson, P., 1961, "The Apparent Decline in Capital-Output Ratios," QJE.

Arrow, K., 1962, "The Economic Implications of Learning by Doing," REStud.

Arrow, K., Chenery, H., Minhas, B., and Solow, R., 1961, "Capital-Labor Substitution and Economic Efficiency," RES.

Asher, A., 1956, "Cost Quantity Relationships in the Airframe Industry," The RAND Corp., R-291.

Asimakopulos, A., 1963, "The Definition of Neutral Inventions," EJ.

Asimakopulos, A. and Weldon, J., 1963, "The Classification of Technical Progress in Models of Economic Growth," Ec.

Atkinson and Jones, 1954, *The Survey of Current Business*, August 1954.

Aukrust, O., 1959, "Investment and Economic Growth," PMR.

Aukrust, O., 1964, "Factors of Economic Development: A Review of Recent Research," *Weltwirtschaftliches Archiv.*

Balogh, T., 1958, "Productivity and Inflation," OEP.

Balogh, T., 1964, "Education and Economic Growth, Comments on Professor Tinbergen's Planning Model," *Kyklos.*

Banerji, H., 1956, *Technical Progress and the Process of Economic Development.* The Hague: Netherlands University Foundation.

Bardham, P., 1963, "A Short Note on Technical Progress and Terms of Trade," OEP.

Barr, J., 1965, "A Note on Heterogeneous Capital and Smooth Production Functions," ditto, Carnegie Institute of Technology.

Barton, G. and Loomis, R., 1961, "Productivity in Agriculture," U.S.D.A. Tech. Bulletin No. 1238, April 1961.

Barzel, Y., 1963, "Productivity in the Electric Power Industry 1929-55," RES.

Becker, G., 1964, *Human Capital*, NBER. New York: Columbia University Press.

Bell, F., 1964, "The Role of Capital-Labor Substitution in the Economic Adjustment of an Industry across Regions," *Southern Economic Journal.*

Bergstrom, A., 1962, "A Model of Technical Progress, the Production Function and Cyclical Growth," Ec.

Bernard, G., 1964, "Notes on Production Models," *Revue d'Economie Politique.*

Bhagwati, J., 1964, "The Pure Theory of International Trade," EJ.

Bhalla, A., 1964, "Investment Allocation and Technological Choice—A Case of Cotton Spinning Techniques," EJ.

Bierwag, G., 1964, "Balanced Growth and Technological Progress," OEP.

Black, J., 1962a, "Technical Progress and Optimum Savings," REStud.

Black, J., 1962b, "The Technical Progress Function and the Production Function," Ec.

Blaug, M., 1960., "Technical Change and Marxian Economics," *Kyklos*.

Blaug, M., 1963, "A Survey of the theory of Process Innovation," Ec.

Blitz, R., 1958, "Capital Longevity and Economic Development," AER.

Bowen, H., 1954, "Technological Change and Aggregate Demand," AER.

Brakel, L., 1962, "A Comparison of Productivity and Recent Productivity Trends in Various Countries," RES.

Bray, J. and Watkins, P., 1964, "Technical Change in Corn Production in the U.S., 1870–1960," JFE.

Brems, H., 1959, *Output, Employment, Capital, and Growth*. New York: Harper.

Brems, H., 1963, "What Induces Induced Investment?," *Kyklos*.

Bronfenbrenner, M., 1960, "A Note on Relative Shares and The Elasticity of Substitution," JPE.

Brown, M., 1962, "An Iconoclastic View of the New View of Investment," Netherlands Econometric Institute, EI Report 6402.

Brown, M., 1965, "The Share of Corporate Profits in the Postwar Period," United States Dept. of Commerce.

Brown, M. and Conrad, A., 1962, "Fundamental Variables in a Generalized System of Production," Report of Netherlands Econometric Institute, Balanced Growth Division.

Brown, M. and deCani, J., 1962, "Technological Change in the U.S., 1950–60," PMR.

Brown, M. and deCani, J., 1963a, "Technological Change and the Distribution of Income," IER.

Brown, M. and deCani, J., 1963b, "A Measure of Technological Employment," RES.

Brown, M. and Popkin, J., 1962, "A Measure of Technological Change and Returns to Scale," RES.

Brozen, Y., 1957, "The Determinants of Technological Change," AER.

Brozen, Y., 1958, "The Economics of Automation," AER.

Brune, M., 1964, "Estimation of Production Functions and Factor Contributions to Growth Under Structural Disequilibrium," Abstracted in EM.

Budd, E., 1960, "Factor Shares, 1850–1910," NBER, SIW, *Trends in the American Economy in the Nineteenth Century*. Princeton.

Burton, H., 1956, "Innovations and Equilibrium Growth," EJ.

Cairncross, A., 1955, "The Place of Capital in Economic Progress," in *Economic Progress*, Proceedings of International Economic Association Conference, edited by L. Dupriez. Louvain: Institute de Recherches Economiques of Sociales.

Carter, C. and Williams, B., 1957, *Industry and Technical Progress*. London: Oxford University Press.

Carter, C. and Williams, B., 1958, *Investment in Innovation*. London: Oxford University Press.

Carter, C. and Williams, B., 1959, *Science in Industry*. London: Oxford University Press.

Chakravarty, S., 1964, "Optimal Investment and Technical Progress," REStud.

Champernowne, D., 1958, "Capital Accumulation and the Maintenance of Full Employment," EJ.

Chandler, Cleveland, 1962, "The Relative Contribution of Capital Intensity and Productivity to Changes in Output and Income," JFE.

Charnes, A. and Cooper, W., 1952, "A Model for Product Optimization in New Item Production," Proceedings of the 2nd Annual Logistics Conference, George Washington University, Washington, D.C.

Charnes, A. and Cooper, W., 1954, "Silhouette Functions of Short-Run Cost Behavior," QJE.

Charnes, A. and Cooper, W., 1962, "Optimizing Engineering Design Under Inequality Constraints," ONR Research Memo 64, August 1962, Carnegie Institute of Technology.

Chenery, H., 1949, "Engineering Production Functions," QJE.

Chenery, H., 1953, "Process and Production Functions from Engineering Data," in Leontief, W. (ed.), *Studies in the Structure of the American Economy*. London: Oxford University Press.

Christensen, R. and Yee, H., 1964, "The Role of Agricultural Productivity in Economic Development," JFE.

Clark, Colin, 1958, "Comparisons of Productivity Trends," JB.

Clemhout, S., 1963, "The Ratio Method of Productivity Measurement," EJ.

Cole, H., Holland, D. and Posner, M., 1960, 1961, "Factor Productivity and Efficiency, I, II, III, and IV," BOIS.

Comandor, W., 1965, "Research and Competitive Product Differentiation in the Pharmaceutical Industry in the U.S.," Ec.

Cragg, J. 1963, "Total Productivity, Innovation and Full Employment Growth," Canadian Journal of Economics and Political Science.

Cyert, R. and Lave, L., 1965, "Structural Unemployment: A Lesson in Classical Analysis," ditto, Carnegie Institute of Technology.

Denison, E., 1962, *The Sources of Economic Growth in the U.S. and the Alternatives Before Us;* New York, Committee for Economic Development.

Denison, E., 1961, "How to Raise the High-Employment Growth Rate by One Percentage Point," AER.

Denton, F., 1964, "In Defence of Kendrick: A Comment on S. Clemhout's "The Ratio Method of Productivity Measurement," EJ.

Department of the Census, 1960, *Historical Statistics*, Washington, D.C.

Department of the Census, 1964, *Statistical Abstracts*, Washington, D.C.

Dhrymes, P., 1963, "A Comparison of Productive Behavior in Manufacturing and Service Industries," RES.

Dhrymes, P. and Kurz, M., 1964, "Technology and Scale in Electricity Generation," Em.

Diwan, R., 1964, "An Empirical Estimate of the CES Production Function," abstracted in Em.

Domar, E., 1961, "On the Measurement of Technological Change," EJ.

Domar, E., 1962, "On Total Productivity and All That," JPE.

Domar, E., Eddie, S., Herrick, B., Hohenberg, P., Intriligator, M., and Miyamoto, I., 1964, "Economic Growth and Productivity in the United States, Canada, United Kingdom, Germany and Japan in the Post War Period," RES.

Drandanakis, E., 1963, "Factor Substitution in the Two-sector Growth Model," REStud.

Dunlop, J., 1962, *Automation and Technological Change*. Englewood Cliffs N.J.: Prentice-Hall.

Education, 1962, JPE Supplement.

Edwards, H., and Drane, N., 1963, "The Australian Economy, July 1963," ER.

Edwards, H., and Drane, N., 1964, "Notes on Technical Change in Australian Manufacturing," ER.

Eels, F., Hazelwood, A., Knowles, K., and Winston, C., 1959, "Innovation and Automation: A Discussion Based on Case Studies," BOIS.

Eisner, R., 1956, "Technological Change, Obsolesence, and Aggregate Demand," AER.

Eltis, W., 1963, "Innovation, Technical Progress and Economic Growth," OEP.

Enos, John, 1958, "A Measure of the Rate of Technical Progress in the Petroleum Refining Industry," Journal of Industrial Economics.

Ewell, R., 1955, "The Role of Research in Economic Growth," Chemical and Engineering News.

Fabricant, S., 1959, *Basic Facts on Productivity Change*, NBER. New York: Columbia University Press.

Fellner, W., 1958, "Automatic Market Clearance and Innovations in the Theory of Employment and Growth," OEP.

Fellner, W., 1961, "Appraisal of the Labour-saving and Capital-saving Character of Innovations," in Lutz and Hague, *The Theory of Capital*.

Fellner, W., 1962, "Does the Market Direct the Relative Factor-saving Effects of Technological Progress," in Universities-NBER, *The Rate and Directions of Inventive Activity*. Princeton: Princeton University Press.

Ferguson, C., 1963, "Cross Section Production Functions and the Elasticity of Substitution in American Manufacturing Industry," RES.

Ferguson, C., 1965a, "Substitution, Technical Progress, and Returns to Scale," AER.

Ferguson, C., 1965b, "Time-Series Productions Functions and Technological Progress in American Manufacturing Industry," JPE.

Ferguson, C. and Pfouts, R., 1962, "Aggregate Production Functions and Relative Factor Shares," IER.

Findley, R., 1960, "Economic Growth and the Distributive Shares," REStud.

Findley, R., 1963, "The Robinsonian Model of Accumulation," Ec.

Findley, R. and Grubert, H., 1959, "Factor Intensity, Technological Progress, and the Terms of Trade," OEP.

Frankel, M., 1955, "Obsolescence and Technological Changes in a Maturing Economy," AER.

Frankel, M., 1962, "The Production Function in Allocation and Growth, A Synthesis," AER.

Frisch, R., 1965, *Theory of Production*. Chicago: Rand McNally.

Fromm, G., 1960, *Prices. Profits and Productivity*, unpublished Ph. D. Thesis, Harvard University.

Fuchs, V., 1962, "Capital-labor Substitution: A Note," RES.

Fuchs, V., 1964, *Productivity Trends in the Goods and Service Sectors, 1929–1961: A Preliminary Survey*, NBER. New York: Columbia University Press.

Gaathon, A., 1960, *Capital Stock, Employment, and Output in Israel 1950–1959*, Jerusalem.

Galenson, W. and Leibenstein, H., 1955, "Investment Criteria, Productivity, and Economic Development," QJE.

Gallaway, L., 1964, "The Theory of Relative Shares," QJE.

Gasser-Stäger, W., 1964, "Growth and Change in Swiss Agriculture Since the 19th Century," SZVS.

Gordon, D., 1956, "Obsolescence and Technological Change: Comment," AER.

Gordon, R., 1961, "Price Changes: Consumers' and Capital Goods," AER.

Gourvitch, A., 1940, *Survey of Economic Theory and Technological Change and Employment*. WPA, Washington, D.C.

Grant, A., 1963, "Issues in Distribution Theory: The Measurement of Labor's Relative Share: 1899–1929," RES.

Green, H., 1964, *Aggregation in Economic Analysis*. Princeton: Princeton University Press.

Griliches, Z., 1957, "Specification Bias in Estimates of Production Functions," JFE.

Griliches, Z., 1957, "Hybrid Corn: An Exploration in the Economics of Technological Change," Em.

Griliches, Z., 1958, "The Demand for Fertilizer: An Economic Interpretation of a Technical Change," JFE.

Griliches, Z., 1963, "The Sources of Measured Productivity Growth: U.S. Agriculture 1940–60," JPE.

Griliches, Z., 1964, "Research Expenditures, Education, and The Aggregate Agricultural Production Function," AER.

Griliches, Z. and Grunfeld, Y., 1960, "Is Aggregation Necessarily Bad?" RES.

Grossfield, K., 1962, "Inventions as Business," EJ.

Gruen, F., 1961, "Agriculture and Technical Change," JFE.

Haavelmo, T., 1954, *A Study in the Theory of Economic Evolution*. Amsterdam: North-Holland Publishing Co.

Habakkuk, A., 1962, *American and British Technology in the 19th Century*. Cambridge: Cambridge University Press.

Hahn, F. and Matthews, R., 1964, "The Theory of Economic Growth: A Survey," EJ.

Hamberg, D., 1959, "Production Functions, Innovation, and Economic Growth," JPE.

Hamberg, D., 1964, "Size of Firm, Oligopoly, and Research: The Evidence," CJEPS.

Harrod, R., 1939, "An Essay in Dynamic Theory," EJ.

Harrod, R., 1957, "Professor Fellner on Growth and Unemployment," *Kyklos.*

Hart, P., and Prais, S., 1956, "The Analysis of Business Concentration: A Statistical Approach," JRSS.

Heady, Earl O., 1962, *Agricultural Policy Under Economic Development.* Ames: Iowa State University Press.

Heady, E. and Dillon, J., 1961, *Agricultural Production Functions.* Ames: Iowa State University, Press.

Heertje, A., 1963, "On the Optimum Rate of Savings," *Weltwirtschaftliches Archiv.*

Helmut, W., 1963, "Technical Progress and Factor Substitution," Jahr.

Hicks, J., 1932 (revised 1963), *The Theory of Wages.* London: MacMillan.

Hicks, J., 1910, "Thoughts on the Theory of Capital—The Corfu Conference," OEP.

Hildebrand, G. and Liu, T. C., 1965, *Manufacturing Production Functions in the United States, 1957.* Ithaca: Cornell University Press.

Hirsch, W. Z., 1956, "Firm Progress Ratios," Em.

Hirshleiffer, J., 1962, "The Firm's Cost Function, A Successful Reconstruction," JB.

Hodjera, Zoran, 1963, "Unbiased Productivity Growth and Increasing Costs," OEP.

Hogan, W., 1958, "Technical Progress and the Production Function," RES.

Horowitz, I., 1962, "Firm Size and Research Activity," SEJ.

Houthakker, H., 1955, "The Pareto Distribution and the Cobb-Douglas Production Function in Demand Analysis," REStud.

Howrey, P., 1965, "Technical Change, Capital Longevity, and Economic Growth," AER.

Hultgren, T., 1960, "Changes in Labor Cost During Cycles in Production, Business," NBER, Occasional Paper No. 74.

Hymer, S. and Pashigian, P., 1962, "Firm Size and Rate of Growth," JPE, LXX, 1962. See also comment by H. Simon and rejoinder LXXII, 1964.

Hymer, S. and Pashigian, P., 1962, "Turnover of Firms as a Measure of Market Behavior," RES.

Ijiri, Y. and Simon, H., 1964, "Business Firm Growth and Size," AER.

Inada, K., 1964, "Economic Growth Under Neutral Technical Progress," Em.

Intriligator, M., 1965, "Embodied Technical Change and Productivity in the United States 1929–1958," RES.

Iulo, W., 1961, *Electric Utilities—Costs and Performance.* Pullman: Washington State University Press.

Jewkes, J., Sawers, D., and Stillerman, R., 1958, *The Sources of Invention, 1958.* London: Macmillan.

Johansen, L., 1957, "Substitution vs. Fixed Production Coefficients in The Theory of Economic Growth: A Synthesis," Em.

Johansen, L., 1960, *A Multisector Study of Economic Growth.* Amsterdam: North-Holland.

Johansen, Lief, 1961, "A Method of Separating the Effects of Capital Accumulation and Shifts in Production Functions Upon Growth in Labor Productivity," EJ.

Johnson, G., 1954, "The Functional Distribution of Income in the U.S., 1850–1952," RES.

Johnston, J., 1960, *Statistical Cost Functions.* New York: McGraw-Hill.

Jorgenson, D., 1961, "The Development of a Dual Economy," EJ.

Kaldor, N., 1957, "A Model of Economic Growth," EJ.

Kaldor, N., 1961, "Increasing Returns and Technical Progress—A comment on Professor Hicks' Article," OEP.

Kamien, M., 1965, "Technological Progress and the Demand for Factors of Production," ditto, Carnegie Institute of Technology.

Kendrick, J., 1958, "Productivity Trends in Agriculture and Industry," JFE.

Kendrick, J., 1961, *Productivity Trends in the U.S.* Princeton: Princeton University Press.

Kendrick, J. and Sato, R., 1963, "Factor Prices, Productivity, and Growth," AER.

Kendrick, J., 1964, "The Gains and Losses from Technological Change," JFE.

Kennedy, C., 1961, "Technical Progress and Investment," EJ.

Kennedy, C., 1962, "The Character of Improvements and of Technical Progress," EJ.

Kennedy, C., 1964, "Induced Bias in Innovation and The Theory of Distribution," EJ.

Kindleberger, C., 1961, "Obsolescense and Technical Change," BOIS.

Kmenta, J., 1964, "On Estimation of the CES Production Function," Read at the Econometric Society Meetings, December, 1964.

Knowles, J., 1960, "Potential Economic Growth in the U.S.," Study Paper 20, Joint Economic Committee, Employment, Growth, and Price Levels, Washington, D.C.

Komiya, R., 1962, "Technical Progress and the Production Function in the U.S. Steam Power Industry," RES.

Kravis, I., 1959, "Relative Income Shares in Fact and Theory," AER.

Krelle, W., 1961, "Income Distribution and Technical Progress," *Kyklos.*

Krelle, W., 1964, "Investment and Growth," Jahr.

Kuh, Edwin, 1960, "Profits, Profits Markups, and Productivity," Study Paper No. 15, Joint Economic Committee, Study of Employment, Growth, and Price Levels, Washington, D. C.

Kuh, E., 1965a, "Cyclical and Secular Labor Productivity in United States Manufacturing," RES.

Kuh, E., 1965b, "Income Distribution and Employment over the Business Cycle," in J. Duesenberry, G. Fromm, L. Klein, and E. Kuh (eds.), *The Brookings–SSRC Quarterly Econometric Model of the US Economy.* New York: Rand McNally–North-Holland Publishing Co.

Kurz, M., 1963, "Substitution versus Fixed Production Coefficients: A Comment," Em.

Kurz, M. and Manne, A., 1963, "Capital–Labor Substitution in Metal Machining," AER.

La Tourette, J., 1964, "Technological Change and Equilibrium Growth in the Harrod-Domar Model," *Kyklos.*

Lave, L., 1963, *Measurement of Technological Change in Agriculture, 1850–1960,* unpublished Ph.D. dissertation, Harvard University.

Leontief, W. *et al.,* 1953, *Studies in the Structure of the American Economy,* New York.

Leontief, W., 1964, "An International Comparison of Factor Costs and Factor Use, A Review Article," AER.

Lerner, A., 1944, *The Economics of Control.* New York: Macmillan.

Lerner, A., 1965, "On Some Recent Developments in Capital Theory," AER.

Levine, H., 1960, "A Small Problem in the Analysis of Growth," RES.

Levy, Ferdinand, 1964, *An Adaptive Production Function and Its Economic Implications,* unpublished Ph.D. Thesis, Carnegie Institute of Technology.

Ling, S., 1964, *Economics of Scale in the Steam-Electric Power Generating Industry.* Amsterdam: North-Holland.

Little, A., 1963, *Patterns and Problems of Technical Innovations in American Industry,* New York.

Lomax, D. S., 1950, "Cost Production Functions for Great Britain," JRSS.

Lomax, K., 1952, "Cost Curves for Electricity Generation," Ec.

Lundberg, E., 1961, *Produktivitet och räntabilitet.* Stockholm: P. A. Norstedt and Söner.

Lutz, F. and Hague, D., 1961, *The Theory of Capital.* New York: St. Martin's Press.

Lydall, H., 1959, "The Growth of Manufacturing Firms," BOIS.

Machlop, F., 1934–35, "The Common Sense of the Elasticity of Substitution," REStud.

Mansfield, E., 1961, "Technical Change and the Rate of Imitation," Em.

Mansfield, E., 1962, "Entry, Gibrat's Law, Innovation, and the Growth of Firms," AER.

Mansfield, E., 1963a, "The Speed of Response of Firms to New Techniques," QJE.

Mansfield, E., 1963b, "Intra firm Rate of Diffusion of an Innovation," RES.

Mansfield, E., 1963c, "Size of Firm, Market Structure, and Innovation," JPE.

Mansfield, E., 1964, "Industrial Research and Development Expenditures: Determinants, Prospects, and Relation to Size of Firm and Inventive Output," JPE.

Mansfield, E., 1965a, "Rate of Return from Industrial Research and Development," AER.

Mansfield, E., 1965b, "Innovation and Technical Change in the Railroad Industry," *Transportation Economics.* New York: Columbia University Press.

Mansfield, E., 1965c, "The Economics of Research and Development: A Survey of Issues, Findings, and Needed Future Research," University of Pennsylvania Conference on Technological Change and Government Regulation of Industry. Homewood, Ill.: Irwin.

Mansfield, E. and Brandenburg, R., 1965, "The Allocation, Characteristics, and Success of the Firm's R and D Portfolio: A Case Study," Ford Foundation Conference on Technical Change.

Marcus, M., 1964, "Capital-Labor Substitution Among States: Some Empirical Evidence," RES.

Markham, J., 1965, "Market Structure, Business Conduct and Innovation," AER.

Massell, Benton, 1960, "Capital Formation and Technical Change in U.S. Manufacturing," RES.

Massell, B., 1961, "A Disaggregated View of Technical Change," JPE.

Massell, B., 1962, "Another Small Problem in the Analysis of Growth," RES.

Massell, B., 1962, "Is Investment Really Unimportant?," Me.

Massell, B., 1962, "Investment, Innovation, and Growth," Em.

Massell, B., 1964, "Aggregative and Multiplicative Production Functions," EJ.

Matthews, R., 1964, "The New View of Investment: Comment," QJE.

McCarthy, M., 1965, "Embodied and Disembodied Technical Progress in the Constant Elasticity of Substitution Production Function," RES.

McFadden, D., 1963, "Further Results on CES Production Functions," REStud.

McFadden, D., 1964, "Notes on the Estimation of the Elasticity of Substitution," Read at the Econometric Society Meetings, December, 1964.

Meade, J., 1961, A Neo-Classical Theory of Economic Growth. London: Allen and Unwin.

Meiburg, Charles, 1962, "Nonfarm Inputs As a Source of Agricultural Productivity," JFE.

Michaely, M., 1964, "Factor Proportions in International Trade: Current State of the Theory," Kyklos.

Mills, F., 1952, Productivity and Economic Progress, NBER Occasional Paper 38. New York: Columbia University Press.

Minhas, B. S., 1963, An International Comparison of Factor Costs and Factor Use. Amsterdam: North-Holland.

Mirrlees, J. and Kaldor, N., 1962, "A New Model of Economic Growth," REStud.

Morishima, M., 1964, Equilibrium Stability, and Growth. Oxford: Oxford University Press.

Morrissett, I., 1953, "Some Recent Uses of Elasticity of Substitution: A Survey," Em.

Mukerji, V., 1963, "Generalized SMAC Function with Constant Ratios of Elasticities of Substitution," REStud.

Nelson, R., 1959, "The Economics of Invention: A Survey of the Literature," JB.

Nelson, R., (ed.), 1962, Rate and Direction of Inventive Activity, NBER. Princeton: Princeton University Press.

Nelson, R., 1964, "Aggregate Production Functions," AER.

Nerlove, M., 1963, "Returns to Scale in Electricity Supply," in Christ et al., Measurement in Economics. Stanford: Stanford University Press.

Neville, J., 1964, "Technical Change in Australian Manufacturing," ER.

Newman, P. K. and Read, R. C., 1961, "Production Functions with Restricted Input Shares," IER.

Nicholson, R. J. and Gupta, S., 1960, "Output and Productivity Changes in British Manufacturing Industry 1948–54," JRSS.

Nield, R., 1963, *Pricing and Employment in the Trade Cycle*. Cambridge: Cambridge University Press.

Niitamo, O., 1958, "The Development of Productivity in Finnish Industry," PMR.

Nordin, J., 1947, "A Note on a Light Plant's Cost Curves," Em.

Pasinetti, L., 1960, "On Concepts and Measures of Changes in Productivity," RES.

Peston, M., 1959, "A View of the Aggregation Problem," REStud.

Phelps, E., 1962, "The New View of Investment: A Neoclassical Analysis," QJE.

Phelps, E., 1963, "Substitution, Fixed Proportions, Growth and Distribution," IER.

Phelps, E. and Yaari, M., 1964, "Reply to Matthews," QJE.

Phillips, A., 1956, "Concentration, Scale, and Technological Change in Selected Manufacturing Industries, 1899–1939," *Journal of Industrial Economics*.

Phillips, A. W., 1961, "A Simple Model of Employment Money and Prices in a Growing Economy," Ec.

Pitchford, J., 1960, "Growth and the Elasticity of Factor Substitution," ER.

Posner, M., 1961, "International Trade and Technical Change," OEP.

Pyatt, G., 1964, "A Production Functional," abstracted in *Econometrica*.

Railway Productivity, 1962, BOIS.

Rapping, L., 1965, "World War II Ship Building Production Functions," RES.

Rasmussen, W., 1962, "The Impact of Technological Change on American Agriculture, 1862–1962," JEH.

Reddaway, W., and Smith, A., 1960, "Progress in British Manufacturing Industries," EJ.

Resek, R., 1963, "Neutrality of Technical Change," RES.

Riese, H., 1964, "The Balance of Growth in Neo-Classical Theory of Equilibrium," *Kyklos*.

Robinson, J., 1938, "The Classification of Inventions," REStud.

Robinson, J., 1952, *The Rate of Interest and Other Essays*. London: Macmillan.

Robinson, J., 1956, *The Accumulation of Capital*. London: Macmillan.

Robinson, J., 1962, "Comment," REStud.

Robinson, J., 1963, "Learning by Doing: A Further Note," REStud.

Robinson, J., 1964, "Solow on the Rate of Return," EJ.

Rogers, E., 1962, *Diffusion of Innovations*. New York: Free Press of Glencoe, Inc.

Rosenberg, N., 1963, "Technological Change in the Machine Tool Industry, 1840–1910," JEH.

Rosenberg, N., 1963, "Capital Goods, Technology, and Economic Growth," OEP.

Rosenberg, N., 1964, "Neglected Dimensions in the Analysis of Economic Change," BES.

Rostow, W., 1960, *The Stages of Economic Growth.* New York: Cambridge University Press.

Rothbart, E., 1946, "Causes of the Superior Efficiency of U. S. A. Industry as Compared with British Industry," EJ.

Ruttan, V., 1956, "The Contribution of Total Productivity to Farm Output: 1957–75," RES.

Ruttan, V., 1959, "Usher and Schumpeter on Invention, Innovation, and Technological Change," QJE.

Ruttan, V., 1960, "Research on the Economies of Technological Change in American Agriculture," JFE.

Ruttan, V. and Stout, T., 1958, "Regional Differences of Technical Change in American Agriculture," JFE.

Ruttan, V. and Stout, T., 1960, "Regional Differences in Factor Shares in American Agriculture," JFE.

Salter, W., 1960, *Productivity and Technical Change.* Cambridge: Cambridge University Press.

Samuelson, P., 1959, "A Modern Treatment of the Ricardian Economy," QJE.

Samuelson, P., 1961, "A New Theorem on Non-Substitution," in H. Hegeland (ed.) *Money, Growth, and Methodology.* Lund, Sweden: Gleerup.

Samuelson, P., 1962, "Parable and Realism in Capital Theory: The Surrogate Production Function," REStud.

Scherer, F., 1965, "Size of Firm, Oligopoly, and Research: Comment," CJEPS.

Schmookler, J., 1952, "The Changing Efficiency of the American Economy, 1869–1938," RES.

Schmookler, J., 1959, "Bigness, Fewness, and Research," JPE.

Schmookler, J., 1965, "Technological Change and Economic Theory," AER.

Schultz, T., 1956, "Some Reflections on Agricultural Production, Output and Supply," JFE.

Schultz, T., 1960, "Capital Formation by Education," JPE.

Schultz, T., 1962, "Some Reflections on Investment in Man," JPE.

Shen, T., 1961, "Innovation, Diffusion, and Productivity Analysis," RES.

Sheshinski, E., 1964, "Estimation of Technical Change with CES and Leontief Models," Read at Econometric Society Meeting, December, 1964.

Simon, H., 1951, "Effects of Technological Change in a Linear Model," in Koopmans, T., *Activity Analysis at Production and Allocation.* New York: Wiley.

Simon, H., 1960, "The Corporation: Will it be Managed by Machines," in M. Anshen and G. Bach (eds.), *Management and Corporations, 1985.* New York: McGraw-Hill.

Simon, H., 1965, "The Long Range Economic Effects of Automation," in *The New Science of Management Decision,* Revised edition. New York: Harper.

Simon, H. and Bonini, C., 1958, "The Size Distribution of Business Firms," AER.

Simon, H. and Levy, F., 1963, "A Note on the Cobb-Douglas Function," REStud.

Soligo, R., 1963, "The Short Run Relationship Between Employment and Output," unpublished Ph.D. thesis, Yale University.

Solow, R., 1956, "Contributions to the Theory of Economic Growth," QJE.

Solow, R., 1957, "Technical Change and the Aggregate Production Function," RES.

Solow, R. M., 1958, "The Constancy of Relative Shares," AER.

Solow, R., 1960, "Investment and Technical Change," in *Mathematical Models in the Social Sciences*, edited by K. Arrow, S. Karlin, and P. Suppes. Stanford: Stanford University Press.

Solow, R., 1962a, "Technical Progress, Capital Formation, and Economic Growth," AER.

Solow, R., 1962b, "Substitution and Fixed Proportions in the Theory of Capital," REStud.

Solow, R., 1963a, "Heterogeneous Capital and Smooth Production Functions: An Experimental Study," Em.

Solow, R., 1963b, "Capital, Labor and Income in Manufacturing," in *The Behavior of Income Shares*, SIW, Vol. 27, NBER.

Solow, R., 1963c, *Capital Theory and the Rate of Return*. Amsterdam: North-Holland.

Sraffa, P., 1960, *Production of Commodities by Means of Commodities*. Cambridge: Cambridge University Press.

Stigler, G., 1963, *Capital and Rates of Return in Manufacturing*, NBER.

Stoleru, L, 1965, "An Optimal Policy for Economic Growth," Ec.

Strassman, W., 1959, *Risk and Technological Innovation: American Manufacturing Methods During the 19th Century*. Ithaca: Cornell University Press.

Streeter, P., 1962, "Prices and Productivity," *Kyklos*.

Sturmey, S., 1964, "Cost Curves and Pricing in Aircraft Production," EJ.

Sutherland, 1959, "The Diffusion of an Innovation in Cotton Spinning," *Journal of Industrial Economics*.

Swan, T., 1956, "Economic Growth and Capital Accumulation," ER.

Terleckyj, N., 1958, "Factors Underlying Productivity: Some Empirical Observations," JASA.

Terleckyj, N., 1959, *Sources of Productivity Change, A Pilot Study Based on the Experience of American Manufacturing Industries, 1899–1953*, unpublished doctoral dissertation, Columbia University.

Terleckyj, N. and Halper, H., 1963, *Research and Development: Its Growth and Composition*. New York: NICB.

Theil, H., 1954, *Linear Aggregation of Economic Relations*. Amsterdam: North-Holland.

Theil, H., 1957, "Specification Errors and the Estimation of Economic Relationships," *Review of the International Statistical Institute*.

Tinberger, J., 1959, "Zur Theorie der lang tristigen Wirtschaftsentwickluns," *Weltwirtschaftliches Archiv*, 1942, translated as: "On The Theory of Trend Movements," in *Selected Papers*, Amsterdam.

Tinberger, J. and Corveg, H., 1962, "Quantitative Adaptation of Education to Accelerated Growth," *Kyklos*.

Tolley, G., and Smidt, 1964, "Agriculture and the U.S. Economy," Em.

Tostlebe, A., 1957, *Capital in Agriculture*, NBER. Princeton: Princeton University Press.

Towne, M. and Rasmussen, W., 1960, "Farm Gross Product and Gross Investment in the 19th Century," NBER, SIW, XXIV, *Trends in American Economy in the 19th Century*. Princeton: Princeton University Press.

Tsuru, Shigeto, 1962, "The Effects of Technology on Productivity," KK.

Tweeten, L. and Tyner, F., 1964, "Toward an Optimum Rate of Technological Change," JFE.

United States Department of Agriculture, 1961, "The Balance Sheet of Agriculture," Agricultural Information Bulletin No. 247.

Usher, D., 1964, "The Welfare Economics of Invention," Ec.

Uzawa, H., 1961, "Neutral Inventions and the Stability of Growth Equilibrium," REStud.

Uzawa, H., 1962, "Production Functions with Constant Elasticities of Substitution," REStud.

Uzawa, H., 1965, "Optimum Technical Change in An Aggregative Model of Economic Growth," IER.

Valavanis—Vail, S., 1955, "An Econometric Model of Growth, USA 1869–1953," AER.

Verdoorn, P. J., 1949, "Fattori che regolano lo sviluppo della produttività del lavoro," L'Industria.

Villard, H., 1958, "Competition, Oligopoly, and Research," JPE.

Wall, B., 1948, "A Cobb-Douglas Function for the U.S. Manufacturing and Mining, 1920–1940," Em.

Walters, A., 1963a, "The Accelerator and Technical Progress," REStud.

Walters, A., 1963b, "Production and Cost Functions: An Econometric Survey," EM.

Walters, A., 1963c, "A Note on Economies of Scale," REStud.

Weintraub S., 1958, *A General Theory of the Price Level, Income Distribution, and Economic Growth*, Philadelphia.

Whitaker, J., 1964, "A Note on the CES Production Function," REStud.

Williams, B., 1964, "Investment and Technology in Growth," *The Manchester School*.

Wilson, Thomas, 1960, "Productivity and Output in the Postwar Period," Technical Note No. 2, Joint Economic Committee, Study of Employment, Growth, and Price Levels, Washington, D. C.

Wilson, Thomas and Eckstein, Otto, 1964, "Short-Run Productivity Behavior in U.S. Manfuacturing," RES.

Woodruff, W., 1962, "Enquiry into the Origins of Invention and the Inter-continental Diffusion of Techniques of Production in the Rubber Industry," ER.

Worley, J., 1961, "Industrial Research and the New Competition," JPE.

Worswick, G., 1958, "Prices, Productivity, and Incomes," OEP.

Zweig, F., 1936, *Economics and Technology*. London: T. S. King and Son.

Index

Index

223